FILLING THE HEAD

PUBLIC CULTURES OF THE MIDDLE EAST
AND NORTH AFRICA

Paul A. Silverstein, Susan Slyomovics, and Ted Swedenburg, editors

FILLING THE HEAD

Listening to Rap in Arabic

Rayya El Zein

INDIANA UNIVERSITY PRESS

This book is a publication of

Indiana University Press
Office of Scholarly Publishing
Herman B Wells Library 350
1320 East 10th Street
Bloomington, Indiana 47405 USA

iupress.org

© 2025 by Rayya Sunayma ElZein

All rights reserved
No part of this book may be reproduced or utilized in any form or by any means, electronic or mechanical, including photocopying and recording, or by any information storage and retrieval system, without permission in writing from the publisher.

First Printing 2025

Cataloging information is available from the Library of Congress.

ISBN 978-0-253-07296-2 (hdbk.)
ISBN 978-0-253-07297-9 (pbk.)
ISBN 978-0-253-07299-3 (ebook)
ISBN 978-0-253-07298-6 (web PDF)

For my parents and their parents

CONTENTS

Acknowledgments ix

Note on Transliteration xi

Intro: Learning to Listen *1*

1. Revolting *26*
2. *Istifzaz* *45*
3. Listening *63*
4. Yearning *89*

Outro: Politics in Motion *110*

Appendix 123

Notes 127

Bibliography 149

Index 159

ACKNOWLEDGMENTS

This project has been cooking for a long time. The tender object in your hands is a feast of relief for a solid few whom I now have the pleasure of acknowledging. Obviously, the book's faults are my own, but its existence is indebted to many.

Once I articulated my intention to write it, my parents did not let me give up on its completion. They were steady and ever insistent that I not let it go. The further along I advance in my own parenthood journey, the more I am aware of and touched by how they are (still) parenting me. This book is for them.

Muqataʿa, El Rass, Edd Abbas, Osloob, Shahid, Mohamad Ali Nayel, and many other musicians, artists, writers, and curators were generous and patient with me. I hope they find something useful in these pages.

CUNY as an institution appeared in my life by accident and housed an initial politicization of my thought and imagination around collective care. I would be a different person without having been a student and a worker at that institution. I had no idea at the time how precious the student mobilizing in 2011 and 2012 and in the Free Universities of NYC in the years after would later appear to me.

I was lucky to encounter, over the course of graduate study and postgraduate employment, a wealth of generous and thoughtful mentors where most students and early professionals are happy to find one. At the CUNY Grad Center, Maurya Wickstrom was the most careful, exacting reader I have had. She was a mentor who saw me as a whole person and who saw the whole work I could create (and that I was not yet creating it). She pushed me in ways I desperately needed in a particularly trying time in her own life, and she shared with me some of the warmest and most exciting moments in my own. Also at CUNY, Tony Alessandrini, Ammiel Alcalay, and Christopher Stone showed me warmth and generosity as I was getting my footing as a writer and as an adult. I remember their kindness often.

Even before I graduated, Marwan Kraidy and Tarek El-Ariss fondly and uncondescendingly adopted me, extending opportunity, support, and affinity. I can't imagine how lonely postgraduate work must be without the kind of warmth and positivity they offered. This is to say nothing of the structural support Marwan also extended at the University of Pennsylvania. This book would be a simpler, duller contribution without having been incubated at CARGC. At Wesleyan, Kēhaulani Kauanui received me with expansive attention for my writing and my positioning as a Palestinian scholar and thinker.

Christine Sargent and Samira Rajabi read more of the manuscript than anyone but the editorial team and shared my ups and downs throughout. Ted Swedenburg caught this manuscript when I had all but given up that it would materialize at all. He has been a steady and encouraging champion since it was only a research project. The two anonymous readers similarly inspired and pushed me to carry this project into its current form. I am grateful to Huda Fakhreddine for generously lending attentive counsel in the project's final moments. Chapter 4 is stronger because of her. Adam Faruqi's sharp ears and musical expertise helped to bring some of the music to life on the page. Sarahh Scher made indexing a breeze. At IUP, Bethany Mowry was a delight to work with.

I gave birth twice during the time that this project moved from a draft of a prospectus to a revised manuscript. Given the proximity, I have the opportunity to affirm childbirth is much easier than writing a book, but it is also a completely different creativity and intensity. Lana and Miro reinvent daily what gratitude means. Together with my parents, they cemented my determination to complete this project. George never put himself between me and this project, despite carrying it with me for over a decade.

My transition out of the academy has been as smooth as I could ask for, which is not to say it was easy. Every so often, I hear from a student who remembers something we read or some feedback on a paper. I am always surprised something in a classroom can last that long, yet I know how marked I am, still, by various classrooms I have been a part of. Students contributed to this text in so, so many ways.

As much as anything else, the initial months of 2024 have shown that the shape of our educational institutions and how we engage them are neither predetermined nor infallible. As this project concludes, I catch myself looking forward to the teaching and learning that are inevitably to come—in whatever form they come.

NOTE ON TRANSLITERATION

I USE A SIMPLIFIED VERSION OF THE *International Journal of Middle East Studies* (IJMES) transliteration from Modern Standard Arabic. I omit dots under certain letters for readability; I use the ʾ for the *hamza* and ʿ for the letter *ayn*. I use the most common English spellings for proper nouns, and I use the transliteration patterns the artists themselves use. For example, I write El-Farʿi, the Jordanian rapper, as El Far3i, as he does, using the numeral 3 commonly used for the *ayn* in bilingual Arabic English popular culture. The *alif-lam* appears as "al-" except in proper nouns commonly written with an *el* or without the - as in El Rass or Metro Al Madina.

FILLING THE HEAD

Intro

LEARNING TO LISTEN

I FIRST HEARD "MIN AL-KAHEFF" ("FROM THE CAVE") by the Ramallah Underground during a morning commute.[1] It was the very beginning of 2011, with all the excitement of the early days of the Tunisian and Egyptian revolutions. I was living in Brooklyn, New York, and teaching at City College in Harlem, and I perceived the hour-plus commute underground as an excruciating removal from the livestream of protest occupations in Cairo's Tahrir Square. I can still feel my numb arm hanging onto the pole above me, crammed in with everyone else, half awake, half asleep, fumbling with playlists to keep me distracted on the way. On one such playlist, I tuned in and out of the first verse of Ramallah Underground's 2007 track, allowing myself to swing with the jolts of the subway car and in time with the synthesizer. When Asifeh spit the line "*bi al-demoqratiyyah samamouna* (they poisoned us with democracy)," I felt my heart beating faster.[2] But everything else on the subway car ceded to the background when I heard the following refrain:

بحاول اطنش بس السياسة بتشدني
بقولها افلتي! ما بدي
بتقولي انا جزء من حياتك
مش حتقدر تمشي ضدي

I try to pay no heed, but Politics, she draws me back.
I tell her, 'Let go of me! I am not interested.'
She responds, 'I am a part of your life, you won't be able to resist me'

I spent the rest of the ride listening to that track on repeat. By the time I climbed the station steps into the full morning light, the length of Manhattan later, the torn plastic cushion on my headphones was wet from the tears on my face.

Experiences of listening like this one catalyzed the research in this book. For a long time, I did not know what to make of the reaction I had to Ramallah Underground's track.[3] The recognition and voiced articulation of an internal debate over political engagement was both comforting and devastating. But what kind of rap was this? And what kind of reaction was I having to it?

Nearly three years later, I was driving from a café on Rainbow Street to the UNRWA university campus in the Jordanian capital, Amman. In the café, I had bought the CD of *Adam, Darwin, and the Penguin*, the 2014 collaboration album by Lebanese rapper El Rass and the Syrian electronic musician Munma, and had it playing in the car. Listing in and out of the minimal, ambient electronica, I wove with other vehicles around the traffic circles. But the fourth track, a three-way collaboration that additionally includes the Jordanian rapper El Far3i, made me turn up the volume and focus my listening.[4] In "Fi al-Jaleed" ["In the Ice"], rappers El Rass and El Far3i recount traveling to Scandinavia for a concert, a complicated experience navigating the exoticized orientalism of the concert organizers, the Islamophobia and anti-Arab racism of visa application processors and border guards, and the overwhelmingly warm reception they received from an expansive Arabic-speaking diaspora settled in Stockholm.[5] The two rappers relate these experiences in overlapping puns, switching between physical and affective renditions of cold and warmth, distance and stasis.

Focusing to keep up with El Rass's sharp lyrical twists, I felt my heart thudding in my ears when, in the second verse, he recounted a Syrian listener greeting him at this concert *in tears*. I can still feel how his spitting of these lyrics raised the hair on the back of my neck. I pulled off the road, rolled up the windows, and turned off the engine. *What was this? Other people cry in response to this music? And rappers know about it?* I hit "repeat" and played the track again; this time the skin of my arms raised completely into gooseflesh despite the Jordanian sun.

As these linked vignettes illustrate, my initiation into rap in Arabic began with hair-raising invitations to listen closely. I often did not know what I was listening for when I downloaded mixtapes, poked through SoundCloud profiles, or slipped CDs into laptops and car drives. Not knowing what I was looking for, I nonetheless distinctly felt when I heard it, my body reacting with a mix of delight, surprise, and relief.

A single phrase emerged over and over in my discussions with both performers and fans. As we talked about why they liked the music, how they got into it, who influenced them, why they made rap, or why they listened to it, many noted how this or that artist or track ʿ*abba rasshom*—Arabic for *filled their head*. What was important about this album? What did you like about this rapper or that song? Why do you like to listen to this group? *I don't know, Rayya, it fills my head.* What did this metaphor mean? What kind of visceral metaphor was this, and what ineffable experience did it represent?

Learning to Listen

"To listen politically," the anthropologist Anna Tsing writes, "is to detect the traces of not yet articulated common agendas."[6] This book is an archive of such listening to experimental Arabic-language rap in three Arabic-speaking cities. Moving between Ramallah, Palestine; Beirut, Lebanon; and Amman, Jordan, *Filling the Head* is about the different ways fans and musicians listen to rap in Arabic and what those experiences feel like.[7] I note how the music moves listeners, what gigs artists choose to take and how audiences behave in them, the aesthetics that connect these spaces, and the strategies bar owners and concert organizers use to engender the atmosphere they desire. I believe these exchanges between rappers and audiences have something to teach us about the proposal, heeding, and cultivation of what Ashon T. Crawley calls *"otherwise* worlds."[8]

It was commonplace in the excited years of the Arab Uprisings to hear researchers and journalists pontificate about the connection between protests and music, especially rap music. Mainstream media produced a slate of articles attesting to the power of rap in the "Arab Street." Many outlets published "soundtracks" to the revolutions that foregrounded rappers and rap in Arabic.[9] This coverage explicitly tied the early political roots of rap and hip-hop in the US—rappers like Run-D.M.C., Public Enemy, Talib Kweli, Tupac, and others—with emergent political and aesthetic energy in Arab-majority cities. Such a narrative suggested that, like Black and brown youth in US cities in the late twentieth century, Arab youth in the 2010s were also taking up microphones to nonviolently "speak truth to power." This journalistic literature finds its echo in academic studies that foreground the political symbolism of youth subcultures, and that continue to be widespread in approaches to Arab youth.[10]

As I talked to rappers about the politics in their work, I heard them refuse these frameworks of cultural resistance. For example, in Amman, the producer Nasser Kalaji identified what he called a myth about rap in Arabic. He told me, "[For some researchers] it's like, *you have to be risking your life to do this! There are snipers on the buildings, and they've tapped my phone!* No, man. It's not like this. I always mention my political stance in the interviews. But people's reactions when I tell them this: it doesn't fit their framework. Like fuck, man, this guy is messing up my story."[11] Kalaji recognizes the bind he is placed in by journalists and foreign researchers who project onto him a specific political model: an underground revolutionary fighting against a conservative regime with populist creativity capable of inspiring a mass uprising. Kalaji took pains to distance himself from this narrative by foregrounding his position as a loyalist, a supporter of the Hashemite monarchy in Jordan. While this political stance is not widespread among my interlocutors, my research started by learning to recognize how the tropes Kalaji identified limit what politics in the music could be.[12] This is a question of being alive to myriad ways rappers might be inviting their listeners to think about and act in the world around them—far beyond support for, or resistance to, ruling parties.

Expectations harbored in the Western press and by liberal researchers about the significance of rap in Arabic have also racialized and depoliticized an understanding of how rap, other globalized genres of music, and politics of secular youth cultures generally might function politically. By *racialized* I mean it mobilizes depoliticized racial shorthand—as in Black youth using rap to speak truth to power—as a stand-in for political processes and material struggles over city space. Swedenburg writes that in the early 2000s, Palestinian rap helped to make the Palestinian cause legible to American youth, noting the appearance of Palestinian hip-hop and rap at solidarity events. Rap has been a medium in which Palestinian youth in Israel and Black and brown youth in the US identify shared forms of oppression in urban blight, institutional neglect, and police repression. Listening to and making the music connects members of these communities in aesthetic and cultural as well as political affinity.

While this practice of building solidarity is important, rap and hip-hop in Arabic have not shown themselves to be particularly effective at fomenting local antiracism or even at discouraging anti-Black or other ethnic or linguistic discrimination within Arabic-speaking communities and in Southwest Asia and North Africa (SWANA) generally. There is very little about the genre, from the policies of bouncers to the affective modes of some live concerts (for example, the extremely popular and widely mediated rap battles) to the lyrics or patterns of lyrical experimentation (the recognized influence of Eminem among the younger generation of rappers and DJs), that suggests the development of rap in Arabic has essentially come with antiracist politics.[13] The projection of a presumed affinity between Black and Arab youth through rap, while building some pathways for the legibility of Palestinian liberation on US college campuses in the early 2000s, has often allowed Arab rappers and their audiences in the diaspora and elsewhere to sidestep a critical investigation of the very palpable and culturally specific Arab and regional legacies of anti-Black racism.[14] Alongside anti-Syrian, anti-Palestinian, and sectarian sentiment, anti-Black racism is a harrowing reality across the region, including in its hip-hop and rap scenes. Reckoning with it is long overdue.[15]

As I submit this manuscript, the legibility of politics around Palestine, around global solidarity with Palestine, and perhaps even around patterns of racism within that solidarity are rapidly changing.[16] Ten years ago, when I was in the thick of fieldwork, conversations with my interlocutors revealed that the notion of politics itself was in motion then as well, though perhaps in a way that will feel very different from the present moment. Many musicians I spoke with initially refused to articulate a political resonance to their work at all, preferring an emphasis on sociality, feeling, or connecting with audiences. (When I prodded that all human interaction was political, most acquiesced that in that sense sure, one could read politics in their work.[17]) As pointed to above, some rappers spoke with pointed disdain about using rap as a specific kind of political expression. They plainly resented that they are so often asked to produce populist narratives of regional struggle—about Palestinians under occupation or Syrian migrants or prisoners in that country's devastating civil war. For example, the Syrian rapper Bu Kolthoum highlighted to me the emptiness of using rap to exploit populist sympathy about regional conflicts:

> How many times have I mentioned Palestine in my music? Not a single time. Not once. Why? Because it's enough, Palestine is understood. There's an occupier who has to leave. Period. End of story. There's nothing to talk about. Arm yourself and go fight or shut up about it. . . . You want to talk politics, be my guest. But you want to come and describe to me, and sing me tracks about Damascus, and sigh about Homs, and Aleppo, and whatever, and you are not Syrian, and you do not have any connection to the streets of Syria. . . . What are you coming to write poetry about? That means you just want views, man. And that means you can eat shit.[18]

In this reflection, Bu Kolthoum articulates a politics that is *not* a renouncement of the Palestinian cause (*there's an occupier who has to leave*) but that, at the same time, *is* a rejection of dying and deadening ways of invoking that political struggle (*There's nothing to talk about. Arm yourself... or shut up.*). As such, his refusal to write about Palestine coupled with his disgust at romanticized images of a victimized Syria point to a rejection of particular political narratives and the affective modes associated with them. Bu Kolthoum's disdain for rappers who take up regional issues or who seek to engage a particular affective resonance that they perceive to be widespread or radical is rooted in a critique of authenticity (*that means you just want views, man*).

Drawing from articulated distances from the political like Bu Kolthoum's, this book is concerned with lyrical and musical experimentation that circumvents, inverts, or refuses mainstream narratives of the political, of resistance, and of oppression. These mainstream discourses sometimes take the shape of US or European influence and expectations. But mainstream political discourses also have local roots and histories. Many of the rappers whose work I consider here are also challenging Arabic political discourses around notions of resistance (*mouqawameh*), resilience (*sabr*), and steadfastness (*sumud*), among others. Much of the lyrical content in what follows is thirsty for and actively experimenting with other ways of addressing and enacting politics.

For example, in our conversations, Bu Kolthoum continued that he was looking for discourse that was "*insani mu siyasi*," or "human, not political." He explained:

> You can't translate feelings politically. The feeling of pain—like every time I see a picture of Damascus, I feel like I'm being hacked apart—I don't go express this pain to a politician. I express it to a citizen like myself, who has left their home behind and is struggling [*taleˁ wa akel khara bara*]. Like the Syrian guy that works here. He speaks with my accent. He's from my neighborhood. These are the people I want to address [*ili ana bakhatebhom*]. Feeling can't be studied. It can't be produced [*la yumantiq*]. It can't be industrialized [*la yousalsal*].[19]

Bu Kolthoum's testimony asks for a framework of what anthropologist Yael Navaro-Yashin calls "sensing the political."[20] This affective mode of observation crucially does not seek to translate "political emotions" into specific political projects. Bu Kolthoum's remarks and similar statements by his colleagues and fans demand a formulation about affect and politics that critiques and distances itself from dominant political narratives. Leaning on Navaro-Yashin, the framework I employ reaches for "another sort of sensibility [that] may keep us within the domain of the subjective experience that the political generates so that we may sense it, catch hold of it as it fleets by."[21] What is required is not only attempting to *understand* the points of view of Bu Kolthoum and others and the context that informs those views but *sensing* them as well.[22] I offer in this book a formulation of political motion as a relation of yearning that is inspired by the affective force with which these musicians and their listeners disown and disavow the categories of the political.

Bu Kolthoum's description of his own affective discourse is rife with yearning while it categorically preempts an attempt to suggest *what* that desire reaches for. "Every time I see a picture of Damascus, I feel like I'm being hacked apart," he says, yet in our conversations and in his music he never articulates yearning for a specific *thing*. Instead, he tells me he raps "because I want to release [*a faregh*] a certain kind of stress. Every track I work on is a product of pressure. Each track is an expression of a production of stress [*daghet*]. I get home, suffocated, no one to talk to, I write a track." Such statements mark that the desire to return home or for the war to end could only be pieces of what this yearning encompasses. Rather, what he points to is a more expansive expression of searching for relief in others (felt as distant or imagined) or in other futures, not yet materialized.[23]

The absence of a single thing listeners yearn for is central to this book's proposal to understand yearning not as political positioning but as a political relation built between listeners and MCs. This thread between musicians and fans produces kinds of movement and motion through careful, deliberate, and focused practices of listening. I trace this feeling of yearning without foreclosing upon it a political definition of the kind of future for which such a feeling might reach.

* * *

I spend time foregrounding descriptions of the political and how it is in motion because most of my interlocutors during the period 2012–18 did not focus their political expressions on the kinds of clean trajectories of progress associated with specific changes or resistance against particular political projects. My prodding with suggestions (isn't the problem capitalism? Neoliberalism? The Israeli occupation? Western orientalism? NGOs?) was often scoffed at or brushed off as simplistic. Of course rappers and listeners decried the Israeli occupation; wished for a flourishing creative industry free from the *moukhabarat* of the Jordanian secret police; bemoaned the devastation of the civil wars in Syria and Yemen; criticized the role of the

US, Europe, Russia, and others in regional politics; and yearned to travel or longed to return home. It is not that, at some level, they did not also, as the anthropologist Stef Jansen highlights in his research in Sarajevo, yearn for "normal lives," manifest in a functioning state able to provide social services, more opportunity, or success.[24]

Still, in this book, I take direction from testimonies like that of Bu Kolthoum above, about why he refuses a specific political discourse, to trace other forms of political relationality, affective speech (*khitab*), and the practices of listening that tune them in. Doing so allows me to explore understandings of both motion and yearning that are not reduced to linear narratives of movement or change. It also allows me to formulate a political agency whose emergence is not dependent on spectacular gestures of resistance.[25] Rappers' and others' reflections on the politics in their work centers on everyday encounters, friction, and flow. These affective relations reflect yearning that might be nostalgic, anticipatory, or both.

Filling the Head

Filling the Head summons an interdisciplinary convergence. I draw from debates and analyses in political anthropology, aesthetics, literature, ethnomusicology, performance studies, Black feminist theory, and cultural studies. I have felt that an exploration of music that *fills the head* requires a set of interconnected analytical tools. The yearning that drives listeners and musicians in pursuit of new music and the satisfying release such music promises cannot be attributed to musical or lyrical innovation, the political economy of its consumption, or a theory of agentive subjectivity that underpins its logic alone. The political potency of the experience of finding music that *fills the head* requires tracing threads through adjacent but usually distinct approaches to cultural production, everyday life, and power.

My research began as a critical commentary of ethnographies of youth cultures that reduce politics to performances of resistive agency. For a long time, I was focused on how media representation of protest culture perpetuated simplistic understandings of both resistance and solidarity.[26] There is a normalizing discourse in ethnographies of cultural forms and power that celebrates just-discovered or just-emergent forms of agency. It seems to me that this approach misses the more sound political alternative that agency is widespread, not rare or elusive. My project takes inspiration from anthropologist Saba Mahmood's clarion analysis of the way in which progressive scholarship has imagined agency in the "subversion or resignification of social norms."[27] Her *Politics of Piety* has been instrumental in developing the theoretical framework to understand how pervasive liberal discourses frame individual artists and the experiences of encountering them and consuming their work. The sequence of questions Mahmood elaborates, building off of Lila Abu-Lughod's critical reflections on resistance, has encouraged me to strengthen the ways in which I also can detach "the notion of agency from the goals of progressive politics."[28] In this, *Filling the Head* draws from ethnographic literature that deliberately disavows a romantic interpretation of the political symbolism of cultural producers' choices, attentions, and dispositions.[29]

Exchanges between rappers and listeners reveal an emergent collectivity in concert spaces and across a distributed virtual listening public. In exploring what these emergent politics may consist of, I focus on the practice of listening as embodied attention. I draw on anthropologists of religion and media Charles Hirschkind and Brian Larkin to explore how audience behavior and rappers' reflections on the same point to the cultivation of attention and inattention as emobodied, iterative engagements.[30] As such, *Filling the Head* is a part of the blooming interdisciplinary academic literature achieving what Viet Erlman called a "resurgence of the ear."[31] This resuscitation of a fleshy, sensing agency for listening, inverts the predilection in Western philosophy to understand listening as either disembodied and cognitive or irrational, vulnerable, and passive. Following the important legacy of Steven Feld, I locate *Filling the Head* in a field that understands listening practices as more than mere "sensory aptitudes"—that is, as both culturally and politically situated.[32]

In exploring agentive listening, *Filling the Head* specifically engages a subfield of sound and performance studies that theorize interpellation, or hailing, and the range of ways—public and exuberant, private and introspective—that listeners respond or refuse to be called. In this, my project has been inspired by interdisciplinary analytical experimentation specifically informed by Black feminists Hortense Spillers, Sylvia Wynter, bell hooks, and Audre Lorde.[33] More specifically still, I have been influenced by the way Spillers's and Wynters's works in particular have been taken up by Black literature, media, and performance scholars Kevin Quashie, Ashon Crawley, Legacy Russell, and (more generally) Alexander G. Weheliye to explore processes of subject formation that are quiet, enfleshed, and exuberant.[34] The proposals I develop entering this cypher of theoretical analysis and interpretation also engage recent global hip-hop studies that share some of the same theoretical underpinnings. Imani Kai Johnson's pushing new approaches to embodiment in the cypher, or the circular performance space where breakdancers, rappers, and beatboxers engage, has been particularly inspiring.[35]

The examples I offer of embodied agency as a multivarious and actively cultivated set of possible responses to being hailed are in dialogue with recent critiques of Louis Althusser's understanding of the infallibility of interpellative authority, or his assumption that "the one hailed always recognizes that it is really him who is being hailed."[36] I engage Black and feminist thinkers that respond similarly to this dissatisfied itch in Althusserian theories of subjectivation by exploring the activity of sifting through competing calls of authority.[37] *Filling the Head* contributes to this understated, interdisciplinary conversation exploring the layers of possibility in the misfires of *infelicitous* interpellation, or the necessary instances when subjects recognize *they are not* being called. One of the contributions I make in this book is exploring the space that this glitchy, unsuccessful interpellation opens to imagine agency *as the yearning for being hailed otherwise.*

In the first half of the book, I turn to aesthetics to understand this *otherwise* and the strategies for getting there. In this, *Filling the Head* also contributes to a comparative body of literature that foregrounds how what Sianne Ngai has powerfully formulated as "ugly feelings" are intrinsic to the operation of desire.[38] My analysis mobilizes the aesthetics of experimental invitations into the cypher in voiced *qaraf* (disgust) and *istifzaz* (provocation) to explore how listeners' responses are both a navigation of material contexts in and around concert spaces and embodied yearnings for belonging and collectivity. In particular, *Filling the Head* takes inspiration from recent writing and performance in Arabic where abjection and disgust figure centrally to unseat universalizing assumptions of the power of disruption or break. I have been inspired by the ways in which Rana Issa, Adania Shibli, Rima Najdi, Leila Sakr, Tarek El-Ariss, Ghassan Moussawi, and other writers, scholars, and performance artists are deliberately examining and reconstructing disgust, anxiety, and exhaustion in Arabic.[39] Their experiments have inspired me to center Arabic conceptualizations of qaraf, istifzaz, *tarab* (being moved by music), and *qalb* (the heart) in my own work to deepen understandings of how and where feelings are embodied and to propose understandings of these locations as activities in and of themselves. I mobilize these specific, individually embodied formations toward an understanding of belonging to collectivity otherwise. In this, I am also heeding Lorde's understanding of desire as "providing the power which comes from sharing deeply any pursuit with another."[40]

Filling the Head argues that yearning to be hailed otherwise is integral to the construction of the cypher of the here and now while also precipitating the cypher to come. My formulation of this cypher to come leans on artist, technologist, and glitch theorist Legacy Russell, where the cypher may be understood as a "slippery" zone of political relation and becoming.[41] Drawing from her work, *Filling the Head* argues for a pleasurable listening experience of both surprise and stillness, a process of sedimentation and discovery that contributes to an analytic literature in the tradition of bell hooks, who identifies aesthetics as "a way of inhabiting space, a particular location, a way of looking and becoming."[42]

The relational becoming I develop in the second half of the book also draws from an established anthropological literature exploring boredom, time, anticipation, waiting, and hope.[43] *Filling the Head* proposes to understand yearning as an affective relation to the present and the future that is always in motion—specifically I am concerned with experiences of motion and movement in the feeling of blockage and being stuck.[44] In this, I have been inspired by and draw from Navaro-Yashin's framing of "sensing the political," Sarah Sharma and Stef Jansen's work on the "meantime," Martin Demant Fredericksen's exploration of "boredom," Ghassan Hage's inspirational attention to "waiting," Yakein Abdelmagid's brave writing on "hope," and Maurya Wickstrom's work on the "blockades" of neoliberalism, among others.[45] I argue that understanding the agency in making and consuming this music lies in paying attention to the movement in the stillness required to listen.

One of the questions the book asks is if affective experiences of listening can be used to analyze millennial political life. By this I mean can attention trained on listening draw out emergent textures of movement and relationality obscured by other kinds of ethnographic observation? What would it mean to think about *political motion* not as political movements but as everyday, affective experiences of moving with and being moved by others? This adds a third vector to academic treatments that have read antiphonal music and movement together—like Imani Kai

Johnson's "aural-kinesthetic" or Ashon Crawley's "choreosonic."[46] By this I mean that my focus on political motion gestures toward considering music, bodily motion, being emotionally moved by the music, *and political movement*—at once.[47]

* * *

Between and beyond the experiences of solitary listening I described above, I spent several years attending rap concerts, where I observed a real range of behaviors, audience demographics, rap performance styles, acoustic setups, and venue aesthetics. For example, at a concert in the occupied Palestinian city of Ramallah, I watched as listeners stood in rapt attention as the DJ and rapper Muqataʻa delivered his set. No one moved (see chap. 2). In Amman, I felt the scrambled energy of listless fans gathered from all over the city, groups of boys teasing each other, and event organizers trying to maintain control (see chap. 3). In New York, I watched as Arab MCs struggled to make their audiences feel comfortable responding to them in Arabic and the halting ways in which they asked listeners to flex muscles of belonging and distinction.[48] In Beirut, I listened in as a veteran DJ coached an aspiring rapper for his lack of flow. There, on the sidewalk outside of the bar, crowds of listeners paused, eavesdropped, and rushed by as the veteran underscored for the novice the importance of flow. In all of these cities, I listened to passersby rebuff, refuse, and ignore the new sounds.

Rooted in the experience of this multisited fieldwork, and in pursuit of a political analysis of patterns of affective listening to cities and politics as people move through them, a central political metaphor in this book is what it means *to be moved*. I build from the classical ethnomusicological framework for understanding Arabic music and poetry (*tarab*, literally "to be moved") while diverging from that anthropological and ethnomusicological literature's emphasis on trance, ecstasy, spirituality, specific musical training, and a single genre of classical Arabic music.[49]

In all of this, my ethnography presents an alternative to familiar readings of resistance in youth cultures across the Global South. I do so in conversation with other ethnographers prioritizing how individual artists, entrepreneurs, activists, and minority groups navigate and invert norms and expectations and actively build their futures and reframe the political.[50] This book documents the search for music that *fills the head* as a political process of yearning for different political questions. *Filling the Head* dives deep into concert dynamics and the performers and listeners who exchange within them, to tell the story of political motion that often doesn't look or feel like revolution—but is nonetheless politically alive.

Amman, Beirut, Ramallah

In the years I conducted research for this book, the Arabic-speaking world saw a dizzying spectrum of political opening and closure. While the popular revolutions of 2010 and 2011 seemed to portend incredible possibility, counterrevolution and foreign intervention quickly buried in rubble and drowned in the Mediterranean the routes that many of us hoped had been opened. Moreover, with the exception of the Lebanese revolution in 2019 (which largely took place after this research had concluded; see the outro), life in the cities I focus on here more or less carried on without spectacular protest. Approaching political processes when "nothing" seems to be happening requires, as bell hooks reminds us, that "'we must learn to see,'" where seeing is "heightened awareness and understanding, the intensification of one's capacity to experience reality through the realm of the senses."[51] To put it another way, this seeing is to listen for the traces of not yet articulated agendas—what the sociologist Raymond Williams famously called "structures of feeling."[52] What structures of feeling and what historical, financial, demographic, or otherwise material infrastructures connect Amman, Beirut, and Ramallah?

Amman, Jordan, Beirut, Lebanon, and Ramallah in the occupied West Bank are very different cities. They have specific, divergent cultural histories (from each other and even within each). And they have particular demographic and economic configurations. And yet, Amman, Beirut, and Ramallah nonetheless share a set of political, affective, and geopolitical features that make the three sites complementary nodes through which to track aesthetic innovation and political emergence during the period 2004–15, when most of the tracks discussed in this book were released and performed.

Filling the Head is not the first study to propose comparatively considering cultural production in Amman, Beirut, and Ramallah. Hanan Toukan's *The Politics of Art: Dissent and Cultural Diplomacy in Lebanon, Palestine, and Jordan* also considers a cross section of regional cultural producers—in her case, visual artists—working and presenting in Beirut, Ramallah, and Amman.[53] She identifies that the dynamics that historically shaped Beirut as a capital for art and literature also contributed to significant developments in Ramallah and Amman—developments significant enough to encourage her to read the three cities together as separate but connected sites. I offer a similar approach to understanding the development of the political economy of concerts and nightlife among the three cities in the new millennium. After the Lebanese civil war, Beirut became ground zero for a particular configuration of real estate investment, driving a postwar gentrification with important knock-on effects around alternative cultural production.[54] Similar dynamics also appeared in Amman and Ramallah.

Like Toukan, I acknowledge the role relative stability has played in drawing regional and international capital to these cities and supporting precarious infrastructure for cultural production in them. Similarly, I also identify the impact that the presence of international NGO workers played in these neoliberal economies and their role ensuring the dominance of specific aesthetics within them. Finally, I also identify the outsize role that the combination or contradiction of stability *and* precarity played in developing particular affective relations toward politics and the future shared by denizens of these cities. Of course, these felt and material relationships have local particularities. The feeling of blockage because of the Occupation in Ramallah is not the same as the feeling of blockage because of the corruption of long-standing sectarian political parties in Beirut. At the same time, the felt relationships to the present and the future echo and resonate among the three cities. In addition to the travel and gig-chasing patterns of musicians and festival curators, this combination of geopolitical, economic, and affective dynamics I have been describing link Amman, Beirut, and Ramallah and make of them interconnected nodes and a more or less cohesive site for the research of this book.

During the period 2004–15 Amman, Beirut, and Ramallah all saw a marked influx of local, regional, and international capital. This influx of capital was precipitated in all three cities by inciting moments in the early 1990s. Lebanon's fifteen-year civil war ended in 1990, bringing a new reign of capital in the rebuilding efforts of the downtown area, led by then–prime minister Rafiq Hariri and his construction company, Solidere discussed in more detail in chap. 1. In 1991, Jordan lifted twenty-four years of martial law, held in place since the *naksa* or setback of 1967 and Israel's occupation of the West Bank after the Six Day War, previously controlled by Jordan. And the first part of the Oslo Accords were signed in 1993, initially seen to promise some hope of a future Palestinian state and drawing financial, demographic, and political attention to Ramallah as its interim de facto capital. These three developments laid the groundwork for a sense of relative stability and opportunity for prosperity, where felt calm evoked both the recent history of each country/territory as well as concurrent regional dynamics.[55]

As all three cities saw political developments that promised relative calm, they all became important hosts of international humanitarian aid workers, whose tastes and preferences for patterns of cosmopolitan consumption increasingly dovetailed with the growing local middle class.[56] The demographic influx of largely European and North American students and workers, and in Beirut the renewed interest and sporadic attention of the far-flung Lebanese diaspora, incurred new stresses on these cities manifest in rising rents, a larger paying clientele for cultural production, demand for luxury services including five-star hotels and upscale restaurants, and other forms of globalized cosmopolitan leisure.

In other words, access to American, European, and Gulf capital that this relative stability promised led to the development and expansion of a local middle class prepared for leisure consumption. The total amounts of investment in the three cities differed; some of the players were the same; a lot of it was directed toward real estate and construction. Much of this construction and investment in real estate has been roundly criticized in all three cities for the role it has played in transforming public space into privatized playgrounds for foreign capital. For example, the Solidere projects in Beirut—largely responsible for the post–civil war reconstruction of the downtown and Beirut's Central Business District—have been critiqued for stealing the public downtown and transforming it into a generic cosmopolitan mall, barring access to the city's original consumers, producers, sellers.[57] Hopes to make of Amman a "new Beirut (before 1975)" or "another Dubai" underpinned several development projects, from the new "tech city" to the Jordan Gate Towers to the Abdali Downtown project. These projects mirrored (and in the case of Abdali shared partners with) the same investors and investment patterns behind the Hariri-led reconstruction of Beirut.[58] A notable example in Ramallah of the same kind of speculative construction, with the additional dynamics of collaboration with Israeli authorities, appeared in the self-enclosed Palestinian city of Rawwabi, which promised a tech hub, modern design, English language education, and a "bustling urban core."[59]

The development and expansion of middle-class consumption that played out in the frenetic opening and closing of dozens of restaurants, bars, and art and performance venues in Amman, Beirut, and Ramallah in the first two decades of the new millennium closely followed the spectacular investment in these and other residential real estate projects. The patterns of financialization and investment around this construction are important not only for signaling audiences with capital to spend but also for affecting the transformation of available public space. In all three cities, public space is a fraught and precious commodity long understood as relatively off limits for young women and visibly marked minorities moving outside of the legible homonormative frameworks of family units.[60] The development of private spaces like bars, restaurants, and clubs with alternative aesthetics promised different opportunities for socialization and leisure not available on Beirut's *corniche*, Ramallah's *manara* square, or Amman's Rainbow Street. These openings for alternative sociality sprung up concurrent with the vast remaking of existing working-class public spaces in the transformation of markets, parks, and theaters into shopping malls and gated residential campuses. These real-estate projects inverted the policing of public space, favoring the consuming power of young women, couples, and families, and discouraging, if not completely prohibiting, leisure patterns not centered around consumption—like strolling, fishing, or loitering.[61] This is to recognize that the development of opportunities for expanding subcultural production—like experimental rap in literal venues for concerts—mirrors the role gentrification has played in the expansion of cultural industries in some European and American cities. By this I mean that the increase in opportunity for cultural production like rap concerts accompanied, and was in some ways facilitated by, rising rents, growing economic disparity, displacement of longtime residents, and new patterns of cleaning and policing designed to remake and surveil public urban space.[62]

Moreover, the calm and stability on which this remarkable financialized investment was predicated was always precarious. The outbreak of the Second Intifada, the Occupation itself, the assassination of Lebanese Prime Minister Hariri in 2004, the 2006 war with Israel, spillover from the Syrian civil uprising (2012) and then civil war, and the expansion of the global war on terror in pursuit of the misnamed Islamic State (2014) were only the most spectacular reminders of precarity. Accordingly, denizens of all three cities readily remarked on the cognitively dissonant illusions of growth and progress marked in these openings around leisure and consumption.

In Ramallah, talk cohered about the "Ramallah Bubble," or the felt sense of dislocation or removal from the realities of the Occupation in bars and restaurants catering to cosmopolitan tastes.[63] This bubble refers to both a credit cycle that looked unstable and to a new culture of consumption, luxury, and entertainment that catered to a lively expat community and the Palestinian middle class. Within the "bubble," one could almost forget the continued presence of the Occupation, encouraged by an atmosphere of consumption.[64] The extension of consumer credit helped in part to provide an audience that had time, interest, and spendable capital for a spectrum of leisure and entertainment, including "alternative" musical production like rap concerts. But as the Ramallah-based rapper She'rap told me, "These bourgeois are open to global culture, and they live like the world is a playground built just for them. And if and when anything happens, they pack themselves up and leave. There is a bourgeoisie; and a bourgeoisie doesn't make a state."[65] His *bourgeoisie doesn't make a state* crystallizes the arguments made by scholars and analysts about how the influx of capital in post-Oslo Ramallah has created a real sense of political suffocation and blockage despite the presence of both relative stability and recent growth.[66]

In Amman, corporate sponsors like Red Bull touted their efforts in developing infrastructure to make the Jordanian capital a "cultural hotspot" despite its regional reputation for being a cultural desert inhospitable to experimentation or uncensored expression.[67] The influx of capital in this context is widely understood to be facilitated by the Jordanian monarchy's close ties with the West, the US in particular, and with Israel, which facilitates the free passage of goods while the former buoys the Jordanian state with aid money. This opening of opportunity in new sponsorships and events is widely understood as concurrent with the heavy-handed role of the monarchy and its relationship with the US and Israel.

Finally, seasonal waves of tourism to Beirut in these years supplied capital for a frenzied pace of beachside and open-air concerts and raves. It frequently prompted visitors and long-term residents alike to refer to Beirut as *wal'aneh*, or literally, "on fire," "lit up." Waves of gentrification, rippling out along several main avenues over two decades (Monot, Gemmayzeh, Armenia St., Hamra St.), happened despite and simultaneously with sporadic bombings striking in different parts of the capital. This intensely jarring pattern of opening and closure, excitement and anxiety led the Palestinian rapper Osloob, who grew up Bourj al-Barajneh, a Palestinian refugee camp south of the city, to characterize Beirut as schizophrenic. He offered, "*Fi nouʿ min al-infisam*. The places and sociality are so different from each other. Whole neighborhoods are built around contrasting realities."[68] It's this schizophrenia that leads Lebanese rapper El Rass to rap about Beirut, disavowing its regional reputation as a center of arts and culture and instead offering: "This is no capital of culture. It's a wrestling ring."[69]

The material differences between these cities notwithstanding, the similarly-experienced feelings of disruption, blockage, contradiction, and disgust with this tension connect people who live in or pass through Beirut, Ramallah, and Amman. These felt realities also underpin musical and lyrical patterns of exchange and collaboration among rappers themselves. The Lebanese sociologist Ghassan Moussawi proposes the term *al-wadaʿ* (literally, "the situation") as a concept to describe the affective relationship to the status quo in Beirut. He writes that al-wadaʿ is a "description as well as a metaphor" used to describe the "shifting conditions of instability in the country that constantly shape everyday life."[70] These include "everyday violence, disruptions, and lack of basic services" and other quotidian encounters that "produce feelings of constant unease."[71] For Moussawi, it is a placeholder for a "shared sense of knowledge and feeling" that might invoke despair one day, exhaustion another, anxiety, frustration, anger, and so on, on a third.[72] In this, it is not only, as anthropologist Yael Navaro-Yashin writes of Northern Cyprus, "affect that is discharged in a postwar environment." It is also a relationship to that environment that feels like "a state of everyday war."[73] This condition informs a kind of abjection in the testimonies of many, many of my interlocutors in all three cities. It is a condition in which moving is very difficult. (One recalls Ghassan Hage's reference to the Lebanese expression *mashi al-hal*—an idiom for "I am doing fine" that literally means "my condition is moving."[74]) While the Arabic term al-wadaʿ literally refers to the present, for Moussawi it also refers to the future as "anticipation of the unknown or what the future might bring as well."[75]

Anthropologist Aseel Sawalha also located a lingering affective malaise in postwar Beirut. She identified among her interlocutors a state of "limbo" that operated as an "ongoing 'state of emergency.'" Sawalha suggested that the "postwar case of uncertainty" permeated "all aspects of daily life for most residents of the city" and was echoed in various claims by Beirutis to "wait and see."[76] My own research also documented similar patterns of anxiety and confusion to Sawalha in all three cities. My interlocutors' testimonies mirrored the limbo Sawalha writes about. Many of the individuals I spoke with expressed hesitancy about next steps, iterating that they would also "wait to see what happens." At the same time, however, I also noticed something else in my interlocutors' expressions and analyses. People spoke of leaving these cities regularly, and a pronounced tin-like tone marked even the more hopeful pronouncements about the future. A lingering state of malaise that connects all three cities is the direct effect of temporalities that have been suspended for different reasons.[77]

Although material contexts differ in important ways, shared understandings of a specific relationship to al-wadaʿ (the situation, the status quo) reveal overlapping patterns of cynicism, resignation, and disgust in Amman, Beirut, and Ramallah. Many cultural producers were both proud of the new role their city was playing, especially in alternative music production in the region, and quick to bemoan the felt impossibility of producing culture, including live music, in it. Musicians' anxiety about there not being the infrastructure to receive their work came up often. For example, in a social media post in early 2016, Laith Al Huseini, the Palestinian Jordanian rapper Synaptik wrote, "Always felt like Jordan is just one big waiting room, everyone is waiting for something, some to leave, some to die, some for a better tomorrow and some for the sum of it all, I'm waiting to get out, I guess."[78] In the post, Al Huseini, who grew up in Jordan, surmises that the whole country is in a holding pattern, a situation from which he also wants to exit. This confluence of hope and suffocation, growth and stagnation characterizes Amman's recent and emerging importance as a regional center for cultural production for a specific economic cross section of the population. It is the double bind of wanting to build and wanting to leave, and the quickly successive expressions of hope and despair, that give needed texture to declarations and celebrations of any of these three cities as sites of regional exchange, emerging capital, and homes for alternative music.

In connecting and moving between Amman, Beirut, and Ramallah, *Filling the Head* acknowledges shared feelings of disgust, resignation, cynicism, and disappointment in all three cities. In doing so, it also builds on a body of work exploring affect in the region and its transmission across national borders.[79] It recognizes shared "histories of yearning for movement" while acknowledging the different geopolitical realities that structure the specific obstacles to motion and movement and particular objects of disgust.[80] Built on overlapping geopolitical developments, a palpable and shared affective relationship to the status quo connects these cities and fans and producers in them. This offers the grounding to explore yearning as a political becoming in and across these sites.

Chapter Descriptions

Over the course of my research, I listened to and spoke with rappers; DJs; bar owners; festival curators; culture program officers at corporations, foundations, and government agencies; journalists; musicologists; and fans. I spoke to owners of dozens of pubs, cafés, bars, clubs, theaters, and other performance spaces in Amman, Beirut, and Ramallah. In addition, over the years, I listened to the music of (in no order) Fareeq Al-Atrash, Ramallah Underground, DAM, Haykal, Shuaʻa, Julmud, Dakn, Al-Nather, Makimakkuk, Chyno, Synaptik, Immortal Entertainment, BLTNM, El Rass, Rami GB, El Far3i, Hello Psychaleppo, Munma, Katibeh 5, Osloob, Touffar, Nasserdayn Bu Touffar, Damar, Jaafar al-Touffar, Muqata'a, Asifeh, Sot Gilgamesh, OkyDoky, Malikah, Bu Kolthoum, Edd Abbas, Mehrak, Malikah, Al Darwish, Khotta Ba, LaTlateh, Jnood Beirut, Sheʻrap, El 7ad, Omar Offendum, The Narcicyst, and Deeb. I formally interviewed many of these artists and informally conversed with most of them. The current volume is a selective sampling of this research and observation, which itself speaks only to a small portion of the output of creative energy that is the development of this subculture over two decades.

As such, the book is not a comprehensive cataloging of this music. Nor does it pretend to be a holistic assessment of the scene through the eyes and ears of various players. The testimonies and examples that support the following chapters are—on purpose—a small sampling, chosen to help me craft a specific argument about some of the feelings the music can engender and the political possibilities these feelings can open.

In an effort to avoid the siloization by city of the dynamics I observed, I have adopted a thematic approach across the chapters. I build my argument for what "filling the head" feels like by exploring aesthetics (chap. 1), epistemology (chap. 2), and listening practices (chap. 3). The final chapter uses the previous three to develop a conceptualization of agency in motion and political belonging, *yearning*, that I understand the feeling of *filling the head* to relieve (chap. 4).

Chapter 1: "Revolting" builds on suggestions I have offered here about the limiting frames of the political frequently applied to Arabic-speaking youth and cultural production. I suggest an affective throughline cohering in experimental rap concerts in the Levant today is the deliberate *disavowal* of an appeal to Arab identity, feel-good national or cultural pride, or even regional crises that would engage the largest audience through a sense of righteous indignation. In live concerts, MCs instead incorporate a degree of disdain for the audience or the fact that they are performing into their act. These exchanges are quite opposite the assumption of protest music while courting different modes of political critique.

In chapter 1, I write against the seductive romanticization of resistance by immersing my attention in disgust. I trace an aesthetics of disgust (qaraf) to formulate an understanding of political release without rupture that I understand is central to the ability of this music to *fill the head*. Building from bell hooks's understanding of aesthetics as a way of approaching becoming, I explore how an aesthetic of disgust builds "the foundation for emerging visions."[81] This chapter explores articulations of disgust in the work of Jaafar al-Touffar, Nasserdayn al-Touffar, Katibeh 5, and members of the *saleb wahed* collective in Ramallah. In their work, I explore how rappers articulate distaste or revulsion in their lyrics and perform disgust, annoyance, or irritation in voice and gesture. In doing so, I argue that they initiate cycles of call-and-response that hail emergent subjectivities and collectivities into being. Attention to aesthetics of disgust in this chapter sets the stage for how invitations to listen might be understood politically.

Chapter 2: "*Istifzaz*" builds from the previous chapter's elaborations of qaraf to foreground that a disgusted listener demands to be called differently. In this chapter, experiences of listening at live concerts illuminate an epistemology of experimental Arabic rap that I propose to understand under an umbrella of istifzaz—Arabic for surprise, provocation, insult. Through an istifzaz epistemology, I dig further into how experimental Arab rappers invite listeners into the cypher. Drawing on the work and reflections of Muqataʿa, Sheʿrap, Osloob, El Rass, Haykal, Shab Jdeed, and others, I argue that the rhythmic movement built in many rap concerts is in fact premised on the slightest bit of irritation, which in practice alienates a portion of a given audience. When an MC starts off too loud, or the sound is not clear and audience members disperse, turn in on themselves, or leave, this too is an active call-and-response from which musicians learn and feel with their audience. While a balance is required so as not to alienate all listeners, a successful affective engagement built through istifzaz succeeds in making more engaged intimacy with a smaller percentage of the audience that has gathered. This kind of exchange is deeply cognizant of the modes of interpellation through which Arab listeners are called into frameworks of belonging and the political and is built on initial invitations to *dis*engage. At the same time, as Laila Sakr has argued of millennial culture and politics in the Arab world, it is grounded in an idea of what *the glitch* opens that is communal in nature.[82] In exploring the work that istifzaz does, I sketch an understanding of interpellative practices that recognize already-formed subjects and invite them to relate to themselves and to each other otherwise.[83]

Lyrical patterns of istifzaz all include the invitation to listen very closely. In chapter 3: "Listening," I further explore the search for these relations otherwise by reexamining the calls into the cypher and the listening practices cultivated by different audiences. The tears I experienced while listening to some of the music, a kind of introspection are tied not only to the particular flows of the lyrics and the ideas presented in them but in embodied attention. Analysis in chapter 3 focuses on the work and concerts of Bu Kolthoum, El Rass, Malikah, Satti, Khotta Ba, DJ Sotusura, Ramallah Underground, and DAM. I consider two major festivals in Amman in 2015 (the Al-Balad and Word Is Yours Festivals). My analysis of these concerts should guard against a romanticization of istifzaz (provocation) or qaraf (disgust) as their own aesthetics or expressions of resistance. In lingering on the refusal to listen, this chapter hosts a conversation about listening practices, how they are embodied, what kind of attention they require, and what role both listening and attention play in the experience of *filling the head*. Importantly, this chapter develops the notion of stillness attached to particular kinds of attention as a felicitous embodiment of being called into the cypher.

The fourth and final chapter, "Yearning," is an invitation to understand yearning itself as political agency. I consider that yearning and longing are active doings that are materially and affectively different from a more static hope. I ask how to understand yearning as a practice or even as a cultivated attention that is rooted in the present and oriented toward the future and how to imagine the enactment of that yearning in everyday things like listening to music. This chapter concludes my consideration of the ways in which audiences and musicians experience experimental rap in Arabic through an explicit exploration of the pleasure associated with those experiences. Exploring the work of Nasserdayn al-Touffar, Al-Darwish, Hello Psychaleppo, and others, chapter 4 ties up some open threads in my analysis over the course of this book. I turn to as of yet unsettled pieces like: what (or where) is the head in the phrase *filling the head*? Or, how to understand where this experience is embodied? How to understand the movement that is embodied in this stillness? And finally, what happens once something *has* filled the head? How to understand catharsis as the continuation of this pleasure or further elaboration of the yearning attached to it?

Drawing heavily from Kevin Quashie's inspiring work on *quiet*, in this fourth chapter, I argue that yearning points to belonging in formation. It is an experience of coconstituted becoming, a recognition of relationality and interdependence, and, perhaps most importantly for this study, an anticipation of being hailed *otherwise*. These otherwise hailings into the cypher are part provocation, part affirmation, part aspiration. They stage polyphonic communication (call-and-response) in a cypher that is at once *here and now* and also a *cypher to come*. I argue that this yearning for otherwise is located in the holistic experience of listening—in the way listeners are summoned. This embodied listening includes but is also not reducible to what the music sounds like. It is not a question of the music *sounding like* "the future."[84] As such, learning to listen for the glitch and quiet follows Anna Tsing's proposal to see what is noticeable *if we look around instead of ahead*.[85] When interpellations into the cypher succeed, they open instead of close off possibilities. Ultimately, I argue it is this yearning for being hailed otherwise that marks the experience of listening to rap.

The book concludes with three meditations on motion, movement, and belonging. "Outro: Politics in Motion" centers on the work of the Lebanese rapper El Rass El Rass, and several of his collaborators and competitors. These three episodes point to the ways in which this music circulates: online, through networks of affiliation, through competition with other rappers, sustained in conversation with fans, and reverberating in different political activities and performance spaces. These moments offer ways of thinking about the circulation of experimental rap and hip-hop in virtual spaces, at a remove from but intimately connected to the live concert.

Ethnographic Vacillation

If I believe I share affective experiences of yearning with some of my interlocutors, it does not mean it was all of the same type or intensity, or that my impression of my own experiences necessarily maps onto all aspects of theirs. Anthropologist Ghassan Hage has convincingly argued for "ethnographic vacillation" to account for critical awareness of the political emotions of the researcher and her interlocutors. By this, he means a way of being in touch with but also critical of the emotions one feels as a researcher. Hage offers this critical framework at a time when, he argues, "reflexivity has become a substitute rather than a complement to what is by far the discipline [anthropology]'s most important achievement: instilling in ourselves and in our readers the desire and the capacity to know otherness seriously."[86] As a diasporic researcher, I am compelled to consider my relationship to this *otherness* seriously.

I am a cis Arab American woman of Lebanese, Palestinian, and Northern European descent who grew up in the US. I speak Arabic with an accent that is not quite placeable: outside of Lebanon, the accent is presumed Lebanese; inside Lebanon, it is decidedly not. It is Palestinian, Lebanese, and American. Above all, the Arabic I speak is based on a phonetic understanding of the spoken language and prone to mistakes and mispronunciations not typical among literate adults.[87] At the same time, my relative ease with language compared to researchers who did not grow up in an Arabic-speaking household offers me access I would not have otherwise. My name, some pronunciation, and the fact that I belong to a global Arab diaspora often produced inclinations to trust or intimacy beyond those that I deliberately tried to foment.

Generally, I admit that over the course of my research, I found myself more introverted than usual, relying on the physical business that cigarettes provided during interviews. I was largely unsuccessful, despite the warmth of some of my interlocutors, at mixing socializing with rappers with my research about them. My practice of participant observation was not styled as a part of B-boy/B-girl culture or the other attending stylistic or expressive elements of global hip-hop. Out of respect for the musicians whose work I appreciate, I never attempted my own raps or beats. With the exception of the now-closed studios of Katibeh 5 in the camps of Bourj al-Barajneh outside of Beirut, I confined myself as researcher to the cosmopolitan centers of each city. My research focuses on the districts where gentrification is most obvious and where the great majority of concerts are held.

Like many of my peers—fans of this music and otherwise—I have also been consumed by the political events of the past two decades, from the second Palestinian Intifada through the counterrevolutions that followed the Arab Uprisings through the global uprisings protesting the Israeli genocide in Palestine and beyond. Besides these regional and global pulls, during my fieldwork, which was also the longest sustained period I have spent in the region, I was also navigating a palpable yearning to belong—not only among the social groups through which I moved but to the Arab cities in which I took up residence. This general longing to belong to these places is a product of the positions in the diaspora I have inhabited and from a feeling of being cut off from places and people of import during a lifetime in the US.

I offer these reflections toward what Hage calls "grounding emotional identification in the existing relations of power."[88] In other words, I mean to describe how, despite my name, my background, and where my immediate family lived (Beirut), I continued to be structurally removed from the subjects and communities of my research—sometimes by my own choices and sometimes as a product of circumstances outside of my control. This seems necessary to underscore in reflections about my own positionality. Critical awareness of my role as a diasporic informant asks me to draw attention to my own trajectories of both motion and emotion.

I started this research in a time of great hope and anticipation across the region (2012). I concluded the first bulk of research in quite a different moment (2015) follow-up research in a different time still (2018) and final edits in yet another (2024). Many times over the years, I weighed heavily the point of such an endeavor. With very few exceptions, the ongoing media fascination with the creative expression of Arabic-speaking youth has not been conducive to musicians taking writing about them seriously, or as serious work, or as stemming from serious interest—much less as rising to try to meet them at the level of political curiosity, social engagement, cultural experimentation, or aesthetic innovation they espouse.

In what follows, it is my earnest intention to respond to these musicians' creativity and seriousness with something like the same. If it is nothing else, let it be read as my own testament to and fierce appreciation of the fastidiousness with which they attend their own work.

1

REVOLTING

*Muqrif al-wada' al-'arabi fa qilet la hali
bistafrigh 'ala al-madineh fiha al-qaraf*
(The state of the Arab world is disgusting so I said to myself,
I'll throw up on a city filled with filth.)
—SOT GILGAMESH

I spat and spat and it kept on being me.
—Clarice Lispector in Sianne Ngai

كيف نتحرر ممن نحب ؟
—Rana Issa

IN 2011, *TIME* MAGAZINE NAMED THE TUNISIAN RAPPER El Général one of its top one hundred persons of the year. *TIME*'s profile of the twenty-one-year-old described his song "Rais le Bled" as consisting of "blunt allegations of government corruption," important especially because it "also became the anthem of protesters in Cairo's Tahrir Square."[1] Across English-language media in the heady days of the Arab Uprisings of 2011 and 2012, excited headlines like "The Hip-Rhythm of Arab Revolt," "Tupac Encouraged the Arab Spring," "Inside Tunisia's Hip-Hop Revolution," "A Modern Revolution: Hip-Hop Shines over the Arab Spring," and "The Arab Spring Has a Dope Beat" proclaimed the central role of rap in the revolutions. Network after network excitedly put forth soundtracks of the Arab Spring featuring rappers, rockers, and singer-songwriters responsible for leading crowds into the streets.[2]

As in Edward Said's analysis of Western knowledge production vis-à-vis the "East," these narratives rely on a perception of South West Asia and

North Africa (SWANA) societies as fundamentally delayed in political development and *essentially* inhospitable to either political expression or innovative creative processes. Accordingly, they celebrate seeming anomalies in the characters of Arabic-language rappers speaking truth to power. This coverage is orientalist in that it celebrates these colorful, youthful characters emerging from violent, despotic backdrops without any attempts to understand the material conditions of which they are a part. Media representations of SWANA youth in coverage like this also conjures a particular *neoliberal orientalism* in how it mobilizes sanitized ideas of social justice strategies, racialized identities, and political aesthetics in place of material analysis.

Racialized ideas about Arab youth in mainstream media have oscillated between two caricatures: the nonviolent protester using creativity and mobile technology to speak truth to power and the vulnerable recruit to Islamist terror, seduced by technology into criminal religious underworlds.[3] Elsewhere I identified this as swinging between images of SWANA youth as "hip-hop revolutionaries" or "terrorist thugs."[4] As Ted Swedenburg has put it, the region's "imagined youths" are suspended between tradition and change—primed to be influenced by either American popular culture or Islamist fundamentalism.[5] These two images—nonviolent protester and terrorist—and the two sets of expectations attached to them—enthusiastic excitement and apprehensive disgust, respectively—are two sides of the same orientalist coin.

The shorthand that the "dope beat" of hip-hop offers racializes this imagination. The excitement about the role of hip-hop and rap in protests and the occupation of city squares during the uprisings attempts to approximate the political experiences of young people in Arab cities to a dematerialized and depoliticized rendition of political organizing and militant resistance in Black and brown neighborhoods in US inner cities. These excited and enthusiastic portrayals whitewash centuries of Black resistance and cultural production into caricatures of the haunts of gentrified neighborhoods, violently assimilating the creative capital of Black popular culture into American empire.[6] This kind of romanticized excitement about the political potential of Arab-Muslim youth coheres across a wide range of educational, political, and arts programming across the political center and left in the US and Europe. It has proven especially durable in the contexts of Palestine and Kurdistan, where identity, place, and performative declarations of solidarity regularly stand in for material analysis of imperial influence, especially the imperial flows of liberalism and progressivism. At the same time, these performative declarations of solidarity have also tended to at best overlook and at worst actively dismiss pervasive anti-Black racism in the region. In other words, both liberal imperialists and apologists for Arab and regional forms of anti-Black discrimination have been especially vulnerable to romanticized excitement about the power of hip-hop in Arabic.

To be sure, the most enthusiastic advocates of Arabic rap in the region also hoped the uprisings would be good for the scene. They saw in the wave of protests in 2011–2012 real development in political rap in Arabic. For example, in 2011, Jeddah-based radio host Big Hass (Hass Dennaoui) started a hip-hop radio blog called *Re-volt*.[7] His initial posts were enthusiastic about the "revolting" youth across different Arab countries and the connection of urban culture, hip-hop, graffiti, breakdancing, and other forms of creative expression with the exciting events of the Arab Uprisings.[8] Reading these pieces in 2011 and 2012, I found myself frequently jarred by his use of the word "revolting." Hass used it to mean "rebellious," "revolutionary," and "rebelling." But when I read "revolting," I kept seeing "disgusting." The glitch stuck in my head like a looped sample.

Aesthetics of Disgust

This chapter explores performances of distaste and disgust by Lebanese, Jordanian, and Palestinian rappers and their audiences. I offer this political, aesthetic, and performative emphasis on distaste and disgust as an alternative to the narrative of revolt and resistance most commonly found in writing about rap in Arabic. As Ted Swedenburg and Cristina Moreno-Almeida have already pointed out, locating Arab rappers and their work along a spectrum of resistance or co-optation blocks recognition of a range of political positions, attitudes, and affects rap music is capable of generating as well as a material analysis of the production of the music.[9] My own research, like Moreno-Almeida and Swedenburg's, builds on a growing literature within popular music and subcultural studies that identifies how the expectation of resistance, struggle, or refusal problematically perpetuates liberal visions of subjectivity as the only agents of political change.[10] I take Big Hass's double entendre seriously as a call to redirect an analysis of politics. In this chapter, I write against the seductive romanticization of resistance by immersing my attention in disgust. I explore two ways in which disgust and revulsion emerge as politicized aesthetics in some Arabic rap. In both, I argue that when rappers articulate distaste or revulsion in their lyrics and perform disgust, annoyance, or irritation in voice and gesture, they initiate cycles of call-and-response that hail emergent subjectivities and collectivities into being.

Focusing on an aesthetic repertoire of distaste and disgust shows how rappers mobilize anger, frustration, and annoyance as pleasure and release. My intention is that this focus on aesthetics and feeling centers a discussion of the politics of this music in the experiences of making and listening to it. As Moreno Almeida rightly points out, "Functionalist explanations hide the fact that many produce and listen to rap music because of the emotional experience."[11] That is, what the music invites listeners to feel and how it does so is a central part of its appeal.

Hass uses "revolting" as a catchword for a wide range of political meaning in rap, The political possibility in listening to revulsion, disgust, and distaste is myriad. I identify two very different uses and sets of meanings around articulations of disgust to gesture toward a spectrum of interpellation and the attendant production of political meaning that cannot be reduced to resistance or struggle. In the next chapter, I continue an elaboration of these aesthetics under the framework of *istifzaz*—Arabic for provocation, surprise, insult. There, I understand "revolting" and the feelings of disgust associated with it under a larger umbrella of aesthetic strategies used to frustrate listener expectations as they call listeners in.

Following poet and critic bell hooks, I understand aesthetics as "a way of inhabiting space" and "a way of looking and becoming."[12] To understand aesthetics as becoming—as opposed to a theory of beauty—offers a crucial opening to center the experience of filling the head as a political process. Moreover, hooks's understanding of radical aesthetics as in constant motion, acknowledging "that we are constantly changing positions," reflects the ways in which the search for music that fills the head is also always on the move. As the navigation of pleasure (and disgust) has been a central question of continental aesthetic philosophy since the eighteenth century,[13] the search for music that fills the head as a practice of discernment could be interpreted as a question of forming and performing musical taste. Ultimately, I want to caution against this kind of understanding of the practice of political listening as it seems to me at odds with *the feeling* of finding music that fills the head. The experience of *filling the head* is not attached to any one genre of music and does not always consistently accrue to specific artists. It is fleeting, evasive. If *taste* is the product of a subject being interpellated into a particular economic class, then what political work do performances of distaste do to hail audiences into listening publics? My exploration of disgust tries to push this understanding of push this understanding of (Bourdieu's) distinction by conceiving of taste, as Paul Geary has suggested, as "both socio-political and embodied."[14] Focusing on rap's aesthetics as a primary vehicle to explore politics in the genre means emphasizing that "many produce and listen to rap music because of the emotional experience" of doing so.[15] *Filling the head* centers these experiences and the affects central to them.

Disgust as an aesthetic envelope cuts straight to the heart of an inquiry centered on the experiences of listening to music. In this chapter, I linger on felicitous statements and performances of disgust because they have proven so useful in understanding yearning (chap. 4) and the search for particular kinds of relief associated with it as quite distinct from desire and the aesthetic qualities of beauty. As Sianne Ngai argues, "In its centrifugality, agonism, urgency, and above all refusal of the indifferently tolerable, disgust offers an entirely different set of aesthetic and critical possibilities from the one offered by desire."[16] Understanding the capacity of this music to fill the head hinges on a poetics of disgust and revulsion as much as it relies on a politics that is not revolt.

Constitutive Disgust

Much work in Western philosophy, especially the foundational work of Julia Kristeva, understands agjection — extreme disgust, subjective horror — as a collapse of the ego, a desire for a thing the self cannot tolerate. In this chapter, building on lyrics and performances of Nasserdayn, Jaafar, Katibeh 5, and others, and the literary theory of Tarek el-Ariss, I argue for an understanding of constitutive disgust. Disgust that is constitutive understands that the abject is too close to *threaten* collapse. Rather, the collapse *is already*. It is ongoing, inherited. This is quite a different relationship than a tantalizing return to a rotting corpse. Rappers cannot alluringly invite listeners to peek at and then turn away from an identified object of disgust. Instead, they invite listeners to feel and acknowledge precisely the suffocating collapse. Repressed elsewhere, these invitations to recognize constitutive disgust are felt as release, pleasure, relief.

Recognizing this suffocating condition means acknowledging that there is no subject position from which to spit out or spit back. As Clarice

Lispector writes in a passage quoted by Sianne Ngai in the epigraph of this chapter, "I spat and spat and it kept on being me." Or as Sot Gilgamesh says in the lyrics paired with Lispector, *"Muqrif al-wada' al- 'arabi fa bistafrigh 'ala al-madina fiha al-qaraf* (The state of the Arab world is disgusting, so I throw up on a city filled with filth)." I understand expressions of disgust as a reaching for release *without* desiring rupture—as embodied navigations of yearning. Disgust opens windows to a politics of becoming without break, rupture, or revolt—that is instead all suffocation and impossibility. There is no distance to be claimed here, no inversion of disgust into gritty heroism. Meeting disgust with disgust is rather a commentary on a blocked constitutive reality. The existing frames to call listeners into struggle have stagnated and feel forced; *they too are disgusting*. No alternative is proposed.

My point is that these expressions of disgust illuminate a very different practice of political interpellation than one that invites a listener to rally and resist. Moreover, there is a crystalline relief in political commentary that explicitly doesn't do so. These experiences of listening can have the pleasurable effect of filling the head.

Tfeh!

Around 10 pm there are maybe forty-five people in the Metro Al Madina theatre, some seated, some standing. In and outside the theatre, Hamra is very quiet. Finally, Jaafar bursts from behind the red curtain and straight off the stage. He seems embarrassed or uncomfortable. He moves quickly and sporadically, rapping almost to himself. . . . Osloob stands onstage with a mixer and a laptop. He suggests multiple times, in different tones, some commanding, some more jocular, that Jaafar slow down or repeat a verse so that people can understand the words. Jaafar refuses. . . .

Many audience members already know the new tracks by heart. Despite being treated with ostensible derision by the rapper, they are eager to sing along with him. Jaafar frequently turns his back on Osloob and the audience. He tosses the microphone away dismissively when the sound accidentally cuts out of it and screams his verses into the void of the half-filled house without a mic. The audience shouts their approval. When he has finished his set, he leaves the stage quickly. He seems tired, irritated, fed up. There is no encore.

Afterwards, outside in front of the theatre, a young woman who attended the concert asks to stand next to me until her ride arrives. "It's not safe at night," she explains. "People here [in Hamra] are rude," she says and explains matter-of-factly they'll make fun of her for wearing a veil. I ask her what she thought of the concert and she bubbles over with enthusiasm. She has raps of her own she has shared with Jaafar.[17]

In 2013, the Syrian Uprising was in the process of escalating into civil war. That month, Syrian president Bashar al-Assad used chemical weapons on residents of Ghouta, a suburb of Damascus. The voicing of US intentions to use military options in Syria came the same week residents of the southern suburb of Beirut reeled from a sequence of suicide bombings. The mood was tense, somber, and quiet.

The headliner of the concert at Metro Al Madina in its then home on Hamra Street was Jaafar, formerly of the duo Touffar. Onstage with him was Osloob of Katibeh 5. Jaafar is from Hermel, in the Bekaaʿ, one of Lebanon's notoriously othered geographies. During the concert that night in the capital, Beirut, the lyrics of Jaafar's tracks addressed a range of class-based grievances, incriminating "polite" Lebanese society. On top of these lyrical expressions of distaste, Jaafar enacted physical gestures of disgust that did not go unnoticed by the audience. Jaafar's gesture of *spitting* invited his gathered listeners to reconsider the excitement of the event.[18] The rapper almost seemed to be resisting the audience itself, if not the very fact that he was performing. He turned his back on them, denied requests from them, complained loudly about sound or light onstage, and so forth. But this hostility, which seemed to be understood, was not directed at audience members or sound technicians and was ostensibly part of the concert itself. His disavowals and refusals of performance etiquette were met with rallied support from the audience standing in Metro's stage-level pit. When Jaafar spit with distaste on his colleagues, the crew, and the audience gathered in front of him, he pronounced a specific politics that may have been interpreted in his lyrics but that were not always a part of the aesthetics of the venue. The audience responded with measured enthusiasm to the disgust Jaafar spit (lyrically) and the distaste he embodied (gesturally, physically).

They had gathered in Metro explicitly to hear Jaafar despite the tense and unpleasant political malaise that had settled upon the neighborhood of Hamra that night. When he performed disgust, when he appeared irritated, fed up, disappointed, or otherwise unimpressed with his surroundings, he was specifically connecting with this audience, who may also have been skeptical of the hipster-esque dynamics of the (literally) underground theater in which the concert was held. In the transmission and reception of this spitting, audience and performer embodied a raised middle finger that accompanied the lyrical one, that denounced how cosmopolitan and upper-middle-class Beirut actively others the Bekaaʿ. The vociferous approval that Jaafar gestures of distaste received completed this affective exchange. Distinguished from the lyrical one, it did not merely reflect the meaning of the words that Jaafar shouted. Lyric and gesture together magnified the performance of disgust and furthered the impact of either element in isolation.

Distaste and irritation were also evident in the stance of the young fan outside the theater. As she lingered next to me, a stranger, until her ride arrived, she objected to the notion that the hip district of Hamra, with its then bustling, cosmopolitan vibe, might be inclusive or festive. Instead, she was vocal and deliberate about spitting it out, marking herself off from it. Her initial mode of reaching out to me came from a feeling of distaste or distrust with our shared milieu. This gesture built on the distaste Jaafar had embodied in the theater and helped her navigate what was to her the foreign space of Hamra Street.

Spitting, a practice long recognized in hip-hop and hip-hop studies, is both lyrical and gestural, both literal and metaphorical. In any language, rappers literally spit to enunciate. But rappers also spit into the *cypher*—a physical circle where freestyling between two or more rappers, or breakdancing between B-boys or B-girls takes place, and also an affective relation held between a community of listeners and other rappers. Spitting into the cypher means entering the lyrical, gestural, and affective fray. As such, it is always a practice of calling in, an invitation. These invitations are pathways to other suns. To feel different centers of gravity.

In his work on global breakdancing, Imani Kai Johnson provocatively describes the cypher as "not things but acts" where participants engage in "a multi-sensorial, collective experience cloaked as an individual one."[19] These individual-collective experiences in the cypher are integral to the sensation of filling the head and necessary for the processes of political becoming attached to aesthetics within them. Spitting in an affective mode close to the Arabic colloquial onomatopoeia *tfeh!* interpellates an individual listener into the cypher as a literal spray of water. The listener, finding herself wet with spit, catches herself surprised, refreshed, pissed off, annoyed. Her body responds: tears, heart pounding, clenched fists, eyes wide. She replays the deck; she looks to the side to find others listening. Et voilà: the cypher as a wet zone of relation and recognition. You heard that too? The wetness on your skin also picking up this electricity?

* * *

The first repertoire of disgust I identify finds its power in illuminating the ways in which those cast out of a certain cosmopolitan social fabric might respond. Much literature on the politics of disgust in the US and Europe notes how discourses and expressions of disgust have been concerned with processes of casting off—typically of minorities, the poor, migrants, refugees, and other "undesirables." For example, Sara Ahmed's work on the performativity of disgust notes how disgust sticks to certain groups while the act of saying "that's disgusting!" can work as "a form of vomiting, as an attempt to expel something."[20] This is how ejection of the migrant or the native from the body politic as unclean works to shore up the coherence of the nation.[21]

I frame this first set of examples around rappers expressing disgust with such disgust. I summon the concert of the Lebanese rapper Jaafar Touffar in the underground theater of Metro Al Madina in Beirut's Hamra district, related above, and some of the work of the Palestinian group Katibeh 5 as examples. Touffar and Katibeh 5 deliberately retain and channel disgust, irritation, and anger in their lyrics and affect while they call in the outcast, poor Lebanese from the Bekaaʿ and Palestinian listener, respectively. The effect of listening to these rappers is quite different from that of listening to more popular outfits who have perfected hyping up heterogeneous crowds via unifying chants of revolution or resistance. Touffar and Katibeh 5 deliberately do not hail wide audiences. They instead reach abject minorities and encourage those listeners to recognize their strength in this difference. This rap succeeds in cultivating a longing for collectivity among a specific demographic that is usually cast out, spit out, shat upon. As has been identified in other genres of global hip-hop, this kind of work allows rappers, and by extension their audiences, to *spit back* at dominant narratives and oppressive practices.

Katibeh 5 was a crew of five Palestinian MCs born and raised in the Bourj al-Barajneh refugee camp in the south of Beirut. In 2014, Katibeh 5 was invited to Ireland for a concert. Four of them traveled to and then applied for asylum in the UK and did not return. Separated from each other and their audiences in the camp, the group disbanded. Osloob, the producer and lone member of Katibeh 5 (onstage during Jaafar's set, described above) who stayed behind, now resides in France.

In Katibeh 5's track "Hadini iza feek" ("Hold Me Back If You Can") off their 2010 album *Tareeq Wahed Marsoum* (*One Way Decree*), disgust boils over. It starts with a snare drum playing a simple four-quarter pattern in 4/4, with a roll on each third beat, very much like a military march. There is a piano playing a B-flat (minor third in the tonal center) on the same rhythm underneath. In the second measure, a digital drum layer is introduced with some high hats and cross sticks. Then the rap begins. Their voices are low and guttural while a flute plays a melodic refrain above both the march and their recorded verses.[22] "Hadini iza feek" plays with narratives of explosive discomfort and reactions to expressions of that distaste, but the track also pushes these refusals of politeness further. This piece's beat underscores a militancy echoed in the lyrics throughout.

"Hadini iza feek" reinvents the image of the Palestinian in Lebanon: not as pathetic victim—as principled, defiant. By expressing disdain for and distancing themselves from the abject image of the dispossessed Palestinian common in Lebanese society, Katibeh 5 spit out what Lebanese society has asked them to swallow.[23] Consider when the group raps:

> Great!
> As long as you are taking my point of view seriously
> You're allowed to be taken aback and to show your irritation
> Just like you show your irritation at my presence
> Because I am a friend to all the images that are not desirable
> This is how we live out these images and no one chooses their life specifically
> I'll tell you
> The pressure of bullets and gunpowder does not allow you to move away
> Experience will guide you on the road
> Hold me back if you can[24]

When they say, "As long as you are taking my point of view seriously / You're allowed to be taken aback and to show your irritation," Katibeh 5 acknowledge the Lebanese audience listening, anticipating their surprise and irritation. At the same time, they dictate the terms of that reception, both "allowing" their surprise and framing it with derision (the sarcastic "*'aal!*" ["*great!*"] that opens the verse). Disgust is palpable throughout—first as derision and then as power. This spitting invites listeners into the cypher. The track invites the listener to recognize, acknowledge, decide: hold me back, if you can.

Rapper and producer Osloob explained to me the awkward reception of Katibeh 5 when they performed this piece as part of the Fête de la Musique in Monot, downtown Beirut, in the early 2000s:

> We knew these were not our audiences. The Lebanese are used to seeing the sad, poor Palestinian. We didn't fit that image. The Palestinian that is a little violent: this image bothers lots of people. Not everyone is able to stand this idea. I think like sixty or seventy percent of Lebanese can't stand to see a Palestinian in this image.
> REZ: *Even people coming to your concerts?*
> Of course. Even Touffar, even Jaafar's audience and fans. Even this audience is not always willing to see a Palestinian in a strong position. The Lebanese audience needs to see the Palestinian as a victim.[25]

In these remarks, Osloob recounts how the track, while popular with their fan base in the Palestinian refugee camps in Lebanon, received a chilly reception when the group performed it before a mixed audience during a concert held downtown. In this example, we can see how spitting worked to engage and connect some audiences while deliberately alienating others. This is a call-and-response that is not about hyping up a heterogeneous audience to a syncopated refrain. This spat disgust is an invitation to recognize relationships, a calling into the cypher, a spray of wetness picking up electricity.

These examples in the work of Jaafar, Katibeh 5, and other rappers in Lebanon, Palestine, and Jordan acknowledge specific demographics and places: Palestinian, Lebanese, Bekaaʽ, Beirut, and so forth. In other examples I draw on in this chapter, the embodied refusal in articulations of disgust illuminates a multipolar political force field in which rappers invite listeners to recognize themselves. These performances of distaste and disgust cannot rally a recognizable collective into being and do not promise the retrieval of an abject hero. They cannot do so because they do not identify binaries of oppressor and oppressed, dominator and dominated, neglecting and neglected. Instead, this rap conjures an exhausting, all-encompassing *wadaʽ muqrif*—a disgusting condition—that rappers call on their listeners to recognize themselves within.

Qaraf

I first noticed the graffito on Dbayeh road sometime in late 2011 or early 2012 (fig. 1.1). An anonymous face void of features but greenish with nausea spews forth a rainbow of droplets. A red *X* ensures that we don't see the figure's eyes, emphasizing its cartoonish sickness. Next to the figure, in white balloon text, the word *'arraftouna*, Arabic for "you have disgusted us."[26] Painted on the Dbayeh highway barrier at eye level for those sitting in traffic, the unassuming graffito sits like a quiet reminder of legions of similarly

Figure 1.1. Graffito on Dbayeh road in Beirut. It reads, "*'Arraftouna*" ("You disgust us"). Photograph by the author, September 2012.

fed up, dusty, ignored, exhausted, spitting up people. Every time I saw it, my heart skipped a tiny beat: a spark of recognition in the otherwise drab expanse of billboards advertising cosmetic surgery and cologne; in the endless sprawl of box stores and strip malls; in the dense mob of traffic. From its generic, grayed face and distorted mouth, a spewing forth of a colorful panoply of exhaustion.

The graffito on Dbayeh road is a specific political utterance, a particular iteration of political disgust. Its object is not the pitifully downcast, as in much political discourse of disgust. The Palestinian, the Syrian, the African or South Asian migrant worker, the peasant, the poor all embody a narrow space between victim, object of sympathy, and intruder, burden, and threat. Yet, the "stickiness" of the abject, to borrow again from Sara Ahmed, is more pervasive and not limited to these groups. This is not the disgust of social "pollution and contamination"—to use Mary Douglas's phrase—that conservative commentators invoke, bemoaning the arrival of refugees, migrants, and other "undesirables."[27] Instead, the cartoon's vomit tries to disgustedly eject a whole network of players, actions, and institutions—the pitifully abject failures of the Lebanese state and its ruling oligarchies; the hypocrisy and failure of "the Left," the international community, and "cosmopolitan" society; and progressivism as represented by these. In turn, the *-na* suffix indicating "us" in *'arraftouna* ("you disgust us") is not a *we* demarcated by a specific sect, class, gender, or race. It is all of us sitting under billboards waiting in traffic.

The disgust in the graffito on Dbayeh road, and which I suggest runs through lyrical and performatic experimentation in some Arabic rap and hip-hop, is critical for understanding how yearning connects listeners and musicians through the search for music that *fills the head*. As Ahmed argues, expressions of disgust also function to release or distance the speaker from the object of disgust. But instead of distancing themselves from a particular body or bodies, these collective voicings of *qaraf* ("disgust") work to release the speaker from held tension of bad options in a political impasse. These articulations of exhaustion by, frustration with, and rejections of omnipresent debility and fatigue express disgust while acknowledging loss and longing. Here, disgust cannot be cast out or away from the speaker; it is constitutive of her political reality.

Consider, for example, the 2015 collaboration track "Nihna w al-zibl jeeran" ("We Are Neighbors with Dung") by the Lebanese rappers Nasserdayn al-Touffar and El Rass. Written during the #YouStink protests (2015–2016) sparked by a crisis in garbage collection in Beirut, the track channeled anger directly at the current government, its corruption, and, even more specifically, Solidere[28] by name (*"ma fi reehah bi solidere, ma fi zbaleh bi solidere, hiyeh al-zbaleh solidere"* ("There's no smell *in* Solidere, there's no trash *in* Solidere, Solidere *is* the waste")).[29] While it channeled disgust at Solidere, the track is notable for how it figures proximity with the object of disgust. The *zibl*, dung, manure, shit is not out there, coming closer, threatening us with its arrival. It is here, on the same street, in our building, under our roof: *we are neighbors*. It doesn't smell, portending a rot to come; it is not something to be cleaned or reformed; it is the decay itself, and we are it. The song's title plays on the Lebanese diva Fairouz's famous "Nihna w al-qamar jeeran" ("The Moon Is Our Neighbor," 1960), which evokes a love affair shared under moonlight. The fall from grace invoked in Nasserdayn and El Rass's title makes that situatedness within decay that much more palpable. It deliberately drags the romance of the Fairouz predecessor and associated ideas of Lebanon and Beirut into the disgust and rot of the Solidere-induced trash crisis. The juxtaposition in the intimacy with the garbage vs. proximity to the moon marks the distance between 2015 and 1960 and imagined ideas of belonging to and within the Lebanese state.

In his book *Trials of Arab Modernity: Literary Affects and the New Political*, Tarek El-Ariss analyzes a nineteenth-century travelogue of a Lebanese writer in exile in Britain and France. In making a case for how Arab writers encountered, confronted, and rewrote narratives of modernity not contingent on Western models of the same, El-Ariss focuses in part on descriptions of what he calls Ahmed Faris al-Shidyaq's "aversion to civilization."[30] Al-Shidyaq's descriptions of revulsion to English food, city living, and rural poverty invert the narratives of modernization and civilization British imperialism was at the time forcing on much of the planet. El-Ariss suggests that in al-Shidyaq's writings, "The body of the Arab traveler is staged as a site of ingestion and expulsion, incorporation and rejection of European food and ideological models."[31] In making his argument, El-Ariss rejects a psychoanalytic reading of the retching, fainting, and queasiness al-Shidyaq describes. Referring to the Bulgarian French psychoanalyst Julia Kristeva's work on abjection, El-Ariss suggests that al-Shidyaq's "visceral reaction to rotten meat and disgusting food could not be reduced to a collapse in the ego."[32]

Kristeva's reading of abjection in her essay *Powers of Horror* centers on the distinction of self and other.[33] For Kristeva, the abject threatens a breakdown in meaning because it blurs the boundaries of the self. Hence, expressions of disgust work to protect the ego by distancing it from the abject. Kristeva argues that expressions of disgust are necessary because abjection is a tension of both erotic desire and "primal" revulsion. The abject "fascinates desire" while producing revulsion. Kristeva writes that the abject "simultaneously beseeches and pulverizes the subject."[34] This tension "draws [the subject] towards the place where meaning collapses," where the border between self and other is no longer perceptible.[35]

El-Ariss contends that this reading will not do to understand Al-Shidyaq in Europe. He suggests that the *"shameless"* omnipresence of decay in Al-Shidyaq's writings means that the abject is never really repressed; it is constitutive.[36] There is no hope of "return" to the scene of the abject—the decaying corpse, the rotting meat, and so on—because, in fact, there is no exit from this stage of decay and rot. El-Ariss suggests that disgust in al-Shidyaq's work cannot be read as a Kristevan "collapse" of the self because the thing with "perverse erotic fascination" is in pure view: indeed, it is everywhere, banal, quotidian, sham*eless*.

El-Ariss's identification of an articulation of disgust that is "constitutive" of what the author lives is a useful alternative to a Kristevan reading of the abject. The "constitutiveness of decay" that El-Ariss located in al-Shidyaq's "aversion to civilization" also frames the disgusted spitting laced through disgusted aesthetics in some experimental rap and hip-hop. Which is to say, the ambivalent desire that Kristeva theorizes is not present in expressions of disgust among my interlocutors in Ramallah, Amman, and Beirut. Articulated disgust with the political system or disgusted elaborations of a number of its very real problems does not imply that these speakers of disgust are somehow drawn back, despite themselves, to the scene of corruption, crime, or abuse. Disgusting realities are not fascinating in their morose appeal: They are suffocating in their seeming permanence. Expressed disgust in this context is as much suffocation as it is revulsion, as much exhaustion as it is disavowal.

As such, raps that channel this exhaustion (*inhak*) as articulated disgust do not so much signal abjection as a "collapse of the ego" as they are political performatives that enact the taking in of breath *through*, not away from, the contamination of the pollutant. The "stickiness" of this disgust has less to do with a simultaneous desire for the object of disgust as it does an impossible desire to actually be rid of it.[37] Indeed, one's inability to rid oneself of the disgusting mess is a big part of why it disgusts, thereby driving the lyrical and gestured *tfeh!* of spitting. Spitting on the disgusting thing defiles it further. But when one spits—not on a beggar or the racialized Other but on social filth, systemic corruption, and institutionalized theft—it is not clear how much distance one actually gets from it, especially since there is nowhere to go to be rid of it anyway.

A millennial generation of Arabs increasingly identify the misfires of narratives of pan-Arabism, the relative cosmopolitanism of these capital cities (the oasis of "the good life" in a region plagued by conservative religiosity and authoritarianism), and reject or refuse the optimism these images conjure, identifying them as "cruel" but also as false, disappointing, ineffective, pathetic.[38] Disgust, without trying to be "resistance," productively disavows affects of hope, nostalgia, and romanticism. A rejection of and articulation of disgust with Beirut's pretensions to cosmopolitanism are thread through lyrical and musical practices of spitting in other live concerts and mediated recordings. In the buildup and aftermath of Lebanon's protests against political corruption in 2015 and 2019, these performances of disgust became more acute and more popular. Prominent among these expressions of disgust are those that expel romanticism or idealism. In these, nostalgia and romanticism are spit from the body of the rapper as if illusions contaminate or poison the speaker. In the work of the rap duo Touffar, but also of Katibeh 5, El Rass, and others, we can see the disgust for certain kinds of politicized romanticism as a rejection of what the literature scholar Lauren Berlant calls a "desire for the political." In this sense, the disgust for and articulated disavowal of certain kinds of nostalgia and romanticism are a conscious rejection of "cruel optimism."[39]

Much rap *about* the city of Beirut performs the types of disgust I am discussing here and refuses the romance with the city. "Beirut Khaybetna" ("Beirut, Our Disappointment," 2013) is a another good example.[40] The piece is also a collaboration between Nasserdayn al-Touffar and El Rass, with music and production by Wattar, of the Syrian group Latlatleh. Nasserdayn's verse opens the piece, the beginning of which berates the "left" of Beirut:

> This is talk of [the Right of] Return, it goes best with *mazzeh*,
> Jaffa won't be liberated unless the sushi is fresh
> And the free, leftist revolutionary
> Won't bring up Palestine except when there is cold beer and girls
> You like Najji el-Ali so much?
> The cartoon Handala is turned around gawking at tits
> The hammer and sickle became an umbrella and the white dove of secularism
> But by the order of the religious authorities and history, the color red, blood, and the DshK[41] turned pink from the ground meat of UNESCO
> Tell me how did the Left become "democratic"?
> Money came from Europe to muzzle it
> Brother, return the Left from those who stole it—that guy sweating from his forehead, about to toast his glass of *arak*.[42]

In this verse, Nasserdayn berates a particular kind of Beirut sociality, likely situated in the pubs and restaurants of Hamra street (exactly where Jaafar's concert took place, discussed above), where self-proclaimed leftists engage in political discussion over small plates of traditional Lebanese food (*mazzah*). Here, with Lebanese Almaza (a local beer) and in the company of *sabaya* (young women—open sociality with Lebanese women being another romanticized Lebanese stereotype), these "leftist revolutionaries" discuss the Right of Return to and liberation of Palestine. But Nasserdayn calls out this posturing and cosmopolitanism as invested in only *a sense* of Arabness (mazzeh and *arak*, an anise-flavored alcoholic drink), which is invoked to flirt or, worse, to womanize (Palestinian graphic artist Naji al-Ali's iconic character Handala's back is turned because he is distracted by women's breasts). Nasserdayn continues to spit on the failures of the Left, his voice more loaded with disgust as the verse progresses, announcing that revolutionary red (communism), spilled blood, and engaged struggle has been diluted ("turned pink") by the waste ("ground meat") of the UN. His call "Brother, return the Left from those who stole it!" is both an indictment pronounced with disgust at the failures of the Left and what it has become and a statement riven with longing, wishing for the mobilized return of something worth believing in.

This critique of the Left under the title of "Beirut, Our Disappointment" makes its statement about the selling out of a political idea also a criticism of social posturing particular to Beirut but recognizable in both Ramallah and Amman. In his verse, Nasserdayn clearly expresses disgust with talk and no action but also the posturing of Beiruti liberals as they masquerade as political visionaries. His verse is an example of rap energy in Beirut that specifically invokes the heroes and strategies of the Arab Left in the twentieth century.[43] Musically, the whole track is underscored by a single 'oud. The trills on the stringed instrument counter the disgust of the lyrical spitting with the pronounced expression of loss and longing. As the three musicians declare their attachments to cities and places outside of Beirut, the "disappointment" in the track's title, its chorus, and the disgust in the lyrics stages a disavowal of the romance with Beirut as home of "the good life."[44]

* * *

The Palestinian writer and historian Rana Issa opens her stunning essay "Khatem Izdihar" ("Izdihar's Ring") with the darkly comic metaphor of the young author pissing herself in traffic.[45] A urologist offers the diagnosis that shame and fear are keeping her from regularly emptying her bladder and thus causing these incidents where she finds herself sitting in her own filth. Unable to follow through on the doctor's prescriptions, she instead sets out to identify "the reason, not the solution" to her incontinence. In the essay, Issa explores the linked traumas handed down from grandmother to mother to daughter from the Arab Revolt through the Nakba through the Lebanese Civil War. She tells the stories of her grandmother and her mother, the choices they were forced to make and misfortunes that befell them in the Palestinian refugee camps of Lebanon and, eventually, the hospitals within them. As she does so, she wrestles with her own palpable disgust with her mother and her mother's mother and the men and women around them.

The point is not a litany of the sociocide committed against Palestinian women by the Occupation, the Lebanese, or Palestinians themselves. Instead, Issa's provocation is to ask, "How do we get free of those we love?" How to *navigate*—not break with—a constitutive disgust? A *qaraf* that is of me because it is me. A disgust located in *an inheritance*, in lineage, *in love*—not a rotting corpse or an oozing cockroach—but whose stench, whose ooze is suffocating perhaps because of the impossibility of being rid of it. A disgust that does not make her wretch or gag but that she cannot keep from seeping from her, pooling around her, sinking into the car seat cushion. A disgust that makes disgust. It is no accident that the accident Issa opens her essay with takes place inside a vehicle, in blocked traffic, like the graffito on Dbayeh highway.

Issa's depiction of disgust, shame, anger, and sadness is informative for understanding the political significance of navigating constitutive disgust. Issa is explicit in refusing the possibility that she might be free of the sadness, anger, resentment, anxiety, or depression that her disgust with her maternal forbears provokes. She writes, "It is easy for men to become discontented with inheritance, as Harold Bloom diagnosed in his critique of literary history. It is enough just to kill the father to make James Joyce or any other man a respectable writer. As for women, they cannot be killed as a metaphor for learning to write." In this, Issa offers a feminist approach to disgust and yearning tied to a model for the political that refuses the possibility of rupture. This is a kind of yearning—irritated, annoyed, ashamed, and depressed—that acknowledges the impossibility of being free of the same.

How do we get free from those we love? is a productive question in a discussion of the aesthetics of rap in Arabic. It is so not because the things rappers rap about—failures of the Left, cosmopolitan society, Arab middle classes, and so forth, as described in the tracks above—are things rappers also, somehow, love. It is a productive question because it positions trauma and the experience of inheritance—literal and political patrimony—as a central, inextricable part of political becoming. *How do we get free from those we love?* is a powerful aesthetic and affective frame within which to explore the political. It is an invitation into relation, into a cypher of (im)possibilities. It is a call to imagine political becoming that does not require a death (of the author, of the father); that does not prefigure break, rupture, or resistance. In doing so, Issa's figure, incontinent and stuck in traffic, models political becoming completely free from the search for and appearance of resistive agency. Her essay invites the reader to imagine history and future as inseparable and the present as incurable. The invitation is freeing, riveting, appalling. Something inside sighs, screams, flips over. This is what rap sounds like.

* * *

A disgusted listener listens differently. She demands different strategies, responds to different invitations. The music that fills her head, that provides temporary relief to this listener, is particular. It necessarily invites her to relate to and move through frustration, distaste, malaise, and resentment.

Enter *istifzaz*. The next chapter explores invitations to know and (re)make the world otherwise. I trace an epistemology for istifzaz, Arabic for "surprise, provocation," in experimental rap in Arabic as a way of digging further into how effective invitations to listen work. They are particular invitations that acknowledge a perpetual state of limbo, a depletion of options, and the constant confrontation with disappointment and disgust.

2

ISTIFZAZ

Bastafazzak ʿa beat kharra zay wijjak
(The shitty beat's in your shitty face)
MUQATAʿA

It is the glitch that incites anticipation—that ecstasy of interference.
LEGACY RUSSELL

THE TRACK BEGINS WITH A STRINGED INSTRUMENT, PROBABLY an electric bass or guitar, being plucked and detuned at the same time. Then a repeated harmonic sample, the bass alternating between a C-sharp and G-sharp. The rapper's voice comes in after a distorted ah-ah-ah as if he was quickly hitting his throat with the back of his hand. Maybe because we can almost feel that pressure on the throat, nausea laces the opening of the track. When his voice emerges from this distortion, it is thick with sarcasm. We are in a mirror of the harmonic devices underlying Ramallah Underground's "Min al-Kaheff" ("From the Cave") (see Intro). But in strong contrast with that piece, it seems almost every element here is highly distorted in one way or another. In place of the interference layered on top of Ramallah Underground's voices in "Min al-Kaheff," Palestinian rapper Shuaʿa's voice here is distorted with derision, with contempt, with scorn.[1]

The track is "Qaboor al-Qarn," released by Palestinian rapper Shuaʿa in the middle of the 2014 bombardment of Gaza. Shuaʿa raps about the ridiculousness of staying "patient," specifically lambasting a political imagination that has failed to offer young Palestinians a future. "*Zay al-hamameh ʿal-beit bidalak sabr inta w ana*," he says, offering a cynical inversion of the populist Palestinian narratives of *sabr* and *sumud* (steadfastness and resilience), stripping the humanity from them and rendering them dumb, repetitive, self-destructive. "You and me, like the pigeons on the roof, got to be patient," he raps.² The track is a good example of the dark humor in some experimental rap coming out of Ramallah. Pigeons' inability to move toward another horizon is related as sabr or patience.³ This inverts the romance around sabr in traditional Palestinian cultural production, poking fun at it. Shuaʻa's track is a good place to recognize, as I suggested in the previous chapter, that a disgusted listener demands to be called differently. A listener that is fed up, pissed off, and exhausted needs a different invitation.

In this chapter, I describe experiences of listening in live concerts to illustrate an epistemology of experimental Arabic rap that I understand under an umbrella of istifzaz. Through istifzaz—Arabic for "surprise, provocation, insult"—I dig further into how experimental Arab rappers invite listeners into the cypher. In the previous chapter, I explored performative spitting as part of an aesthetics of disgust that calls listeners into new orbits, new centers of gravity. That chapter concluded with a proposal to understand disgust not as an urge to spit out but as a condition that is constitutive. In this chapter, I explore an epistemology of istifzaz to address practices of staging surprise and frustrating expectation through which rappers navigate authenticity and identity. These negotiations forge collectivity otherwise. Collectivity fomented by istifzaz paradoxically coheres across invitations to *dis*engage and relies on isolating listeners before inviting their relation to larger wholes. These invitations to disengage are acutely aware of, even collaboratively shaped by, the constitutive disgust discussed in the previous chapter.

Global hip-hop has been understood as an interconnected set of creative activities that "do things" to participants.[4] Rapping is one of these activities, alongside tagging (graffiti), beatboxing, breaking (breakdancing), and turntabling (DJing).[5] Across these activities, practitioners and researchers have identified a constellation of meaning-making processes. Marc Lamont Hill identifies a central four among these, including signifying, born of Black expressive culture, using wordplay, and embodying a trickster character[6]; performing authenticity—that is, being "real"; exploring and expressing individual identity[7]; and building patterns of exchange and belonging—what Halifu Osumare has called "connective marginalities,"[8] what H. Samy Alim calls the hip-hop "umma,"[9] and what is more generally evoked as the Hip-Hop Nation. These four meaning-making processes underpin activity across and alongside the cypher and invite participants to know the world and engage in its (re)making. They inform a hip-hop epistemology—a shared way of knowing and making the world.

I am suggesting that the significance of some experimental rap in Arabic lies in understanding an epistemology built on istifzaz. Rappers draw on a praxis that centers surprise and provocation in order to invite listeners into a specific knowing the world otherwise. In this chapter, I center rappers' testimony about their work and their reflections on developments in the scene to highlight the particular ways this rap works as a navigation of authenticity and identity. The proposal I make here is in conversation with global hip-hop studies exploring the connections between aesthetics, belonging and epistemology, especially Imani Kai Johnson's emphasis in *Dark Matter in Breaking Cyphers* on the embodied and performative "ingredients for an alternative sensibility."[10]

I am also drawing from a theoretically rich literature that has sought to nuance and texture some of the practices that make up digital cultures and aesthetics in the millennial Arab world: Tarek El-Ariss's work on how leaking subjects use *fadh* ("exposing, shaming"); Laura Marks on Arabic glitch; and Laila Sakr on how technobodies reveal relational infrastructures underpinning "imaginaries of solidarity," among others.[11] These works importantly do not predetermine politics in the digital or artistic practices discussed. Laila Sakar states that "the glitch is a cloud of unknowing—*there is no* specific ontology, epistemology, or politics."[12] In this way, istifzaz too troubles ways of knowing without forcing ideology or politics.

Notably different from some of these other approaches to glitchy strategies in the region, istifzaz, as I explore it in this chapter, does not take governments, authorities, or other powerful players as its object. Disgust discussed in the previous chapter does not perform rupture or break. Similarly, istifzaz does not hail power. Rather, the provoked object, the recipient of Muqataʿa's *bastafazak ʿa beat kharra zay wijak* (used as the epigraph: "the shitty beat's in your shitty face"), is a fellow rapper, an invited listener. My proposal in this chapter of how glitch may function politically continues my emphasis on reading politics as embodied in rappers' calls into the cypher and audiences' listening practices within it. Ultimately, I argue that istifzaz allows us to see how what Sakr calls a "dialectic of the glitch," which is crucial to understanding yearning as becoming.[13]

While drawing on the legacies of global hip-hop, in this chapter I also turn to tech and art theory to focus specific attention on how a politics of noise, interference, disruption, and static produces frustration that nonetheless succeeds in calling listeners into the cypher and building a specific kind of collectivity. I follow Black feminist Legacy Russell's understandings of glitch as a "point of departure" and a "slippery area" that "incites anticipation."[14] This framing of provoking (as inciting, departing, anticipating) is significant in how it structures political invitations into the cypher. Russell's centering of pleasure in how glitch works is also important—something I return to in chapter 4. In this chapter, her work allows me to underscore moments of reception when "the audience may become aware of preprogrammed patterns. Now, a distributed awareness of a new interaction gestalt can take form."[15] I suggest that this is the opening that learning to listen politically promises.

These navigations of frustration and anticipation do not reach every listener the same way. As such, this chapter lays the groundwork for understanding that listening to experimental rap is very much a practice listeners commit to and develop, the absence of which musicians bemoan. The next chapter, devoted to the cultivation of listening practices, shows how the success of a concert should not be reduced to the political economy of concert tickets or venue aesthetics.

Al-Missfah (The Filter)

Rappers in many languages use call-and-response to energize an audience. Moreover, antiphonal exchange or communication, call-and-response, has been taken up by an interdisciplinary range of research. Hip-hop studies, African ethnomusicology, and African American religious studies, as well as treatments of protest strategies (e.g., the use of the "human microphone" during Occupy Wall Street protests in New York City in 2011), all suggest that call-and-response is significant in how it is able to create community.[16] For example, historian Robert Farris Thompson calls call-and-response "perfected social interaction" in that it brings individuals together to act as one body.[17] Communication scholars Jack L. Daniel and Geneva Smitherman concur, adding, "Call-and-response seeks to synthesize 'speakers' and 'listeners' in a unified movement."[18] The literature on call-and-response assumes a building of audience community when the practice is effective.

Arab rappers and MCs also use antiphonal strategies to connect with and activate their audiences.[19] In contrast with the traditional patterns that usually aim to unite an audience in the same refrain, however, istifzaz as call-and-response exacerbates fractures and fissures within audiences isolating listeners. Aesthetic choices like those under a framework of disgust, discussed in the previous chapter, recognize and deliberately exacerbate heterogeneity among audiences. Moreover, experimental strategies of calling listeners into the cypher under the framework of istifzaz are highly dependent on infelicitous interpellation—when the invitation to a listener falls flat. Istifzaz does not reach everyone the same way. Spitting assumes that some listeners, finding themselves suddenly wet with spit, will be annoyed and disengage. They will opt out. The cypher holds what remains. Istifzaz draws attention to how these invitations work.

This epistemology built on istifzaz distinguishes experimental distinguishes experimental rap in Arabic sonically, affectively, and politically from other forms of political rap and hip-hop. It remakes patterns of interactions with listeners. Unlike much global hip-hop or other forms of antiphonal communication that use call-and-response to rouse, rally, or unite a listening audience, the rappers of the *saleb wahed* collective, of BLTNM group and related informal networks in Lebanon and Jordan, are intentional and strategic about frustrating expectations and not producing what audiences want to hear. They are selective about what audiences they hope to reach and how. Consider, for example, Palestinian rapper Muqataʿa's 2014 album, which opens with the track "Al-Missfah" ("The Filter").

Static. A drone on an open fifth with fluctuating speed, causing the pitch to rise and fall. On top of it, a sample from vinyl with its own static. The strings section of an orchestra, perhaps in a repeated trill. More interference. And the same static from before, but louder. Through the static and the drone, over the sample, the rapper begins. It is hard to hear him and harder to understand. It is as if we are listening to him through a phone line on a bad connection that keeps cutting out.[20] Discussing the piece in Amman in 2015 with producer Al-Nather, Muqataʿa reflected:

> **Muqataʿa:** Lots of people ask me why in the album *Hayawan Nateq* I put the first track first, people say that should have been the last track. Because it's the weirdest one, the one the least people will be able to understand, and the sound on the track is not clear [*wisekh*], the vocals are the least clear, etc.
>
> **Al-Nather:** On the contrary, I think it's perfect.
>
> **Muqataʿa:** Exactly, *you* do. I made it for you. You and people who think like you. The last track on the album is the cleanest and the calmest. And the name of this [first] track is "Al-Missfah" which means "the filter." So this is the concept. It's part of my message [خطابي], part of my "discourse."

In explaining his choices about how "Al-Missfah" works, Muqataʻa describes a call-and-response that specifically works to filter out listeners. Elaborating a strategy of "filtering," Muqataʻa details the use of interference, unclear vocals, and a "dirty" sound as a way of inviting select listeners to engage. He describes opening the album with the track that requires the most of a listener and closing it with the track that is the easiest to listen to. He refers to the surprise or dissatisfaction this provoked from some listeners while Al-Nather affirms how it worked positively for others, like himself. Muqataʻa continued:

> I like filtering [الفلترة] in music. I believe in this. For example, in the show at Jadal [an independent venue in Amman], ten people left because the sound was very loud. And I told the managers, 'Sorry, the sound was too loud!' But inside, I was happy. Because this is a response. To me, this is normal, a reaction. It's not necessary for everybody to like what I'm doing. There needs to be a conscious reaction. It relieves me when there is a real response from people; that they aren't just waiting for me to finish and then clapping politely. No, there are people who like it, and people who don't. It brings out the reality of what's happening. . . . I don't aim to irritate but I like that there are people who aren't able to enjoy it and who are bothered. That it is not possible to reach everybody.

In these reflections, Muqataʻa expresses an avant-garde musical philosophy in the recognition that it is impossible to reach everyone. His strategies of inviting engagement and disengagement in these remarks are less explicitly lyrical and more ostensibly sonic and musical. Like Jaafar's gestures on stage (chap. 1), they ask for a different model of call-and-response to understand these choices politically.

"Muqata'a's filtering is a specific approach to call-and-response. He speaks of learning and feeling with his audiences through what are invitations to self-select into the intimacy of the cypher. Filtering speaks to the balance of knowing that, for some, invitations will effectively be invitations to leave, disengage. Both listener and musician testimonies point to the significance of and pleasure in these challenges to (dis)engage, how they are a part of building concert energy, flow, and climax – differentiating from mainstream aesthetics and lyrical frameworks and ultimately: filling the head. Besides what the music sounds like, some of the dynamics of filtering are performatic—part of the live performance, like spitting, as discussed in the previous chapter.[21]

Istifzaz | 51

Figure 2.1. *Hayawan Nateq* Release Party, La Wain Pub, Ramallah, November 13, 2014. Photo by Alaa Ghosheh.

In November 2014, I attended a release party for *Hayawan Nateq* at La Wain pub above the Qasabah theater in downtown Ramallah.

> I arrived around 10pm with an Italian woman I had met at a capoeira class and a [male, Palestinian] friend of friends I'd been out with before. The cover was 30 NIS [around US$7]. Our male companion left almost immediately upon entering the bar, but after paying the cover. The Italian and I sat at a bar and ordered a beer. By the time Muqataʿa took the mic, I lost track of the Italian. It was very warm; cigarette smoke was thick. Energy was concentrated up by the stage, maybe two dozen people, very close together. All were focused forward, listening.
>
> Despite the warmth, the energy throughout the bar had holes and gaps in it. Even close to the stage, responses were not uniform. A few people danced, a few people smoked, some smiled and tried to make eye contact with the emcees, obviously positively engaged. With others, body language was more reserved. Muqataʿa had their attention. But it was like each of us was in her own space. Arms folded. Straight faces. [See fig. 2.1.]
>
> The crowd was less concentrated immediately behind me. Thin, even. People chatting, laughing, sitting, standing, disinterested, allowing other things to pull them away from the stage. By 11:30 the musicians had stopped. There was no encore.

What I experienced at the release concert at La Wain affirmed the patterns of filtering Muqataʿa described he was experimenting with in this album. None of the people with whom I came into the concert were with me during the musical climax of the event. These exchanges between musicians and experiences in live concerts and listening to recorded tracks illustrate a unique pattern of engagement that is invited and structured by this music. The listening patterns that Muqataʿa invites are the effects of aesthetic and political coordination of surprise, insult, provocation. The effect in live concerts—*Each of us was in her own space. Arms folded. Straight faces*—is a particular dynamic that rappers deliberately foment. It is not a failure to rouse or hype a crowd in more traditional ways.

The aesthetics of disgust discussed in the previous chapter and an epistemology built on istifzaz that I have been identifying here offer listeners new modes of interpellation into politics. I contend rappers *hail* or call out to audiences using a range of aesthetic strategies that result in different "rituals of ideological recognition."[22] Populist politics ask for and receive particular responses: hype, shouting, vocalized call-and-response—specific aesthetic patterns. By contrast, experimental rappers invite disengagement and use static and noise strategically to filter out listeners who have not committed to a practice of listening carefully. The strategies of filtering under an umbrella of istifzaz isolate and encourage reflection. They build a solitary process of listening at a distinct remove from popular (*shaʿbi*) genres for dancing or socializing. These invitations to listen acknowledge and exacerbate existing divisions within listening publics. And they seek to draw attention to difficult questions of belonging and representation without claiming or asserting a common unifying platform, affect, or identity.

Istifzaz as an invitation to know and (re)make the world is significant in how it hails a listener, in how it calls her in. Legacy Russell writes, "It is the glitch that incites anticipation—that ecstasy of interference."[23] In other words, in frustration there is excitement and anticipation. In the next chapter, I explore further how excitement about these glitchy invitations to know and (re)make the world build tentative collectivity through shared anticipation. Before moving on to how yearning is a part of the satisfying experience of the music *filling the head*, I want to explore further the frustration of expectations through aesthetic choices and the specific ways in which rappers understand and perform authentic politics and identity. I quoted Russell describing glitch as "a point of departure."[24] Understanding from where rappers are departing in their mobilization of istifzaz is important. These provocations and surprises are often made clear in navigations of authenticity.

Navigating Authenticity: Between Shaʻb *and* Shareʻ

Many studies of hip-hop have taken up debates over authenticity. These navigations of authenticity center race, place, experience, language, and commerciality, among others.²⁵ Debates over authenticity are also commonplace in Arabic-language rap scenes. What being *real* constituted differed among the rappers and fans I spoke with. But many rappers articulated authenticity in proximity and distance from "popular" (shaʻbi) events or spaces and "the street" (al-shareʻ). Not all registers of this distance were the same—some bemoaned it, some treated it as obvious, some resisted the frames of this distance entirely. All of these assessments of authenticity illustrate how rappers approach expectations of their listening public(s). These navigations of distance and authenticity are important in situating how aesthetic strategies like spitting or filtering work as an invitation to engage.²⁶

In Arabic, "popular" (shaʻbi) encompasses a range of meanings. It can be popular (widely liked), commercial (widely available), public (as in, free public space), or populist (of "the people").²⁷ The last two less often map onto the term in English. Experimental rap in Arabic music doesn't sound like "popular" (commercially successful) music in these cities, and it is rarely played in "popular" (public, populist) venues or events. Rappers readily distance and distinguish themselves and their work from the aesthetics and audience demographics of popular culture and musical events.

For example, when I asked Ramallah-based rapper Sheʻrap if he considered that the rap he makes is shaʻbi, he laughed. Then he said, "It's difficult to talk about rap being shaʻbi. Can you imagine, in the middle of a *hafleh shaʻbiyeh* [a popular party], like at a wedding, someone taking the mic and singing a rap song? That'd be hilarious!"²⁸ His location of the absurd in rap at a shaʻbi occasion is important in how it recognizes a marked distance between the two. Other rappers more specifically located authenticity in the distance between the rap they wrote and "the street." Palestinian rapper Haykal told me, "I never wrote about myself "I am resisting" or "I am resistant" [*mouqawem*]. The looks you will get from the street here will be like: Who are you kidding, man? [*Inta esh tithabal?*] It's impossible for someone to come down [and rap] "I am resisting" if the street [*al-shareʻ*] rejects you [*tafef ʿaleyk*]."²⁹ Haykal's comments affirm a refusal that his work is understood "as resistance." And his reference to *al-shareʿ* complements Sheʿrap's comments about hafleh shaʿ biyeh and the distance between them and the rap they write.

Importantly, rappers in the mid-2010s clearly identified a progression of rap sounds and aesthetics *in Arabic*. While Haykal was marking the distance between his work, expressions of resistance, and the street, he was also telling a story about the sounds and aesthetics of Arabic rap—those he incorporates and develops in his own work and those from which he was trying to distance himself. He told me he was reluctant to embrace the first Palestinian rap to emerge in Arabic in the early 2000s—MCs like Rami GB and DAM, which he had access to as a teen and preteen in Ramallah. He explained, "[This music had] a very strong Palestinian character [*tabaʿa*] that was very close to the general taste, or the taste of weddings, etc. As part of the middle class, my taste was closer to pop and Western music. I wasn't accepting wedding music, to me that was trash, even though I grew up in Al-Bireh [outside of Ramallah]. Rami GB and DAM were close to this Palestinian character that I didn't use to like." Haykal's distancing of himself from "Palestinian character . . . [and] general taste, or the taste of weddings" can also be interpreted as a refusal of the stereotyped images and affects of Palestine, and "Palestinian-ness" that have long framed both Palestinian cultural production and politics, and which Haykal distinctly felt did not represent him.³⁰ This can be read productively alongside discussions in the previous chapter of Nasserdayn al-Touffar's lyrical work specifically calling out the failures of pan-Arabism.

Experimental rappers largely avoid performances or associations of *turath*—Arabic for "heritage" or "folklore." Rappers are largely not interested in being identified first by national cultural markers. More localized identities, especially if they are marginalized locales, show up in interjections between verses—for example, Tripoli, Hermel, or Homs. The emphasis here is also on the connections or flows of people and ideas between them, in addition to the collaboration between musicians. These stagings of identity and solidarity are a filtering out of an audience that would expect or primarily respond to hackneyed presentations of national culture or belonging and the politics attached to these.

In the reflections above, Haykal admits he felt more at home in more globalized cultural contexts "closer to pop and Western music"—and was less interested in the outward representations of Palestinian identity and culture in some popular culture. Crucially, in these remarks, Haykal demonstrates that it is not that Arabic rap *itself* is not or cannot be shaʿbi, or of the street. These new iterations of it in particular are distancing themselves aesthetically, socially, and politically from shaʿbi aesthetics and practices. His statement "to me that was trash" is a declaration of taste that simultaneously marks positioning and progression of the genre *in Arabic*.[31] I will return to this progression of the genre in more careful detail in the next chapter to explore what it means for this music to *fill the head*.

Other rappers referred to the work required to *take rap to* shaʿbi spaces and audiences. The Palestinian rapper and producer Osloob (of the crew Katibeh 5,) offered the following reflections on changes to the scene in the fall of 2014. It is important to read these alongside Haykal's distinctions about the kind of he's producing and that he grew up hearing in the mid-2000s. Osloob told me:

> Rap developed a lot the past ten years. Rappers stopped using simple [*tafha*] rhymes—like *makan, zaman, hanan, hunan*—what everybody can think up. Now there is serious playing with words. This is a development in the brains of the rappers. But something else is happening. Hip-hop is leaving the street. It's becoming more "white collar" [*maktab*] and "cultured" [*muthaqaf*]. These lines like: *ithab muhajaran ka al-qurunful w inta al-seif w al-qamar*.[32] What? What are you talking about? Someone in the street can't understand this. Not all rappers are able to get their voices to the street, to *shaʿabi* society or *shaʿabi* neighborhoods.
>
> So when they can't do this, they take it elsewhere. A neighborhood like Hamra (in Beirut, see chap. 1, outro), the people in it are more ready to accept hip-hop than other quarters in the city. And there's a lot of rappers who are not interested in this experience, in the trial [of getting the street to accept hip-hop]. It's hard, and sometimes it tears you up inside. But it's worth going through with it.[33]

Osloob gestures broadly to the development of lyrical wordplay in the scene. He suggests a double bind—rappers are improving lyrically, but to him this has also meant that the music is less shaʿbi, further from the street. His comments offer another angle to understand the distance from populist aesthetics that younger rappers Haykal and Sheʿrap articulated. Osloob draws attention to the work of selecting concert venues in hip parts of town as a refusal of the work of "getting their voices to shaʿbi society and neighborhoods." His understanding of the artist as taking up this "trial" to carry a message to specific audiences is also a framing of authenticity related to confronting listeners' frustrations as they are invited into the music.

Osloob's understanding of the rapport between rap and the street, probably closest to an understanding of authenticity and hip-hop in some US contexts, was specifically refuted by other rappers, especially those whose music and rhythms were less in conversation with aesthetic trends in global hip-hop. The Lebanese rapper El Rass's position on rap's relationship to "the people" also framed his understanding of his authenticity as an artist. He distrusted the notion of "the people" and instead suggested that across aesthetic and material differences, individual listeners self-select into listening practices, if they can be reached by willing artists.

> I think we should take advantage of every line we can have to every kind of people we can access. I don't believe in this big "other" as in, "I want to sing for 'the people.'" Who are 'the people?' Everyone is the people. I don't necessarily want to perform for rich kids all the time, but rich kids are people too, they have minds, you know? And I think it's not necessarily linked. Obviously the hip places want to get acts to perform in their venue. When they see an act being successful, they draw them in. This creates a circle of people that, for example, look like each other and belong to the same thing that is linked to this artist in some way or another.
>
> I cannot say that my listeners are from one social group at all. It's very obvious in my gigs. Even the shows I do in hip places, there are people there who never come to these venues. Who only come to watch our gigs. People who sometimes come from remote regions in the countryside, who come from Tripoli, normal people, students, people who don't really go out at night—they come. And that's what's really cool. It's not like they are concerts for rap aficionados and hip-hop heads. It's not.
>
> There are people in these concerts that I can assure you don't listen to rap. And besides the few names of Arabic rap that they've discovered and are attached to, they don't listen to any rap outside of this.[34]

In these comments, El Rass articulates authenticity in a selective engagement with audiences across class, aesthetic preferences, and other demographic markers of taste. His remarks defend his own interest in reaching a hipster, cosmopolitan, "rich kids" audience as its own kind of authentic endeavor ("we should take advantage of every line we can have to every kind of people we can access"). But he's not talking only about elites. His music does draw an eclectic crowd, including listeners—men and women—who would otherwise avoid bars and clubs at night. He also makes a case for understanding success that is not a success of the *genre* at all ("I can assure you people [in these concerts] don't listen to any rap outside of this"). In underscoring these individual listeners "who only come to watch our gigs," El Rass highlights how *individuals* who are not attracted by the genre and who in fact refuse to be hailed by a hip-hop nation are nonetheless called into this music.[35] This framing allows El Rass to circumvent the question of what Osloob called the work of getting rap to shaʿbi contexts. But his comments also point to a fluidity of "the street" and popular politics in it, suggesting that cosmopolitan aesthetics and social practices (of venues, for example), musical experimentation (in electronic or hip-hop sounds), lyrical development (in rhyme schemes—what Osloob called "development in the brains of the rappers"), and the offering of exciting political frameworks and ideas are not mutually exclusive. Al-shaʿb (the people) is not a monolith but a fluid constellation, and constituents may successfully be invited into the cypher by aesthetics, consumption practices, or lyrical expression they might otherwise refuse. El Rass's comments illustrate how he understands authentic rap as the hailing of a heterogenous collectivity, not unlike what the queer performance scholar José Muñoz referred to as "belonging-in-difference."[36] Central to this understanding of slippery, fleeting relation is the sense of the listener and audiences as always in motion, heeding calls into the cypher on the go—selectively responding to some and ignoring others. This is the call into the cypher that istifzaz portends and, in its most powerful form, the fleeting collectivity it offers.

* * *

A selective tour of understandings of al-shaʿb ("the people"), al-shareʿ ("the street"), and authenticity in rap would be incomplete without a consideration of Shab Jdeed, the prominent rapper at the center of Ramallah-based record label BLTNM. The label and the rapper made a splash after the bulk of my research had concluded, but he and they are an important node in the trajectory of rap in Ramallah to date and in this consideration of populist authenticity in particular.

In 2019, the Arabic-language music platform Ma3azef released a twenty-six-minute video interview with Shab Jdeed showcasing the Ramallah rapper's ostensible middle finger to interest about him and his work as art.[37] The interview's appeal is clearly Shab Jdeed's authenticity, an aura even his collaborators hold in deep reverence. (They are crouched on the floor in one corner of the room, out of the camera's view, filming the filming of the interview with their phones while Shab Jdeed sits on the sofa, in front of the camera, alone). This authenticity is located in the rapper's working-class-ness as much as his personality or skill: his isn't an intellectual project born of diasporic travel patterns or globalized consumption. And it is in part embodied in the blatant refusal of any sort of politicized appeal in the music.

Shab Jdeed declares at the outset of the interview, "If any of you think you know what [my work] is about, you'd be wrong." He contends that his primary consideration is that his lyrics "can't be lame [*bayekh*]" but that all of it is "fucking around [*manyakeh*]"—"not something you could explain to just anyone, like my mother, for example" ("*mish ishi wadha feek tishrahha la immi masalan*"). The interview paints a picture of the rapper and his collaborators (Al-Nather and Haykal) as down-to-earth guys who are "over the bullshit" media hype about rap in Arabic. The appeal of the interview is undeniably how Shab Jdeed irreverently frames his answers to the straightforward questions of the interviewer. He refuses a political meaning to his work, not only but especially vis-à-vis the Occupation; he refuses a cogent narration of an artistic process; he refuses an aspiration to "make it" as a rapper, saying he'll only do it for "four years," and after that, he's out (he wants to get married and have a proper job). Characteristically, he even refuses his own answers, saying, "Ask me again tomorrow and I'll give you a different answer." This ostensible "fuck you" to the expectations or interest in the rapper as an artist are not separate from the content of the work. It's refreshing to a viewer and a listener bored by the same tired tropes of framing the music or its impact. The enthusiasm of his peers, recorded in the interview, is reflected through the interviewer to the anticipated listening audience.

"Kohl wa 'Atmeh" ("Charcoal and Darkness") is a track by Shab Jdeed released in 2018.[38] The tagline for the song is "*min al-nass lal-nass*" ("from the people for the people"—specifically using the less politicized nass over sha'b). The piece relates the everyday experiences of preparing to cross into and moving within Israel as a Palestinian living in the West Bank. Shab Jdeed relates getting up extra early (when it's still dark and everything is black, the color of charcoal) in order to have enough time to get through the Qalandia crossing and still get to work on time. How to sit and stand in the bus or the train in Israel so as not to get searched, and so on. Stripped of platitudes, not entreating solidarity or support, obscure to anyone who is not commuting into Israel to work, the track recounts the grind in an acknowledgment of everyday life as the soundscape of the post-Oslo occupation. The piece is a notable, relative hit (fifteen million views as of December 2023).

Another track, Haykal's "Sot Ramallah" ("The Sound of Ramallah") is a denouncement of the individuality, competition, and hypocrisy that have become the mark of agency of the de facto Palestinian capital.[39] Haykal's indictment of the city while simultaneously claiming himself to be part of it points to a declaration of autonomy that is embedded within the very thing he critiques or seeks distance from. The piece is in dialogue with a lineage of Palestinian rappers critical of celebrations of Palestinian resistance.[40] The music video is shot entirely at night, echoing the lyrics of Shab Jdeed's piece, above. In both pieces, the listener can imagine the drone of noise in a Ramallawi soundscape: horns in traffic; restless people waiting (babies crying, overheard phone calls, exasperated sighs); but also the relentless discussions of peace, development, and the future that seem to go nowhere and the circulation of shame, pride, and entreaties to resilience to and for a Palestinian audience in the West Bank and across the diaspora.

"Kohl w ʿatmeh" and "Sot Ramallah" defamiliarize the shaʿbi soundscape of Palestinian resistance and turath by turning the microphone instead to everyday life in post-Oslo Ramallah under Occupation. This is a kind of glitch in the scoring of Palestinian politics as the rhythms of *sabr* (resilience) and *sumud* (steadfastness) and a refreshing centering of the everyday material failures of Oslo as the beat of Palestinian life. In them, and in the work of the *saleb wahed* collective and the BLTNM group, the next generation of Palestinian rappers is sketching out new proximity and distances embodied in different class recognition, different historical referents, different aesthetic inspiration.

* * *

Legacy Russell writes about the glitch as "a blooming of particularity and selfhood," and it is in this sense that the disavowals of the proximity or propriety of rap to shaʿbi events or aesthetics discussed above can productively be read.[41] That is, in the declarations of slippage, distance, and disavowal to shaʿbi events and aesthetics I've just discussed, I see declarations of authenticity that are commitments to preserving aesthetic experimentation, to lyrical and sonic becoming. Phrases like *That'd be hilarious* (Sheʿrap) and *to me that was trash* (Haykal) and how it's indecipherable to *just anyone* (Shab Jdeed) hold space for "a blooming of particularity" that is a kind of anticipation and an invitation to other kinds of populist belonging.

These pieces build on, borrow, and refine aesthetic and political experiments made across a history of rap in Arabic. They build on Muqataʿa's experiments with filtering and other reframings of the political. Rosa Menkman writes, "Glitch . . . searches for the unfamiliar while at the same time it tries to de-familiarize the familiar."[42] In different ways, BLTNM and their peers and forbears excel at this kind of defamiliarizing while the sounds and scoring of their work explicitly speak to affects and effects of alienation, exhaustion, and disgust. This combination of familiarizing and defamiliarizing is sometimes navigated as authenticity and the ability to and appeal of reaching audiences across felt differences. For listeners, the possibility of a glitchy interpellation carries the crucial option of refusal. Audience responses—especially refusals of these sounds—are critical for fully understanding the impact of this epistemology built on istifzaz on audiences and potential audiences. In the next chapter, I turn to listening practices and how audiences refuse the call into the cypher. Together, these explorations of authenticity and identity inform the ways in which istifzaz invites listeners into collectivity otherwise.

The Shitty Beat's in Your Shitty Face

In this chapter, I used Muqataʻa's strategy and philosophy of filtering to deepen a reading of a repertoire of choices designed to provoke and irritate under the umbrella of istifzaz. I explored rappers' reflections on authenticity, especially in navigating proximity and distance to a range of popular formations—shaʻbi (popular), al-nass (the people), and al-shareʻ (the street). I argued that unlike populist music and performance that seek to engage the largest audience through the experience of collective loss and resilience in the face of it, the rhythmic movement built in many rap concerts, as we began to see in the previous chapter, is instead premised on the slightest bit of irritation. In practice, this mismatching of expectations around volume, harmony, lyrical meaning, and rhythmic flow effectively alienates a portion of a given audience. These designed glitches can be understood as a particular kind of call-and-response. The aesthetics of alienation and provocation built around these choices are central to the development of alternative types of flow and related pleasure associated with this music, and its ability to *fill the head*.

Some of the ways rappers invite listeners to listen—how they call you into the cypher—consists of frustrating listener expectations. This filtering is a strategic gamble that is intrinsic to the surprise, delight, and success of specific pieces and whole collectives: too much and nobody will respond, not enough and it won't be interesting. Rappers narrate this quest of reaching audiences as a navigation of authenticity and identity.

Consider Muqataʿa's line of lyrics, included as the epigraph to this chapter: *bastafazak ʿa beat khara zay wijjak*. Roughly translated, it might read, "The shitty beat's in your shitty face." Bastafazak points to a practice of interpellation, of hailing an individual listener, that actively negotiates solitude, movement, and emotion. The root *fazza* [فزّ] is related to unsettling and means "to become frightened." Consider *fazza qalbho* [فزّ قلبه], "his heart was shaken," as in, by fear. Lane's dictionary follows this example with *fazza ʿanho* [فزّ عنه], "he turned away from him, he separated himself from him, became alone." The tenth form of the verb, *istafaza* [اِسْتَفَزَّ], from which the verbal noun *istifzaz* [اِسْتِفْزَاز], the title of this chapter, derives, is sometimes translated as "incitement." Lane's dictionary translates this form of the verb as "excite to lightness and unsteadiness."[43] This *exciting to lightness and unsteadiness* finds an echo in the "positive departure," the "ecstasy of anticipation," and "unstable assemblage" of the glitch. I return to these echoes, drawing out pleasure in that lightness and unsteadiness, in chapter 4.

As in the concert at La Wain, istifzaz can be seen in how listeners are invited into a practice of careful listening. They are together but each in her own space, arms folded. Moreover, the awareness of other listeners, similarly interpellated, as well as others who refused the call (as I will show in the next chapter) is central to the development of that listening practice. As Menkman writes, "Glitch art is not always just a personal experience of shock, but also (as a genre) a metaphor for a way of expression, that depends on multiple actors."[44] This dependence on multiple actors is the promise of collectivity that istifzaz in experimental Arabic rap offers.

Invitations into the cypher under the framework of an epistemology built on istifzaz should not be understood as an attempt to reach *a certain demographic* but an invitation across them into *a kind of practice*. Importantly, as such they are easily accepted or rebuffed *across* demographics. Audiences do not perceive these musical hailings to ask for familiar allegiances in terms of class, identity, and other familiar frameworks of belonging. These invitations do ask for willingness to adopt specific listening practices, modes of attention, and postures of bodily comportment. In this way, listening to experimental rap in Arabic invites a kind of self-fashioning, similar to what anthropologist of media and Islam Charles Hirschkind has described as a disciplinary practice. I turn to this in the next chapter.

At a distance from building uniform crowd energy into hype, istifzaz is an aesthetic development, a shift in the affective and performative patterns with which many rappers communicated with their fans in the early 2000s. This practice of interpellation, or calling the listener and seeking a particular response from her, is central to how politics *moves* (changes position) in the genre and how a particular track or performer *moves* the listener (makes her feel something). This intersection of political motion and emotion is the subject of the last chapter. Strategies of call and response, rapper testimony about patterns of listening, and listener testimony about responding to music when they felt hailed (when a perspective *filled the head*) come together in a political reading of listening as a practice of shifting how one relates to politics as is. This relationship to the political itself becomes the material that rappers affect when successful; it is the horizon within which engagement is possible, exciting, yearned after.

3

LISTENING

> Aren't you coming to listen?
> BU KOLTHOUM

THE THRILL OF ISTIFZAZ, THE FRISSON OF PROVOCATION. And yet, feminist artist and technologist Rosa Menkman offers a salient reminder: "Glitch art exists within different systems." I begin this chapter by considering how rap reaches audiences differently. Menkman offers that "glitch art is not always (or by everyone) experienced as an art of momentum."[1] Rap does not present a thrill, a challenge, an excitement for all listeners. To materialize istifzaz (as discussed in the previous chapter, filtering, interference, the glitch as an invitation), it is important to linger on the reality that many who hear these invitations refuse them. I use this to guard my analysis against a romanticization of istifzaz (provocation) or qaraf (disgust), as elaborated in the previous two chapters, as their own aesthetics or expressions of resistance. In lingering on the refusal to listen, this chapter opens a conversation about listening practices, how they are embodied, what kind of attention they require, and the roles that both listening and attention play in the experience of *filling the head*.

This chapter continues my analysis of what making, seeking out, and participating in this musical subculture feels like. I collect listening practices I observed and those described to me by musicians and fans. In doing so, patterns of listeners refusing the call into the cypher and patterns in rappers' disappointment with how audiences engage construct a horizon of possible listening practices as choices. The spectrum of options confirms that these are not passive reactions but active engagements with the music and the material contexts within which concerts take place. As such, the experience of experimental rap in Arabic is clearly not only about the politico-aesthetic innovations of the artist. It is not only about the rappers rapping. Listeners cocreate concerts and the scene itself.

Global hip-hop studies has long recognized the coconstruction of the cypher, or the circular performance space shared by competing breakdancers, rappers, beatboxers, and turntablists. Imani Kai Johnson relays that cyphers are "not things but acts": they are coproduced by the many collaborators and coparticipants within it.[2] This is true at the level of a physical cypher in a specific venue and the metaphorical one connecting the larger hip-hop community. Johnson continues, "Cyphering is a multisensorial, collective experience cloaked as an individual one.... There is more going on than a mere competitive back and forth."[3] Her argument draws attention to the fact that while individual musical and dance acts in global hip-hop are collaborative and polyphonic exchanges (relying on call and response), the importance of those exchanges extends beyond the literal performance space to and beyond other literal performance spaces, creating a larger metaphorical hip-hop cypher. Rap in Arabic can also work like this.[4]

I am interested in what listeners are doing, what they create. But my ethnographic perspective in this chapter is a little different from these approaches to global hip-hop. I keep one ear open for felicitous exchanges with fans and engaged listeners during concerts. At the same time, I propose to let the other ear follow *in*felicitous exchanges with listeners who hear the call into the cypher but decline to engage. I am curious what potential audiences, seemingly less excited by these sounds or aesthetics, can tell us about the experiences of filling the head. In my fieldwork and in my interviews, *infelicitous* listening emerged as an unignorable part of what was unfolding. Failed calls into the cypher, misfires between rappers and audiences, and competing expectations of what concert time or concert spaces should be used for help illustrate what felicitous listening in the experience of filling the head feels like.

I do not think this is the familiar penchant for conflict or resistance creeping back into my analysis. I am not pointing to refusal of this music as its own resistance to global cosmopolitanism. The interactions and exchanges that develop within a concert space are important. So too are how those concert spaces are connected to other concert spaces within hip-hop culture and other musical and artistic genres. But it is also revealing to consider the interactions and exchanges just outside the concert: in the street outside the venue, in the park across the street, in the alley that serves as the backstage. It is important to consider how the concert speaks to its neighbors, in its own neighborhood.

How the concert speaks to its neighborhood is the flipside of the trial, described by Osloob in the previous chapter, of taking rap to the street. Concerts often provoke responses that are quite different from the exchanges musicians and fans seek. These responses around and outside concert sites are not typically understood as part of the cypher, but they certainly contribute to it. They are not examples of the experience of filling the head. But they can tell us a lot about what the experience of filling the head might consist of. Specifically, these exchanges near the concert, at the time of the concert but importantly removed from it, make a copracticed, cocreated *stillness* in some concerts very obvious. This stillness is a kind of listening practice that is deliberately cultivated—a kind of listening that is sought after and practiced. This stillness is essential to the experience of filling the head.

* * *

In his work on the cultivation of listening practices in the context of recorded religious sermons in Cairo, anthropologist Charles Hirschkind underscores the agency of the listener.[5] He explains that in certain Muslim religious contexts, the failure of a delivered oration is not attributed to the speaker (whether God himself or his messengers or mediations). Rather, agency is attributed instead to an individual or group's "inability or refusal to hear."[6] Hirschkind writes, "*Samʿ* [hearing, listening] . . . is not a spontaneous and passive receptivity but particular kind of action itself, *a listening that is a doing.*"[7] Hirschkind explores how pious working-class Muslims in Cairo in the 1990s cultivated listening as both a cognitive and bodily act that draws on overlapping emotional, affective, and aesthetic dimensions. In this context, he understands listening as a disciplinary practice where "listening with attention" is a "complex sensory skill" that "recruits the body in its entirety."[8] This practice assists the listener in developing a set of ethical practices and moving through the world. The framework Hirschkind builds to develop listening as an active engagement is useful in deepening my own discussion of listening practices to live and recorded rap.

The rappers I focus on in this text are not religious mediators, nor are raps religious texts or messages. Unlike Hirschkind, I am not interested in developing an ethics of rap or of hip-hop culture. Nonetheless, his understanding of the activity in listening, how this activity recruits the whole body of the listener, and how listening as a practice can be understood as a process of *sedimentation* shares important central features with the listening processes I also observed in the subcultural musical scenes in which I participated.

To further explore the embodied activities listening entails, I turn to the question of the cultivation of attention. To make sense of infelicitous calls into the cypher, I argue that audiences deploy attention against a backdrop of a material and affective context of constant disruption—what the sociologist Ghassan Moussawi has theorized as *al-wadaʿ* in his work in Beirut. I link Amman and Ramallah to Beirut in this felt affective urban constellation of constant change and disruption that is coupled with stagnancy and impossibility. This feeling contributes to electricity in the air when concerts open public space for different kinds of interactions. In such conditions, the cultivation of *in*attention is a specific engagement with musicians and concert spaces that is also a wider navigation of affect, materiality, and political possibility.

Testifying against the examples of audience inattention I foreground in the first part of the chapter, rappers and audiences in these same cities identify very different kinds of attention as ideal and desired. The stillness they value is not a response *to* the music or an easy catharsis produced by it either. Rather, the stillness rappers seek points to listening as a process of sedimentation, an entering into and layering within the cypher. As I will show, sifting through material revealed in a process of sedimentation is a very different kind of embodied attention than expressed in less felicitous calls into the cypher. It is hard to see things build up and hard to discern their layers without the kind of embodied attention found in stillness. This chapter concludes by returning to the strategies of musicians to explore different ways that rappers invite stillness as a conscious alternative to other ways of engaging in polyphonic interactions—other kinds of call-and-response.

Stillness, reflecting as it does a process of sedimentation, an active and intentionally cultivated listening practice, is embodied very differently from inattention, but it is hardly still. Stillness is itself the effect of being in pursuit, a sort of driven wandering. That motion, that searching, is the yearning of the next and final chapter.

Refusing the Call

In order to materialize the reality of istifzaz, it is important to linger on the reality of the refusal of that invitation by many who hear it. I offer here observations during, before, and after concerts to recognize the space between two kinds of audiences—what I call *concert goers* and *concert observers*. Concert goers are the audience members typically imagined in live events: those who buy tickets or otherwise commit to attending. Concert observers are another kind of audience who obviously note and acknowledge the existence of the live event—they hear the call—but refrain from engaging in the way organizers intend or refuse to participate at all.

Learned familiarity with sites of leisure and the representation and performance of selfhood within them has been the subject of fascinating ethnographic work in all three cities in this study. In Beirut, Lara Deeb and Mona Harb have explored how café culture in Shi'a Beirut allows youth to perform and navigate morality and moralized expectations in a conservative suburb of the capital.[9] In Amman, anthropologists Jillian Schwedler and Sarah Tobin have addressed how "aspiring cosmopolitans" and enacted "middle-classness" function politically among youth coming into the cosmopolitan center of the city.[10] Schwedler has argued that learning cosmopolitan behavior—how to consume global brands and enact pleasure in elite leisure spaces—is central to the identity of both Ammani elites as well as segments of the middle and lower classes employed in the service sector in West Amman. She calls "aspiring" cosmopolitanism those "practices of survival, creativity, and reimagination" produced "at the blurry boundary of inclusion/exclusion."[11] Her study works to reinsert texture—and agency—into neoliberal critiques of exclusion.

What happens when we consider how some denizens observe but *refuse* the invitation to participate in cosmopolitanism that is specifically *not* staged in elite spaces? By this, I mean, how to interpret the affective and material choices of those who hear the call but elect not to respond in ways musicians, other fans, or venue or event curators expect? I do not mean how religious or state authorities oppose certain concerts or festivals. I mean instead how residents of Amman, Beirut, and Ramallah decide to participate, or not, in outdoor festivals in public space. Specifically, I consider how refusals to participate are noticed by and affect the participation of others.

I consider two outdoor festivals in Amman in 2015: the Al-Balad Festival, held in the Roman Amphitheatre downtown, and the Word Is Yours Festival held in the Seven Hills Skatepark on Arar Street near Al-Weibdeh. The Al-Balad Festival features an eclectic range of regional and diasporic

Arabic musical acts. It is run by the Al-Balad Theatre, directed by Raed Asfour, and was launched in 2009. The Word Is Yours Festival (WIYF) in 2015 was the first iteration of that gathering, a two-day "urban street art festival" featuring graffiti, skateboarding, and breakdancing. WIYF was organized by Shermine Sawalha, Tia Thorpe, Nereya Otieno, and Samantha Robinson in October 2015.[12] Day one of the festival hosted live rap, skateboarding competitions, a B-boy battle, beatboxing challenges, and skateboard building and painting workshops in the newly opened Seven Hills Skatepark in the Al-Weibdeh neighborhood.[13] Day two largely focused on film screenings and artist talks at the Laconda Hotel, also in Al-Weibdeh.[14]

Al-Balad Festival ticket prices ranged by act. Concerts in the Word Is Yours Festival were free. The two festivals are distinct in terms of how they were funded and organized and in how they reached different audiences. They are paired here as public festivals that palpably transformed the use of public space in Amman, bringing audiences into public areas they didn't typically use and bringing genres of music and particular concert etiquette to places that didn't typically host them. As such, I discuss them here as illustrations of the differences between concert goers and concert observers.

Concert goers and concert observers are aware of each others' decisions to participate or not and how they choose to do so. These behaviors mark constant negotiations over proper behavior in and the use and meaning of urban space. I noticed it first when crossing the square toward the Odeon Theatre for the concerts of Al-Balad Festival.

> Crossing the street into the park, we dodge boys and girls with soccer balls, veiled women and young fathers holding babies and young children, toy vendors sending lit plastic tops spinning on the stone ground or flashing boomerangs soaring into the air. On benches or against the walls of the large theatre, young men and teens sit spitting seeds and smoking. As we neared the Odeon (the smaller of two roman theatres), flags advertising the festival marked a sort of fabricated entrance corridor. These flags built a queue for audiences, who stood in between the flags as they arrived and waited to enter or to buy tickets.[15] Opposite the queues, folks clearly not intending to enter, mostly young men and boys, sat on stone structures and quietly watched the queues of people entering. Exiting the theatre, the scene was similar to when we entered it. . . . I wished to use the restroom before and after the concert, something my companions advised me against doing, but waited patiently when I insisted, lest I be left to traverse the square alone[16] [see fig. 3.1].

Dressed up for a night out, the parade of concert goers waiting to purchase tickets for the Al-Balad Festival concerts was something of a spectacle for

Figure 3.1. Dhafer Yousef during the closing concert of the Al-Balad Festival, which was held in the larger Roman Amphitheatre. Note the continuation of regular use of the downtown space outside of the theater (beyond the proscenium walls). Entrance to the auditorium is through the proscenium walls for both musician and audience. There is no enclosed backstage space. August 3, 2015. Photo by the author.

the regular users of the space, many of whom informally queued themselves to watch this crowd. While they used the same space, the delineations between these groups were obvious. My female companion's dress (more conservative than she would wear otherwise) was designed to downplay this difference whereas the queue of those watching the actual concert queue made no effort to mask the difference they observed.

In our interview, Raed Asfour, the artistic director of the Al-Balad theater and of the biannual music festival of the same name, was keen to emphasize that the festival was for "everyone."[17] Specifically, Asfour told me that the festival's ideal audience was "the people [al-nass] . . . in every shape and form: age, economic class, education level."[18] He was keen to emphasize the role he believed the festival played in exposing people to different kinds of music. Over the course of our conversation, Asfour denied any outward characteristic that could delineate the makeup of al-nass (age, economic class, education level). When our conversation turned to the relationship between the festival organizers and attendees and the ordinary frequenters of the downtown plaza where the Roman theaters are located, however, Asfour automatically made a distinction between concerts goers and concert observers. He told me, "No one goes there to build relations with them, to teach them about art . . . and unfortunately their economic level doesn't allow them to attend a play regularly."[19]

Despite asserting that the festival's target audience had no "economic level," Asfour identified real differences between the Ammani citizens who notice the festival is taking place—concert observers—and those who actually attend, or the concert goers. Asfour related to me how this difference has historically been embodied in animosity when the concert goers arrive and "steal" the plaza from those forced to observe the dispossession: its everyday users. The concert goers' arrival, typically accompanied by the police, internal security, and secret police (because the festival is an official event), affects the layout of the public space: corridors are constructed, as described in the notes above, and the theaters are roped off. As tickets are implemented, the festival also affects who has access to which parts of the plaza. All of this happens without "us" [the festival organizers and concert goers] asking "their" [everyday users of the space] permission. Asfour concluded, "Of course they don't have the power for you to ask their permission anyway. These things are tied up with the municipality."[20] Asfour's remarks stage a kind of middle-class consumption as "inclusivity." Organizers are keen to draft an "inclusive" cultural product, staging it against the stunning backdrop of Jordan's ancient heritage.[21] This is despite the obvious divisions the festival stages between audiences and potential audiences in the downtown plaza.

Asfour related to me that organizers offered free tickets to interested parties once they sold as many as they could. He described to me one preadolescent girl who attended five concerts for free, accompanied by a female festival volunteer who would "pick the girl up" from her mother (who was in the park around the theater but did not wish to enter) and return her to her family once the concert was over. With the exception of Mounir Troudi (Tunisia), Morabba3 (Jordan), and Tarraband (Sweden/Iraq), however, the venue for the Al-Balad Festival in 2015 hovered around half capacity.[22] During the hip-hop acts performed by Muqata'a (Palestine), Khotta Ba (Jordan), and El Rass (Lebanon), the theater was less than half full (see fig. 3.2). Tickets for Muqata'a and Khotta Ba's concert was 7 JD (just under US$10), the cheapest

Figure 3.2. Muqata'a in the Odeon theater performing as part of the Al-Balad Festival, 2015. Photo by the author.

concert in the festival.[23] My own perception, shared by some of the musicians who performed, is that more could have been done to lessen the very obvious class barriers operating in a public Ammani space. Khotta Ba told me, "To be honest I'm against doing a show in a place like this and not letting the neighborhood kids in. These kids were running around behind the backstage and throwing stones [at us]. Man, let these kids in, the theatre was empty anyway. But that's how the organizers think. At the end of the day, they want to break even. They're not here to solve society's problems."[24]

The point is not only about exclusion at the point of ticket pricing, however. The large refusal to enter the concert space (think especially of the mother of the girl Asfour mentioned, who preferred not to enter, even to accompany her young daughter) does more than highlight the misfires of the inclusive intentions of the festival organizers or middle-class bias. In the refusal to engage the concert staged in the downtown area, we can see a pattern of deliberation, calculated negotiation, and affective tension conducted between Ammanis in and around concert venues. Importantly for the effect it has on musicians and their ability to communicate with their gathered audiences, these tensions do not stay outside the theaters but enter concert spaces as well.

Related dynamics appeared during the Word Is Yours Festival (WIYF), the two-day festival of hip-hop acts held in the Seven Hills Skatepark in October 2015. The day before the festival, I noticed the familiar distance between concert organizers and local workers gathered at a neighborhood store. I was volunteering with another woman and some of the festival coordinators to clean up the park before musical acts and audiences arrived. Organizers were expecting young people and children in an open grassy space that was not regularly cleaned or tended to. The concern was mostly broken glass.

> Carrying a black trash bag between us, Rana and I set out along the South end of the park, which runs up on Arar Street.[25] We each wore one of the pink plastic dish gloves I had brought. We were talking as we worked, ignoring the shouts and beckoning of men drinking coffee outside the shop across the street. At one point in my gathering of trash, I picked up something heavy. It felt like a rug perhaps, but I could not tell what it was. I lifted it at arm's length to see it more clearly. It was a dead cat. I dropped it and yelped. Rana screamed. Peals of laughter rang out from across the street, where the men had obviously been watching the whole time.[26]

These moments illustrate a distance and difference between concert goers and concert observers. Concert goers (and concert organizers, volunteers, and other participants) come to the public spaces where concerts take place infrequently. But they come with firmly held, specific expectations of how to act and what to do in public space. They are noticed by concert observers, who are everyday users of the space. Concert observers notice the incursions of concert organizers and attendees but markedly avoid participating. In this example, the men across the street clearly noticed my and the other volunteers' presence and recognized what we were doing. To the men, who worked in an auto mechanic shop across from the park, the sight of the individual female volunteers cleaning the park with their hands was ridiculous.[27] Obviously, this was a bad idea, whatever the intentions of these newly arrived do-gooders were—a perception that was confirmed when Rana and I both screamed in fright at the sight and touch of the dead animal. Similarly, she and I both quietly tolerated the taunts and jeers while remaining fixated on tidying the park, which we both perceived was in the best interest of the neighborhood users, despite not having used the park previously ourselves. None of us—neither Rana and I nor the group of men—directly confronted the other. Still, our awareness of their recognition of our intrusion marked the volunteers' attitude in and toward the space. Their laughter and jeering made us aware of our foreignness in the space despite our own perceptions of the value of our presence.

* * *

In many ways, the first day of WIYF was a success: for an entire day, the park was full of a mix of people—local and expat, from different neighborhoods, men and women, with the knowledge of the police and local religious authorities. People came and went in what was obviously for some their first exposure to an event of its kind (see fig. 3.3). In many other ways, the festival fell short. The structure of funding meant that traveling musical acts were paid while the local acts weren't. There were last-minute changes, cuts, substitutions, and contingency plans, leading to mistrust among the performing artists and the organizational team. For example, the time and duration of their sets were changed multiple times. Despite having secured the permits from local authorities to play music in the park, police arrived with the intention to close the event. When festival organizer Sawalha managed to convince the police to allow the event to continue, local religious figures protested the continuation of music, dancing, and gender mixing in a public space, leading to a muted confrontation between the police and the religious authorities.[28]

When dusk fell on day one of the Word Is Yours Festival, the environmental challenges of the day (the sun, schedule changes, negotiations with local authorities) faded. But audience attention remained divided. The gathered crowd nearly erupted in fistfights more than once. As rappers Satti, Malikah, and Bu Kolthoum took the stage for their final sets, groups of boys took to teasing each other. One teenage boy in particular nearly found himself knocked out more than once after repeatedly spraying water at strangers in the crowd. Sawalha herself intervened several times. Even at the climax of the event, three of the scene's most experienced rappers—two of which were then based in Amman (Satti and Bu Kolthoum)—still did not hold the audience's attention (see fig. 3.4).

This seemed obvious enough to the performing rappers. Onstage, Malikah mostly seemed removed, not connected to her audience, an irritation she expressed vis-à-vis problems with sound, rolled eyes at mic problems, sarcasm about the (small) size of the stage (making it difficult for her and

Figure 3.3. Panoramic of the Word Is Yours Festival at the Seven Hills Skatepark in Al-Weibdeh around five p.m., October 2, 2015. The central stage for rap performances was under the black Red Bull umbrella, far left. Shade was limited to where most people were seated, along the near back wall. Photograph by the author.

Bu Kolthoum to move), and frustration with the crowd itself. She seemed to be rapping over them, above their heads, not with and to them. Months earlier, under rain in the garden of the Jadal cultural center, Bu Kolthoum was able to hold an affective exchange that was much more focused and powerful than the much larger, sprawling audience at Seven Hills at night.[29] The Word Is Yours Festival, despite being truly accessible, held in public space, free, and inviting a range of audiences and modes of interaction, was not able to provide the conditions for real focused attention among rappers and the gathered audience.

Awareness of how others were using the space constantly absorbed audiences' attention. The teen teasing the audience by spraying listeners with water observed and attempted to take advantage of how some were using the space. At the same time, others noted with apprehension the behavior of this teen and those who responded to him. These contests operate below and beyond the more official deliberations between organizers and musicians and between organizers and different Jordanian authorities. Nonetheless, these attentions compete with that which rappers seek from their listeners.

Similarly, the refusal to ignore, overtly reject, or embrace the Al-Balad Festival and the new arrivals to the downtown space points to fissures in organizers' discourse about reaching as wide an audience as possible, not to mention obvious class tension. Recognitions of the *other*—for concert goers of concert observers and vice versa—under the watchful eyes of different

Figure 3.4. Malikah and Bu Kolthoum struggle to hold the audience's attention after dusk at the Word Is Yours Festival in the Seven Hills Skatepark. October 4, 2015. Photograph by the author.

kinds of security are indirect and muted. Importantly, these interactions are largely not direct confrontations.

The affective configuration of concert access and audience behavior described here helps to recognize a flip side of aspiring cosmopolitanism and middle classness. Especially in Amman's expanding music scene, there are staged opportunities for the performance of cosmopolitanism—in venues that are *specifically not exclusive* (both spaces described here are public parks)—that citizens actively refused. That is, when privately run festivals clearly trading in the "cosmopolitan international" enter and appropriate lower-middle-class and working-class space, they are pointedly not greeted by the frameworks of aspiring cosmopolitanism Schwedler talks about.[30] This is not to suggest that aspiring cosmopolitanism does not exist in other places and at other times. It is, however, to note that in particular it did not seem to exist here, at the intersection of bifurcated East and West Amman, among ordinary users of park spaces. This was so despite or perhaps because of the framework mobilized by concert organizers.

* * *

Louis Althusser's widely cited framework of subjectivation in interpellation, is famously illustrated by a policeman calling out to someone in the street. The policeman calls out, "Hey there!" And the intended subject turns around. For Althusser, this response, this interpellation by authority, is subject formation. The political subject becomes so in how she responds to being called. For Althusser, when she turns around in response to the police's shout, the subject acknowledges that she hears and responds to the authority of the state. She becomes a subject in response to that call.

In considering a range of embodied responses to live concerts, I am pointing to a spectrum of listening practices. In doing so, I am leading to the recognition of stillness as a particular kind of attention. The cultivation of inattention is an active, political navigation of these Arab cities and the political and affective milieu of a kind of constant disruption, an unpredictable constancy in the second decade of the twenty-first century. Politically, I am interested in the subjecthood of the subject and her agency before the call. Surely the woman who turned around when she heard the policeman's call, is a political subject before she hears the policeman. She is a caregiver, a worldmaker; she is going somewhere.

In considering how concert observers acknowledge but refuse the call into the cypher or, more specifically, *how concert observers acknowledge the call but refuse to enter the cypher*, I am proposing a specific theoretical pivot. I am pivoting away from an agency delivered in a theory of subjectivation and toward a political becoming understood in the rhythms of collective movement. The patterns of hearing the call, entering the cypher and passing through, stopping outside, turning around, or cautiously entering to stay reveal syncopated pulses of agency independent of—preceding and continuing after—the invitation, the act of interpellation, the call. These syncopated pulses are felt in the embodiment of attention by concert goers and concert observers. The texture of this attention is politics in motion.

In the provision of cultural activity like concerts and festivals, there are clear attempts to discipline audiences into specific kinds of behavior and patterns of relation. These are manifest in the reflections of bouncers, event owners, and festival curators. The expectations and disciplining practices are important.[31] Here, I have suggested that refusing the call into the cypher is a kind of listening in and of itself. It is the cultivation of another kind of attention: *in*attention. Understanding this inattention is important for understanding one of its contrasts: stillness, which figures repeatedly in the testimonies of music that fills the head.

Inattention

Musicians, concert organizers, festival curators, even bouncers expect a range of behaviors and reactions to and within live concerts. During my fieldwork, cultural producers related to me the cultivation of listeners' attention as a question of exposure and training. Even when the focus is not policing inappropriate behavior, artists and curators often frame good attention as an issue of knowing or not knowing how to show up. For example, the Jordanian rapper Khotta Ba told me that despite the growth in music production in Amman, "[People] aren't used to coming to concerts. They're not used to knowing what to do in a concert. They don't know if they're supposed to clap at a punchline or what. Some people want the song to be over at a punch line and start clapping. They're not accustomed to a hip-hop show where you come and enjoy and bob your head and go home. Lots of people understand hip-hop as poetry, like they want to come listen to a reading. Others come *too* hyped up."[32]

In his remarks, Khotta Ba frames good listening as a question of "knowing what to do" and showing you know what to do through a set of appropriately timed and proportionately scaled behaviors. I too have observed the kinds of dynamics that Khotta describes and find the attribution to "not knowing" what to do plausible. But I'd like to consider another possibility undergirding the kinds of interactions described in the previous section: a framework of *inattention*. This focus acknowledges that the complaints rappers have about the development of a "scene" in any of these cities is not only that "there is no fan base," as the rapper and producer Mohammed al-Hijazi of Obsolete Records recounted;[33] it is also that the desired modes of communicating and feeling with the audience are regularly stymied even when audiences do gather. I want to caution against a reading of these audience and would-be audience dynamics as a question of cosmopolitan know-how or exposure. What changes in an understanding of the audience reception when we attend to *inattention* as an active practice as opposed to a passive by-product? And how does an understanding of audience behavior change when ignorance is not prefigured as the cause?

78 | Filling the Head

Media anthropologist Brian Larkin has described inattention as "the skill one develops in uncertain situations where one pays attention, but only in order to realize that one does not have to pay attention."[34] In his work on the religious soundscape populated by both Christian sermons and Muslim calls to prayer in Jos, Larkin draws out the ways in which individuals sift through competing claims on their attention. Drawing on fieldwork on loudspeakers in urban Nigeria, Larkin crafts an understanding of the idea of attention intervening between the anthropology of religion and the anthropology of media.[35] Larkin suggests that in certain contexts, "one has to cultivate a technique of not attending."[36] In other words, attention is not a continuum with ignorance on the one side and knowledge on the other. Inattention is a practice as much as attention is. This is useful for understanding listening to rap that does not figure ignorance and appreciation as the only possible responses. In other words, inattention allows for the agency of *knowing* what to do and still *doing something else*. I find this useful in building an understanding of agency and political subjectivity as attached to listening.

Larkin's own contribution is to understand inattention as a modern practice of navigating urban contexts deeply affected by the possibility of sudden eruptions of religious conflict and strife. His analysis of how residents of Jos and Kano cultivate "techniques of not attending" or "attending enough to know one does not have to attend,"[37] like Julia Elyachar's work on "attunement" in millennial Cairo,[38] draw out how listening is a deeply material process of sifting through specific environmental stimuli. Larkin's analysis underlines how listening practices are intimately connected to urban space: where citizens sift through not only the content they hear or the quality of the sound—not only its content or aesthetics—but the material social, cultural, and political context unfolding on a given corner or alleyway.

Drawing on Larkin's work, I want to suggest that audience inattention embodied by concert observers as described above is a navigation of both constant change and constant lack of change in Beirut, Ramallah, and Amman. In infrequently staged public events like open air concerts, inattention is a conscious, willful act and not simply ignorance about how to behave at concerts. It is a riding of the opening concerts offer in otherwise hyperstructured and heavily policed public space. This surfing is also not a refusal—or not primarily a refusal. It can more appropriately be read as a taking advantage of, a *yes, and*, or an entering to skate through the cypher.

The youth spraying water at strangers in the gathered crowd during Malika's set at the Seven Hills Skatepark, the kids throwing rocks at rappers backstage at Al-Balad, and the heckling of the men in the mechanic shop across Arar street are examples of listening practices embodied as a deliberate and practiced *inattention*. This cultivated inattention is a tactic built of confronting both inconstancy and stagnancy in these urban spaces.[39]

This inconstant constancy is akin to what Ghassan Moussawi theorizes as *al-wada'*, or the situation. Al-wada' literally means "circumstances," or "the state of things." Moussawi claims that citizens in Beirut use al-wada' to refer to "feelings of constant unease, anticipation of the unknown or what the future might bring, and daily anxieties" that are the result of everyday threats of violence, economic precarity, omnipresence of corruption, and lack of basic infrastructure and services.[40] Moussawi's contribution in theorizing al-wada' as the context or backdrop for queer strategies in Beirut is to underscore how queer theories of normativity presume the constancy and stability of normativity. In recognizing al-wada's essential disruption as normative, Moussawi highlights strategies of survival and thriving that develop in response to and must intervene in conditions and contexts of constant disruption and precarity.

What is the value of disruption as a strategy of refusal in a context of constant disruption? What other strategies of survival and thriving are made necessary when normativity is felt as a constant state of unpredictable disruption? Moussawi's work helps to illustrate how the provocation of istifzaz (discussed in chap. 2), felt as a welcome invitation to some, will feel unwelcome or annoying to others when experienced alongside a litany of provocative or suppressive openings and closures that listeners also constantly encounter. The felt state of constant disruption that is al-wada' provides material grounding for how the glitch, to return to Rosa Menkman, with whom I started this chapter, is not "experienced as an art of momentum" by everyone.[41]

Practiced inattention in rap concerts is a cultivated response to these material conditions. The meaning of the concert or the opening it offers cannot be easily dissociated from geopolitical, intimately felt conditions of constant disruption and precarity. Recall the fan wearing hijab who asked to stand next to me outside Jaafar's concert in Hamra, Beirut, in chapter 1. Her assertion about how unsafe the space *outside* the theater was for her in this (then) liberal milieu is another affirmation of the different systems within which glitch work moves. Her return to the politics of what is outside the theater, despite having come to be inside it, is another example of how both concert goers and observers are navigating city space with different embodiments of attention and how they actively move through these different attentions as their interests and assessments of risk dictate. Finally, the behavior of concert observers is felt as inattention when compared to the kind of interactions that musicians claim they work toward. This listening is quite another kind of attention, embodied as a practice of weighing what is heard, an inward-focused, careful turning over.

Stillness

The artistic efforts to defamiliarize the familiar through istifzaz, discussed in the previous chapter, are missed or misinterpreted when audiences are only peripherally listening, when other factors compete for their attention. Given that rappers are increasingly invested in more abstract and less explicit navigations of politics, their work suffers when audiences are distracted or when the kind of inattention described earlier in this chapter outweighs other listening practices. Moreover, musicians frequently identified listeners' bodily comportment as the outward manifestation of success. I understand this to include, but also be greater than, a simpler consideration of concert etiquette and whether audiences understand when to clap.

For example, when I asked Syrian rapper Bu Kolthoum about ideal responses from an audience in a concert, he responded, "I hate dancing. Not breakdancing, and of course head banging is part of the process. When you hear a beat, and you move to it, that's part of it. But I mean *dancing*, dancing, that: No. Like, aren't you coming to listen?"[42] His emphasis on listening that cannot happen at the same time as other activities or movement (like *dancing*, dancing) points to a specific embodied attention. Like Hirschkind's interlocutors who debated if it was possible to listen well and perform other activities like driving or working while listening to sermons,[43] Bu Kolthoum's question—*aren't you coming to listen?*—points to specific bodily comportment attached to listening, manifest in a kind of stillness.

This search for a particular kind of engagement is important in that it distinguishes rapper frustration about how listeners engage from their observations about the growth of the scene. *Aren't you coming to listen?* points to an expectation of engaging in relation to others—both the performing rapper and other concert goers—that cannot be reduced to decorum during concerts. I hear his *Aren't you coming to listen?* as an *Aren't you coming to be differently in the presence of others?* or even as *Aren't you coming to be becoming?* It is clear this practice of listening is not only about knowing what to do at a concert. It is also not reducible to the power of the artist onstage. It is about the creation of something in the concert space that didn't exist before and that cannot exist without the concert.

The Lebanese rapper El Rass's description of his ideal concert climax intersects with and expands Bu Kulthoum's:

> When you see a hall of three hundred people, and you're spitting your shit, and no one is moving a thing. They're staring and you can see that they really want to get every word you're saying? You can feel that. Compared to a public, for example, that only reacts when you say something provocative or very catchy. You can see the difference between the different kinds of reactions. And it's not only a question of different kinds of publics. *Sometimes it's your responsibility to take the public to this kind of place.* As opposed to keeping them in the "shout out" place, in the "hype" thing. A lot of people would see a successful show as a super hype thing. For me that is not the case. Like you know when it gets shouting and people going crazy and put your hands up [in the air] and whatever. For me this is not the ideal show. For me the ideal show is when people individually and internally are most affected by what I am proposing to them. And not on a simplistic, basic, bond of punchline/reaction, insult/reaction.[44]

El Rass's description of something palpably felt when "you're spitting your shit and no one is moving a thing" points to a space of emergence when listeners enter the cypher intending *to be still*. El Rass offers three important things in his account. First, a disavowal of "the shout out place" as the desired climax of an effective call-and-response with a live audience. Second, an articulation of stillness—when you're spitting your shit and no one is moving a thing—as a preferred alternative. Third, his assertion that it is his "responsibility" as a musician to "take them there." Testimonies like his and Bu Kolthoum's point to a deliberate avoidance of more traditional models for concert momentum. These accounts are in contradistinction to repeated refrains, chanted lyrics, synchronized gestures, and other iterations of polyphonic communication or an MC "working" the crowd documented in much global hip-hop literature. My own participant observation in experimental rap concerts (like at the concert at La Wain; see chap. 2) affirms the importance of an acute focusing of audience attention, practiced and embodied as stillness.

Moreover, the ideal engagements rappers describe also point to processes of sedimentation in the kinds of attention they seek from listeners. It is this process of sedimentation and the corresponding implications it has for stillness that I want to turn to now. Bu Kolthoum's *Aren't you coming to listen?* could be misinterpreted, I think, as an ask for a specific kind concentration. It might be more accurately framed as a desire to be considered, sifted through. Where the sedimentation around istifzaz is not unlike Rana and my steady picking through the park above Arar Street, and our surprise at the dead cat.

Hirshkind's work is again helpful in understanding how this kind of invitation to listen works. He describes listening as a process of sedimentation. Again writing about listeners to Islamic sermons, he writes, "The ability to both recognize and take delight in small differences in the telling of a story one has heard many times before, to grasp the workings of providence or the effects of sin in the actions of characters, to register with appropriate awe and surprise the appearance of the miraculous: these define the outline of a practice, one that requires honed sensory skills and the criteria for their assessment."[45] This is the kind of practice that also is embodied in stillness and that is integral to the experience of filling the head associated with rap in Arabic. This stillness offered by listeners feeds back to musicians about what kind of momentum or toward what kind of peak their concerts might move (sometimes it's your responsibility to take them there). El Rass told me, "When I realized, every time I go on stage, I see people crying: this changed my conception of my own work." Being listened to with stillness invites musicians into different conceptualizations of their roles as central conduits in concert spaces.

Inattention is an acceptance of the concert that rides the exhilaration of the opening that concert offers, knowing the precarity of the moment. Cultivated inattention knows nothing is certain except the constant disruption of al-wadaʿ, and prepares to ride the energy of the opening, to stay on top of it. In contrast, stillness is an acceptance of the concert that enters to stay. It is an attention that says, "I believe this will happen again, despite of al-wadaʿ. I make myself still to discern what I can from this opening, as I move toward the next one."

Recall the sequence of concerts—Bu Kolthoum, Satti, and Malikah at the Word Is Yours Festival; and Muqataʿa, Khotta Ba, El Rass, and others at the Al-Balad Festival—and the patterns of divided audience attention that greeted musicians there. I proposed understanding this inattention as neither ignorance about proper concert etiquette nor resistance to the festivals' cosmopolitan restaging of public space. I drew on Moussawi theorization of al-wada' to understand audience inattention as a navigation of the constant felt context of disruption, precarity, and stagnancy in these cities. Inattention allows observers to engage openings like concerts from the side of the concert space, from across the street, or in the backstage alley without reflecting or positioning themselves within the opening the concert stages.

Bu Kolthoum and El Rass identify a very different kind of attention, manifest as a kind of stillness, at a pronounced remove from dancing or hype as their desired mode of audience engagement in rap concerts.[46] This stillness is a markedly different comportment of both bodies and attention. It is central to the feelings of pleasure I am associating with the genre, the experience of filling the head, that is the subject of the next and final chapter. Before moving there, I will explore a few more examples of the practice of stillness through accounts of listening to the Ramallah Underground.

Sedimentation

The track opens with the orchestral sample and the bass both on a C-sharp (C#), a single note. There is no tension. The sample is the refrain "*khaleeni 'ayeesh*" from Umm Kulthoum's "Amal Hayati." As it plays, the bass moves down a whole step to a B natural and then moves a further whole step down to A natural, accompanied by a new orchestral sample, a trill on a minor second. Then the bass and the sample climb back up to B, and finally both lines return to the C#. This harmony repeats itself over and over for the duration of the track. It is a constant push and pull, pulling tension and resolving tension, over and over. Umm Kulthoum vocals are layered over this as well as the orchestra doubling her melody on B, D#, E, C#, which contains a similar theme of approaching tension and releasing it. This dialogue between the bassline and the sample makes the track feel like it is starting and stopping. Umm Kulthoum's plea sounds like it may be allowed to play out each time before the sample is cut short and replaced by reverb.[47]

Mirroring the musical tension in the opening and interludes just described, the lyrics in Ramallah Underground's "Khaleeni 'Ayeesh" ("Let Me Live") also stage tension in the constant interruption of expectations. The listener hears Umm Kulthoum's plea in the sample and expects the Palestinian crew to address their lyrics to the Occupation. But no, the lyrics castigate the global Palestinian community for the hypocrisy in frameworks of resistance that require austerity for young people in the West Bank while Palestinians in diaspora live wealthy, carefree lives. The plea to be allowed to live is to fellow compatriots, to imagine lives that are not overdetermined by performances of "resistance." In the track, the rapper Muqataʿa directly confronts the hypocrisy of the Palestinian diaspora for holding forth about "resistance" from afar while Palestinians like him, enduring the Occupation, just want to live life without asking for handouts. It is a track laced with anger, the disgust in Muqataʿa's verses contrasting cuttingly with the yearning in Umm Kulthoum's voice. Listening to this track and sifting through the starts and stops, who it is addressing, the tension, the istifzaz, and the proposals it offers is a good example of how experimental rap invites the cultivation of stillness. You need this stillness to sift through the layers the piece offers.

Listeners frequently describe the piece as "dark." The Jordanian DJ Sotusura remembers Arab audiences in London being visibly upset by it. He told me, "Everybody who hears this outside of Palestine feels like it's directed at him."[48] I knew this piece but was surprised when DJ Sotusura brought it up in our interview in 2015. He used it as an example of what he called "two schools of Palestinian hip-hop." Examining these two schools is my final exploration of the cultivation of different kinds of attention in rap in Arabic, through different kinds of calls into the cypher offered by rappers.

I was asking Sotursura about audience reactions to rap, skating around the question of *tarab*, or a kind of musical ecstasy (which I will explore more in the next chapter). Relaying what rap could do, DJ Sotusura drew my attention to the influence and legacies of two Palestinian rap and hip-hop crews. The first was DAM (Tamer Nafar, Suhell Nafar, and Mahmoud Jreri). DAM are from Lod, a Palestinian town inside Israel (what Palestinians call '48) and are the subject of numerous academic studies on youth, subculture, music, and rap in Palestine as well as the documentary film *Slingshot Hip-Hop*.[49] The second crew Sotusura brought up was the Ramallah Underground (Muqataʿa [whose solo work is discussed in chap. 2] and Asifeh [Stormtrap] and Aswat [Basel Abbas]). Ramallah Underground split up in the early 2010s, but all three members are still making art/music (other tracks of theirs discussed in the intro.).[50] Basel Abbas (Aswat) is a sound/visual artist who collaborates prominently with Ruanne Abu-Rahmeh.[51] Both DAM and the Ramallah Underground were active during the Second Intifada (2000–06).

In our conversations about different kinds of concerts and audience reactions, about hype and stillness, DJ Sotusura told me, "Ramallah

Underground is a school when it comes to Arabic hip-hop. DAM is a school and Ramallah Underground is a different school."[52] In saying so, Sotusura identified aesthetic and political differences between the two groups, differences that can be traced as aesthetic lineages within the Palestinian rap scene and beyond.[53]

Both older musicians and producers and younger ones recognize important aesthetic differences between DAM and the Ramallah Underground. Sotusura explained, "DAM are good performers, they're good onstage, capturing the crowd, and communicating with the crowd. I think in this part of it they're stronger than the others. They're the first crew that did live shows and had a proper interaction with the crowd and had a proper live show." The Ramallah-based rapper Haykal described it like this: "DAM have, like, signatures. Like 'Rrrrrrramallah!' all the time. They want to keep people hyped, in a fun way. '*Yalla!* Let's have fun!' 'Yalla heyyyy!' [he claps]." He described this style of DAM's stage presence as "more like comic" and nationalistic.[54] Al-Nather called it "acting."

In contrast to this, Haykal offered that "the way [that Muqataʿa, formerly of Ramallah Underground] delivers, it's not his concern if people like him or not. He's informing. There is informative behavior in both of them [Asifeh and Muqataʿa]. They like for the effect on people to come from . . . the words themselves, how they control the sound, and how they use hip-hop for what it is, as music. DAM do it up more like a show."[55] This "informative behavior" is critical for understanding what kind of listening experimental rappers invite. It is this informative behavior that is especially conducive to Hirschkind's "process of sedimentation." Moreover, these differences between how performance styles invite attention are precisely what excited a younger generation (cohering, for example, around the *saleb wahed* collective in Ramallah) about the music while also making up what Sotusura considered to be the foundations for "two schools" of rap in Palestine. These noted differences in how rappers invite audiences into the cypher—comic, nationalistic, acting versus informative—and the attendant listening practices each expect—I could say hyped up or sedimentative—are so important for an understanding of the aesthetics, experiences, and ultimately political promise of the genre I have been laying out in this book.

Another related example draws on the differences between DAM and the Ramallah Underground. Al-Nather and childhood friend Dakn were twelve when they first heard the two crews perform, a concert they remember vividly. Dakn described it like this:

86 | Filling the Head

I came with my neighborhood club [نادي] where we had been playing basketball. I was very young and most of the crowd was my age. I'd heard of DAM, I knew some of their tracks. DAM took the stage and everybody got on their feet and started dancing, and I did too. Their track "Meen Irhabi" ["Who's the Terrorist?"] in the middle of the *intifada* really captured people's imaginations [كثير بتعقد كانت]. Every line was like what we wanted to hear.

But then Ramallah Underground took the stage. And they played "Khaleeni 'Ayeesh" ["Let Me Live"]. And that was like, wow [وكانت يعني احا]. It was from the street. It was different: a different approach to people.[56]

The two tracks were released around the same time. The first, DAM's popular anthem, "Meen Irhabi," has been written about extensively. The piece revolves around the question and answer "Who's the terrorist? / You're the terrorist!" and proceeds to outline the ways in which Zionist Israelis are terrorizing the indigenous Palestinians, who, far from being terrorists themselves despite global accusations, are defending their homes. The piece is by far DAM's most popular track. In the 2010s, they were still being asked to play it in concerts, requests they only grudgingly entertained during my fieldwork, a decade after its release.[57]

In the second track, the one discussed above, Muqata'a's verses are set between Umm Kulthoum's samples. Umm Kulthoum's piece "Amal Hayati," from which the sample is taken, is about a love affair that is ending. The refrain "let me live" (khaleeni 'ayeesh) is a plea to be allowed one more day in the company of her beloved. Her refrain takes on a very different meaning sampled under Muqata'a's verses. I mentioned earlier how DJ Sotursura recalled how the Palestinian diaspora were called into this piece. Dakn, who grew up in and heard the piece live in Ramallah as a teenager, recounts that he felt the piece was written for him. "It reached out and shook me," he recalled.[58]

Moreover, how Dakn juxtaposed live performances of the two pieces is a critical articulation of the role of interpellation in how rap in Arabic works. While Dakn and Al-Nather both admit that while they were excited by DAM's piece in performance, it was Ramallah Underground's track that really touched them.[59] Dakn concluded that the Ramallah Underground simply "saw things differently, and this perspective filled my head ['aba rasi]. You know what I mean?"[60] Dakn's identification of Ramallah Underground's different perspective as the thing that felt satisfying in their music comes in an expression to stop and be still, an expression of wonder (*wa kanat ya'ni aha*: it was, like, wow). Stillness results from a recalibration of thought, energy, attitudes. Stillness is the result of being asked to and

Listening | 87

agreeing to enter, to listen; it is the practice of cultivating an engagement with "a different approach to the people."

Like his peers, Haykal also constructs a contrast of the experience of listening to the two bands. His account is additionally telling for how the experience of filling the head differs from other pleasurable reactions induced by listening.

> DAM have this lyric, "Why are the children of the world free, but I don't have freedom?" [ليش اطفال العالم حرة بس انا ما الي حرية؟] in the song "Ma Ili Hurriyyeh" ("I Don't Have Freedom"). I used to repeat this line for like six months after I heard it. But then I thought about it some more, and it occurred to me that the children of the world *aren't* free, and actually this phrase is really dangerous. Your capacity [استيعابك] for resistance itself really disappears here. You erased the idea that there are children who are much more oppressed than the Palestinians, and you've made it so that the Palestinian deserves more respect than the rest. Now you've become like everybody else. You didn't *take me anywhere*. You're repeating the same thing, like Najwa Karam. You didn't *do anything with my brain*. You just repeated what everyone says and got me to repeat it. [Added emphasis]⁶¹

Haykal's association of DAM's lyrical framing of Palestinian suffering with pop music (Najwa Karam is a Lebanese pop star) is telling for how Haykal understands mainstream political narratives as objects of disgust (you've become like everybody else) that work to close off the imagination. The refrain of "I Don't Have Freedom" is meant as a rallying cry of conscience and resistance, relating the Palestinian child to an indifferent global public. But Haykal comes to understand this very rallying cry as an obstacle, saying it didn't *take him anywhere*, and worse, it stopped him from imagining alternatives: *It didn't do anything with my brain*. Instead, it encouraged him to fall in line with a popular iteration of Palestinian politics ("you repeated what everyone else says and got me to repeat it"). DAM's lyrics in this piece survey a range of popular images associated with Palestinian resistance and end with the recording of a child's voice singing the refrain.⁶² It is precisely this that Haykal relates with distaste: "Now you've become like everybody else."

In contrast, Haykal describes Ramallah Underground and the lyrics of Muqata'a a very different way: "When Muqata'a delivers this line, 'We [Palestinians] are the biggest consumers, that's why they keep us alive [اكثر مستهلكين للبضاعة فا تركونا الحياة],' he solves a lot of personal problems for me. He tells me basically 'don't think that you've performed some great resilience [ان صمدت]. Don't think that you are strong.'"⁶³ Haykal's description of Muqata'a telling him that *he is not* strong, that he is not resilient, that he is just a consumer being *allowed* to live, inverts populist political narratives in Palestine. Muqataʿa's inversion of expectations—his use of istifzaz—underscores for Haykal the economic dependency of Palestinians on Israel and asks for a consciousness that is not content with getting the listener to "repeat" what everyone else says. Listening to this, Haykal suggests, produced a feeling of surprise and relief; it invited him to relate to the status quo differently—it *solved a lot of problems for me*. It is precisely this kind of reaction that is the experience of *filling the head*.

Conclusion

This chapter began by considering infelicitous calls into the cypher—those invitations to listen that are ignored by potential audiences or listeners who hear the call but decide not to heed it. I argue that these are important in understanding not just a range of aesthetic choices used by rappers and DJs, but a range of listening practices cultivated by audiences and potential audiences and rappers themselves. In the production of concerts and music festivals, there are clear attempts to discipline audiences into specific kinds of behavior and patterns of relation. These are manifest in the reflections of bouncers, event owners, and festival curators. This chapter builds on the previous one, exploring an epistemology built on istifzaz and the affective, social, political relations engendered within the cypher. It is important that relations in the cypher seemed to be preconditioned by the bodily comportment of their audiences—in *how* they listen. This *how* is not only a precondition to *but a result of* listening.

I concluded the chapter with reflections on stillness and how this felt suspension of time and energy in a concert space is often indicative of success—of the conditions of the music filling the head. In the next chapter, I explore that stillness and what helps to engender it. As I will show, stillness is not void of but born of movement and motion. I turn to Kevin Quashie's notion of quiet and Jose Muñoz's work on cruising to further unpack stillness and the political motion embodied within it. That final chapter explores yearning as the affective underpinning of music and listening that *fill the head*.

4

YEARNING

In October 2023, a few days before the Israeli assault on Gaza began, the Lebanese standup comedian Shaden Fakih joined the podcast *Sarde (After Dinner)*.[1] The conversation was wide-ranging in the style of the show, touching on the Lebanese comedian's recent tour across Europe, Arab identity, religion, Lebanese politics, economics, and colonialism. In response to the hosts' standard closing question—"Is there hope?"—which Fakih begged them not to ask, she eventually responded, "There's no hope. *Khalas* [enough]. We've grown up." But she also said, "We have to struggle. I don't believe anything will change, but there's no other option. We have to struggle."[2] Her remarks encapsulated a disavowal of a hopeful or optimistic orientation toward the future that is nonetheless riven with longing. Fakih's renunciation of hope echoes testimonies from activists, artists, musicians, technologists, and others in the decade that followed the so-called Arab Uprisings.

The heart of this chapter is an invitation to understand yearning as political agency. It is around and toward this center that I move my analysis. Yearning, longing—I consider these active doings that are materially and affectively different from a more static hope. At the same time, yearning is a doing that is informed by other feelings and dispositions, like anger. Audre Lorde reminds us that "it is easier to be furious than to be yearning."[3] And I move in pursuit of that challenge: the more difficult yearning. How do we understand yearning as a practice or even as a cultivated attention that is rooted in the present and oriented toward the future? And how do we imagine the enactment of that yearning in everyday things like listening to music?

These questions conclude my consideration of the ways in which audiences and musicians experience experimental rap in Arabic through an explicit exploration of the pleasure associated with those experiences. My exploration of this pleasure again returns to Audre Lorde, this time to her understanding of the erotic as "the power of our unexpressed or unrecognized feeling."[4] Like the tension built and released over any number of tracks I've discussed in these pages, the power of unrecognized or unexpressed feeling, felt as yearning, is central to the search for music that *fills the head*.

I am looking to understand what listeners and musicians say (and cannot say) they are listening for and what amounts to the relief, excitement, and surprise that first drew my tears in that subway car to Harlem and at other points raised goose bumps or made me shudder. What is, as Palestinian rapper Haykal offered in the previous chapter, the experience of a piece of rap "solving a lot of problems"? Further still, what does the pursuit of that experience look like? To answer these questions, I engage the Arabic ethnomusicological notion of *tarab*, Kevin Quashie's articulation of the *interior*, and Jose Muñoz's dialogue with Ernest Bloch and C. L. R. James in his theorizations of *cruising*. In so doing, I offer a search for the experience of music that fills the head as a model of political subjectivity built on relational movement.

This chapter ties up some open threads in my analysis over the course of this book—as yet unsettled pieces like what is *the head* in the phrase *filling the head*? How to understand where this experience is embodied? Is stillness, as a cultivated attention and practice of listening, static? How to understand the movement that is embodied in this stillness? And finally, what happens once something *has* filled the head? How to understand catharsis as the continuation of this pleasure or further elaboration of the yearning attached to it?

I argue that yearning points to belonging in formation. It is an experience of coconstituted becoming, a recognition of relationality and interdependence, and, perhaps most importantly for this study, an anticipation of being hailed *otherwise*. To return to Ashon Crowley, "Otherwise is a word that names plurality as its core operation, otherwise bespeaks the ongoingness of possibility, of things existing other than what is given, what is known, what is grasped."[5] These otherwise hailings into the cypher are part provocation, part affirmation, part aspiration. They stage polyphonic communication (call and response) in a cypher that is at once *here and now* and also a *cypher to come*. When these interpellations succeed, they open instead of close off possibilities. Ultimately, I argue, it is this yearning for being hailed otherwise that marks the experience of listening to rap in Arabic.

Longing

The expression *'abi al-rass* is commonly encountered in reference to the experience of tarab.⁶ Similar to but distinct from the Spanish *duende*, the Persian *hal*, Albanian wedding singing, the Tunisian *stambeli*, and the Moroccan *gnawa*, tarab describes both a traditional genre of Arabic music production (*tarab al-'arabi* [tarab music]) and the audience-performer interactions and the affective condition evoked by the exceptional performance of live music, often associated with that genre.⁷ Most readily located in the careers and popularity of Umm Kulthoum, Mohammed Abd al-Wahab, and others of their generation, tarab music reached its peak during the mid- to late twentieth century.⁸ Tarab music is associated with songs written in specific modes where the subject is almost always love and is nearly completely dominated by an affective mode of longing. My interlocutors are intimately familiar with this style of popular music. They consistently testify to its presence in their narratives of musical exposure as children and teenagers. Tarab music is consistently sampled across the wide range of Arabic rap, as discussed in a number of tracks in this book.

A great number of contemporary Arabic rap lyrics explicitly articulate longing—not for a sweetheart but for any number of things taken, lost, missing, stolen, or otherwise nonexistent. Without taking a lover as the subject, many lyrics articulate sentiments of betrayal, spurning, or deceit. Most of the powerful tracks I've chosen to discuss as exemplary in this book articulate some form of alienation—from self, from immediate community, from international understanding—that may be the result of local corruption, colonialism, occupation, discrimination, and so forth. While these lyrics are not articulated in an affective register often associated with love, lust, or despair, much of it is written and performed in a mode of longing. These ways of engaging with the world invite the listener to relate otherwise to politics as is.

The affective articulation of desire, betrayal, or slighting in overtly political contexts in rap tracks should not be confused with pieces in which rappers directly address a subject of love or romantic partnership, a growing subgenre. Arabic rap about love has been a favorite suggestion among journalists, enthusiasts, and musicians themselves who declare politics "gets boring." I am not associating the powerful affective modes I think can exist in rap performance with individual songs that discuss love.[9] I am talking about the articulation of longing when the topic is not overtly romance, where it overlaps with anger, exhaustion, or hope. I echo here Claudia Tate's understanding of feeling, desire, and longing to "not simply mean sexual longings but all kinds of wanting, wishing, yearning, longing, and striving."[10]

Tarab music is called such because of the tarab condition it has been associated with producing. At its simplest, to be affected by tarab in a musical context means to be moved by the music. Ethnomusicologist Ali Jihad Racy elaborates an understanding of tarab as a state of rapture, an emotional blending that is transformative for subjects, and a desired state of spectatorship.[11] Distinct from trance though it shares some of its characteristics, the tarab condition is an affective state induced by the processes of careful listening and exchange with engaged performers.[12]

Tarab has been a subject of interest for my theoretical and methodological interlocutors in this book as well. Notably, Charles Hirschkind, in his work on listening to Islamic cassette sermons (discussed in chap. 3), also turns to tarab and the cathartic release understood to be embodied in listening that has been the subject of a range of Muslim commentators. Indeed, the widely recognized power of listening on the heart or the soul in the Islamic tradition has made the reception of music and poetry the subject of some debate. Because listening in the Islamic tradition is recognized to have such an effect, Muslim philosophers have spent considerable energy delineating what kinds of listening are acceptable, what is acceptable to listen to, and how listening should be carried out. For example, the treatises of the twelfth-century Persian philosopher Muhammad ibn Muḥammad Al-Tusiyy Al-Ghazzali are on the proper form of listening: how to be moved (and how not to be moved) by the love of God.

This legacy of philosophical and scholarly attention in the Islamic tradition on proper forms of listening supports Hirschkind's argument of understanding listening to recorded sermons as a modern but historically informed disciplinary practice. That is, listening is something certain believers learn to do as part of developing the attention and orientation associated with living a moral life. Central for Hirschkind is the concept of "listening with the heart." His interlocutors describe a goal of listening with the heart and an attendant a feeling of *inshirah al-sadr* (opening of the chest) as a pleasurable release that can result from proper forms of listening to Islamic sermons. Listening with the heart is something that one learns how to do in order to precipitate this cathartic experience. For Hirschkind, *qalb* (heart) is located at a remove from ʿ*aql* (the mind), and this distance holds important sway in the development of an individual's orientation to the world. He writes that listening "with the heart means to bring to bear on it those sensory capacities honed . . . that allow one to hear . . . what would escape listeners who applied only their 'ears' or al-ʿaql [minds]."[13] A central component of Hirschkind's argument is recentering the senses in modern political subjectivity. Using his interlocutors' understandings of how sermons work on the heart through the ears, he offers, in his own words, "an interrogation of the sensorium as both a condition for and object of an emergent form of ethical-political reasoning."[14]

As discussed in chapter 3, Hirschkind's work has been influential in the development of my own understanding of the relationship between listening and cultivated attention and the possible shapes of political subjectivity associated with or developed through interpellation (the practice of hailing and being hailed). However, I am less interested in the idea that embodied listening practices can reclaim feeling as more important than, or just as important as, reason in the development of political subjectivity. I am more interested in understanding how listening to experimental rap in Arabic can help dissolve the differentiation between feeling and reason as attached to agency. I am trying to understand what blending reason and feeling could imply for recognizing political activity.

It deserves mentioning that while *al-rass* (literally, the head) is clearly associated with the mind (ʿ*aql*) and the brain (*moukh*), the head should not be reduced to the seat of reason or cognitive functioning alone. In Arabic, as in English, *head* is much more physical than either ʿaql or moukh and connotes a sense of leadership (as in *head of a bank*). I have also long privately appreciated the relationship between *shaʿr* (hair) and *rass* (head). Shaʿr (hair) shares its root with the Arabic words for both feeling (*shaʿour*) and poetry (*sheʿr*). So in my mind's picture of the head, there is already a composite of both feeling and thinking.

I have found tarab useful as a framework because it encourages this kind of conceptual blending on multiple levels. Racy argues that the term tarab is "conceptually elusive." For example, especially in twentieth-century tarab al-ʿarabi where the subject is love or matters of the heart, it is all the more compelling that the phrase used to describe the feeling of listening to that music is *filling the head*. In a useful formulation for describing how tarab may be identified, Racy suggests understanding it as "'transformative blending'—the creation of new blends that are no longer identifiable by their inner, mostly emotional ingredients or no longer emotional in the familiar sense."[15] In addition to the easy association with longing, tarab is useful for understanding movement between emotions or affects—for example, from sadness to anger—without reifying or reducing them to each other.

I am also looking for a kind of transformative blending that, as a practice, moves among cognition, intellectual engagement, feelings, emotion, and affect. Tarab itself identifies movement between emotions as integral to how it functions. My own proposal in this chapter is that yearning and the different embodiments and practices that I have been suggesting may be associated with it—listening as a cultivated attention embodied in stillness—can be used to shape an understanding of the political that consists of regular, disciplined, interdependent movement. The point is to explore what kinds of political subjectivity is legible if the criteria for recognition lies in a manifestation of desire that is always in motion. What kind of activity is political when political subjects are understood to be seekers in pursuit of belonging otherwise?

* * *

The patterns of cathartic release documented by a wide spectrum of commentators on tarab in different musical and religious contexts point to relief in hearing an articulation of longing similar to one's own. An episode in Abu al-Faraj al-Isfahani's 10th century *Kitab al-Aghani (Book of Songs)* takes the example of a woman far from her homeland. One day when she is off to gather water, she hears someone singing about their own homesickness. The woman is so moved by the music that she faints and dies.[16] The anecdote highlights how the feeling of homesickness was already present in the woman, but the surprise of hearing someone else articulate it, and set to music, brought that feeling out and moved her. This tarab relieved her of the painful feeling of being far from home. Al-Ghazzali quotes Sufi philosopher Abu Said b. al-'Arabi as saying, "Ecstasy is lifting of the curtain, and witnessing of the watcher, and presence of understanding, and observation of the unseen, and converse with the secret, and *intercourse with that which is missing*; it consists in thy passing away and coming to an end in respect of what thou art."[17] This feeling of relief, this conversing with the secret and the passing of one version of oneself into another, can also be manifested in the longing for something politically evasive and as yet unattained.

To follow the framework of resistance readily projected on the genre of rap in Arabic, it seems at the very least that the anger that performers articulate in their lyrics (rage, I was told more than once) should translate to the audience, inspiring them to pick up rocks and make revolution—or whatever artistic resistance is meant to catalyze. On the contrary, however, most listeners affirm they feel relieved or relaxed after having attended a rap concert. DJ Sotusura offers his reflections having watched audiences for over a decade: "This guy on stage *relieved* them. He said everything that was on their minds so they *relax*. They don't come out of the concert, 'Let's break shit!' I think rather they come out of it feeling like, 'Wow this was *good for my soul* to hear someone say what I can't say.'"[18] This feeling of relief in *hearing someone say what I can't say* mirrors precisely what al-Isfahan and al-'Arabi describe above as "intercourse with that which is missing." This is the yearning and relief that can exist in the experience of listening to experimental rap in Arabic.

I have been suggesting throughout this book that understanding the political experience of listening to this music requires a different model for understanding political agency. Articulating precisely the shape of that agency now depends on locating where it may be traced. Haykal's "you didn't do anything with my brain" (see chap. 3) together with Sotusura's "this was good for my soul" suggest that al-rass (the head in *filling the head*) is best understood as an in-between place—neither 'aql nor qalb but both undeniably inflected by the intellect and irrefutably affected by feeling. A range of interlocutors and inspiration have invoked the chest, the heart, the head, the mind, and the soul, all through specific engagement via the ears. Pushing past this litany of possible places to locate the site of yearning and further flesh out the political subjectivity attached to belonging otherwise, I turn to Kevin Quashie's 2012 book, *The Sovereignty of Quiet: Beyond Resistance in Black Culture*.

In his captivating study, Black literature scholar Kevin Quashie locates something he calls "the interior." His project is to explore the political possibilities for Black subjects beyond the expectation of resistance. He locates this possibility in a set of compartments and practices that are "quiet." Like the stillness I located in the previous chapter, this quiet "is neither motionless nor without sound. Quiet, instead, is a metaphor for the full range of one's inner life—one's desires, ambitions, hungers, vulnerabilities, abilities, fears."[19] *The Sovereignty of Quiet*, like many of the tracks I have described listening to in this book, has also compelled me to be very still and to listen.

Specifically, Quashie's understanding of the interior as an alternative to agency and subjectivity and the external performances of resistance calls me to push my own analysis in welcome ways. His proposal bridges multiple sites of embodiment and feeling and echoes Hirschkind's tracing of an ethics of listening in arguing for the recognition of "an ethic—rather than a politic of resistance" that guides the actions of the fictional Black female characters he analyzes.[20] His articulation of the interior is worth quoting at length. He offers, leaning on Hortense Spillers:

> The interior is the inner reservoir of thoughts, feelings, desires, fears, ambitions that shape a human self; it is both a space of wild sel*full*ness, a kind of self-indulgence, and "the locus at which self-interrogation takes place." Said another way, the interior is expansive, voluptuous, creative; impulsive and dangerous, it is not subject to one's control but instead has to be taken on its own terms. It is not to be confused with intentionality or consciousness, since it is something more chaotic than that, more akin to hunger, memory, forgetting, the edges of all the humanness one has. Despite its name, the interior is not unconnected to the world of things (the public or political or social world), nor is it an exact antonym for exterior. Instead, the interior shifts in regard to life's stimuli but it is neither resistant to nor overdetermined by the vagaries of the outer world. The interior has its own ineffable integrity and it is a stay against the social world.[21]

Quashie's proposal for an introspective, desire-ful, wonder-ful political subjectivity is a powerful alternative to any single physical location (heart, chest, head, mind, soul) as a site of searching and yearning. This interior recognizes the potency of political being in a site of observation, vulnerability, and wonder. Engaging Quashie's work has been marked for me by a sense of relief as I searched for ways to understand the experiences I was having with the music, and that I knew others were also having, but that I struggled to articulate as more than exasperation with the framework of resistance.

Consider Haykal's description of listening to Muqataʻa (see chap. 3) and how it echoes in an uncanny reverberation of Quashie's analysis of Zora Neale Hurston's character Janie in *Their Eyes Were Watching God*. Quashie quotes Hurston, "[Janie] stood there until *something fell off the shelf inside her*. Then she went inside there to see what it was."[22] This is a delightful way to read Haykal's assertion that Muqataʻa's lines "solved a lot of problems for me." The experience is hearing a line and—*sharp intake of air*—feeling the jar fall off the shelf. You make yourself still and think, *Did I hear that?* And then go see what it was. Hurston again: "New thoughts had to be thought and new words said. She didn't want to live like that."[23]

An invitation to relate to politics, otherwise.

Stillness (Coda): Quiet

As mentioned, Quashie addresses the closing off of political horizons in the expectation that Black artists and authors are always performing resistance. He offers, "All living is political—every human action means something—but all living is not in protest; to assume such is to disregard the richness of life."[24] Quashie's alternative to a celebration of resistance is a focus on quiet, which entails attention to the interior and the inner lives of Black protagonists in African American literature. His is a call to "rethink expressiveness" by paying attention to the intimate processes of engaging with the world and the "agency to be had in surrendering to the wildness of one's inner life."[25] The stillness rappers seek out from their audiences (see chap. 3) demonstrates that for them, ideal listening practices are a similar formation. Stillness is not passive or devoid of activity; rather, it is an active kind of listening, of sifting through stimuli, of surrendering, of waiting.

In chapter 3, I explored stillness as the embodiment of a particular kind of cultivated attention by concertgoers, at a remove from the inattention of concert observers. The stillness I have been discussing as a response to the call into the cypher by experimental rappers refers to a kind of bodily comportment, very similar to Quashie's quiet. It is not the stillness referred to in Muslim religious contexts as *sakina*, which means more "tranquility" or "calm." Stillness in chapter 3 was important in how it allowed for listening to take place as a process of sedimentation, a process of paying attention, sifting through layers.

In the previous chapter, I addressed Althusser's theory of subject formation where interpellation features centrally in the subjectivization of political being. Different from these subject-forming hailings, I suggested that invitations into the cypher gesture toward alternative becomings—not in relation to existing authorities but across multiple force fields and in relation to other similarly interpellated listeners. These invitations to listen *hail political being into being otherwise*. This is different from the birth or appearance of political subjects so often sought in political ethnographies of cultural production, underpinned by Foucauldian, Arendtian, or Butlerian frameworks of the political. The reception of invitations to listen by listeners yearning to be hailed otherwise acknowledges that agency is always already there and, more importantly, always already hailed otherwise. To reformulate Althusser's exchange, it is a practice of saying, "Hey, you! *There is something else.*" The listener nods. She makes herself still, to hear. And suddenly, the jar falls off the shelf inside her. There it is: the force field that is other listeners, other concentrated stillness, the recognition of other formations and collective relation to this deeply wounded world.

Quashie's quiet is a productive way to understand the practice of listening for these invitations. He calls quiet "a vibrant, self-aware relationship to the world" that allows for one to "engage life as it comes, to move and be moved."[26] Quashie's point is to locate a political subjectivity—a selfhood—not based on one's subject position, on one's race or gender or one's response to authority. His argument is to locate political being in "the rages of the interior—a subjectivity served and armed by possibility."[27] Recall that Hirschkind's point is for the acknowledgment of the heart as central to political subjectivity, significant in its alternative to the Western location of subjectivity in the mind. One of Hirschkind's central arguments is toward the location of a modern political agency informed by and shaped by a religious, feeling heart.

My own point is first to locate and understand a multisited interior that is both cognitive and feeling, both intellectual and affected. This interior is the felt location of music that fills the head. Second, continuing to borrow from Quashie, I propose to understand this interior as a place of motion and searching. Given the embodiment of stillness I have been outlining as central, the interior as a place of motion deserves further attention. The pursuit of music that fills the head and the felt satisfaction in political invitations of being hailed otherwise, and of, as Haykal offered, *hearing someone say what I can't say*, should not be reduced to an understanding of "listening with the heart" or developing the capacity to hear emotionally. But I also want to offer that these same listening practices should not be disassociated from the Arabic qalb (heart).

The root of the Arabic word for heart, ب - ل - ق, means to flip, turn over, upturn, topple. In this I am not trying to make a tired argument about the inconstancy of feeling. Rather, I am recognizing a practice of turning over, of careful weighing and considering, testing even—the way a very young child examines an object, flips it over, even tosses it aside, only to return to it sometime later—as central to the activity of the interior and the quiet practices that reflect it. Further, this attention, this turning over of learning and discovery, of frustration and excitement, built of but not reducible to curiosity—encouraged in the youngest children and gradually discouraged with age—*is* agency. It is agency that appears not as response to the call of authority or resistance to it. Rather, this agency is apparent in relational observation, attentive discovery, careful consideration, and yearning for otherwise. Quashie writes, "The agency is in the *asking*, in the *pursuit*."[28]

This pursuit is akin to the battle Shaken Fadih mentioned in response to the question I referred to in the beginning of this chapter: "Is there hope?" To steal from the Ramallah Underground (see the intro.), the pursuit is recognizing politics as an irrefutable part of one's life, no matter how much you pretend it doesn't exist.[29] And without leading too much into the musical example of this chapter (discussed below), this agency in the asking is a kind of introspective arousing of oneself (*thawra 'ala al-nafs*), a kind of prayer: listening itself as a calling into being where the listening and the calling are almost indistinguishable. A yearning for being otherwise.

Al-wada' (Reprise): Thoughts on Waiting

In the introduction and again in chapter 3, I included some general framings of *al-wada'*, or the geopolitical and sociocultural context in which I understand experimental rap in Arabic to intervene. As I develop these thoughts on yearning, I am reminded of my interlocutors' reflections on time itself and the role of waiting not only in the completion of my own analysis but as reflected in musicians' conceptualizations of their own work. I argued in the introduction that a confluence of hope and suffocation, growth and stagnation characterizes Amman's, Beirut's, and Ramallah's growing capacities for alternative music production. It is the double bind of wanting to build and wanting to leave, and the quickly successive expressions of hope and despair, that make up the specific texture of "wait and see" in these cities. These feelings of frustration, impatience, anxiety, and malaise often accompany a deliberate retreat from political expression. The Jordanian rapper Satti offered, "I don't want to be just a column in the newspaper, you know? Everybody's really into politics now. People read a lot and they are hearing all sorts of different things already.... What's it going to change if I come and rap about the same things? This stopped being really interesting to me. It's not about getting in trouble or anything. I'm just sick and tired of it."³⁰ Satti's remarks reflect a change in the sociality of political discourse ("everybody's really into politics now"), something Satti doesn't feel his music can compete with ("this stopped being really interesting to me"). Moreover, his decision not to address politics is marked by exhaustion or frustration ("I'm just sick and tired of it"). The Jordanian rapper Khotta Ba expressed similar feelings when he also articulated a retreat from politics, saying, "I no longer have the heart to run after politics or go down to protest. Khalas. You feel like you're not going to have an effect, nor are you going to accomplish anything. Because seriously what you're up against is huge, so don't waste your time. If it's going to work out, it will work out on its own. Not because of me or anyone else."³¹ Khotta's resignation here is laden with exhaustion ("what you're up against is huge, so don't waste your time"). His remarks echo those documented by other anthropologists and ethnographers of millennial Egypt, for example.³² Importantly however, as he continued, he also communicated a pronounced anxiety: "I don't know where I'll be in a year or two years. You really don't know. Maybe you'll find yourself doing great and maybe you'll find yourself with nothing in the street. That's what's happening everywhere around us. Honestly, I don't know what's coming. And I don't feel like what's coming is going to be nice in the end. It doesn't look that way."³³ Thread through these reflections is a palpable disgust laden with exhaustion. These are examples of what anthropologists Stef Jansen and Ghassan Hage identify as the feeling of "not moving well enough," riven with both resignation and disgust.³⁴ These testimonies are exemplary of what Jensen describes in Sarajevo as *ganjati*, as a state of "chasing things." Jansen writes that in his field site of Dobrinja outside Sarajevo after the Dayton Peace Accords, chasing takes place "under the sign of a fragile hope, in need of permanent rekindling, that one was getting closer to the objective."³⁵ As we see above, in Amman, musicians expressed similar patterns, but the "sign of fragile hope" Jensen writes about did not seem to be very present.

Scholarly attention to affect in Arabic-speaking contexts has increased. Moods and emotions like hope, boredom, cynicism, fear, anxiety, desire, and so forth have been theorized as ways of relating to the state (or nonstates, or failed states);³⁶ as ways of relating to architecture and urban geography;³⁷ as products of the circulation of certain media;³⁸ as the entry points to major political events.³⁹ In the Egyptian context, Samuli Schielke has written about boredom and longing in ways that resonate in obvious ways with the moods I also identify in the Levant.⁴⁰ Lori Allen offers an ethnographic picture of cynicism in the Palestinian Territories that similarly resonates with some of my own work in Ramallah. The political scientist Lisa Wedeen offered notes about relationships constructed toward Lauren Berlant's "good life" in Syria that also overlap with my own observations.[41]

Ethnographic research into time and collective attitudes toward the future has been the subject of anthropological work in both the Global South and the Global North for some time. This work has considered neoliberal time through attitudes and behaviors associated with waiting, queueing, traveling, boredom, buying time, and making time, among others.[42] I cannot afford an exhaustive catalog of these here. Nor do I intend to suggest that my own interlocutors comprehensively fit into one or another of these models or that their testimonies cohere instead as a totally unique set of moods, notions of time, or attendant conceptualizations of progress. The testimonies I have included here are intended to put pressure on a notion of the political that locates the objects of dissatisfaction, cynicism, resignation, and disgust not only in a set of players, institutions, or representatives but in a collectively held attitude toward the status quo. The experience of filling the head emerges as a pleasurable experience of relief from this waiting, that acknowledges the exhausting weight of this collective disgust and disappointment. Listening to music cannot end the Occupation or resolve a refugee crisis. But it can offer ways of relating to the present that temporarily invert its exhaustion.

It is precisely this way of relating to politics as is that listening is able to affect. Althusser writes that subjectivity coheres in the *relation* to one's conditions of existence.[43] How individuals relate to their conditions structures how they think about them, act within them, and move to change them. Importantly, then, affecting the relation to these conditions is a significant part of changing them. The possibility of an invitation to shift a relation to these conditions is the promise offered by careful listening. Filling the head is a feeling of relief born of acknowledgment and inversion of politics as is to which the primary relationship is described as exhausting or disgusting, but to which one is largely resigned. Rappers' acknowledgments of identifying and then inverting constitutive abjectness (chap. 1) around them *do things to listeners' brains*, to use Haykal's terminology (chap. 3). Like my own experiences riding the subway in New York listening to Ramallah Underground (intro), these lyrical inversions of politics as is produced marked emotional responses that have the effect of cleansing and relieving—*filling the head*.

To Overthrow Oneself—the Cypher to Come

As I adjust the order of these paragraphs, student encampments are taking seed across the US and around the world. They are occupying spaces of learning and communing in protest of the infallibility of Israeli military action and the efforts the US leads to support the Zionist genocide of Palestinians. The encampments come seven months into a collective global witnessing of brutality all the more terrifying in the knowledge that the violence and depravity being wreaked upon Palestinians today is neither new nor unique to Palestinians. For weeks, as Israeli tanks and troops have amassed in preparation of their declared invasion of Rafah, where more than two million displaced and starving Palestinians have taken refuge, the air has been thick with a perceptible impossible-to-know-what-is-coming and an impossible-to-deny-something-is. We stand on the precipice of something tangibly different, tangibly real. The student encampments are alive with this tipping point. They are pregnant with very material incarnations of care, becoming, and belonging that many of the different cyphers I have sketched here have sometimes promised. By the time these words are printed, this current moment of opening will have transformed to something else. My descriptions will carry naiveté or romance or foolishness. I retain them anyway. They reflect the invitation to possibility that the cypher opened by experimental rap sometimes portends.

In any case, it is impossible not to think of the student encampments as I turn to my next musical example, Nasserdayn al-Touffar and Sayyed al-Darwish's "Kheir al-Shaghab" ("The Rising Riot"). This track, like some of the material I turn to in the outro (and some discussion in chap. 1), is born of a moment of protest but is not what I would call *protest music*. It speaks to the dynamics of the street while also asking for stillness, holding space for quiet deliberations and invocations. It speaks to formations of *al-shaʿb* and *al-nass* ("the people"; see chap. 2) while it also declares a revolution of the self. It does all of this while responding to a very specific set of material formations and openings in widely debated and contested strategies of protest: *the riot*. In all of this, "Kheir al-Shaghab" conjures to borrow from José Muñoz "the moment of the *not-yet-here* that is as vivid as it is necessary."[44]

Indeed, Muñoz's work building an alternative horizon on which to understand queer becoming is helpful to further explore rappers' invitations into the cypher of the here and now and the cypher to come. Like Muñoz, and like the radical Black historian C. L. R. James on which he leans, my intention is also to point to the overlap of the present and the future and question the presumed distance between them. Muñoz asks, "Must the future and the present exist in this rigid binary?" How can we instead recognize, as James suggests, "a future in the present"?[45] As I discuss below, Nasserdayn and Darwish's track is an example of how interpellation in experimental Arabic rap invites imagining a collectivity to come that is rooted in a present individual struggle with oneself. I argue this imaginative move is important in how it "longs for a moment outside of this current state of siege."[46] Like the student encampments today, the cyphers built by experimental rappers and their listeners can also be spaces of struggle despite oneself, over oneself, that, in so doing, lead toward a different collective. The point is not only the ultimate inseparability of the present and the future but also the "transformative blending" of the individual and the collective. Like many of the tracks that inspired this book, "Kheir al-Shaghab" invites a listener to imagine a collective politics to come through a working out of an internal debate about the shape of politics and one's role in them.

* * *

It's 2016. I am running alone along the river in the Georgian capital, Tbilisi. We live some ways from the city center, connected to it by a highway that follows along the Mtkvari river. The water is brown and flows heavily in the opposite direction of the traffic. When it is warm, the fumes from the traffic threaten to smother the open air over the fast, muddy water. It is late morning. I run with the water, against the traffic.

The rush of adrenaline from the 2015 protests against the sectarian regime in Beirut, Lebanon, has not yet worn off for me. The DJ and fixer Muhammad Ali Nayel had uploaded a new playlist. It was called "Musiqah li al-Tamarrod" ("Music for the Rebellion"). Happily putting aside for the moment my skepticism about the romance with protest, I queue up the tracks.

It is a gray day, the clouds are hanging low over the river, and I am feeling far from home, cut off from struggles and conversations I could be a part of. I felt, as we say in Arabic, as if *maʻtouʻa min shajara* (cut off from a tree). I am exhausted by efforts to integrate, restless, and frustrated by a litany of nonthings that is simultaneously the weight of continuous, perpetual real things: the impossibility of rootedness, ever evasive belonging, and frustration with the seeming depleting prospects of living a meaningful life. Over the sound of the car horns and to temporarily drown out my own feeling of strangeness in a city and with a language I don't know well, I crank up the volume and feel my feet pound into the sidewalk.

The opening track of Nayel's playlist is Nasserdayn al-Touffar and Al-Darwish's "Kheir al-Shaghab" ("The Rising Riot"), produced by Hello Psychaleppo.[47] It is not the first time I've heard it, and my pace quickens. Nasserdayn's verse starts; I concentrate. A sequence of permissions to the listener (*sar feek, you can now*), setting up an invitation. My ear catches:

فيك تقول أني مع أني ضدّ و
يلعن كلّ شي و كل حدا

(you can now say I'm with or I'm against and screw everything and everyone).[48]

I run faster. Darwish's verse starts slow and low, and I feel it thundering:

ثورة على النفس //
بس الذليل اذا اكل الشمس بضل تاي //
حيّ على الشعب[49] //
حيّ على خير الشغب //
بآية عالغضب //
الحق شرق على شعر البلد اللي فرد //
على صرخة ما في للأبد //
حيّ على النّاس //
مدد //

> Overthrowing oneself
> But the lowly dog will remain lost, even if he eats the sun
> Heed the call of the people; heed the rising riot
> With a verse on anger
> Truth has risen, on the feeling of the country that was set free
> By the shout "There is no forever!"
> Answer the call: *madad*[50]

I put it on repeat, my strides as long and as wide as I can make them. I feel the yearning in the call Darwish makes in *thawra ʿala al-nafs* (overthrowing oneself): it is a pronouncement, an announcement, a calling into being. And I feel the yearning command, almost shouted, in the *madad, madad, madad!* that the riot and the people expand, grow, and spread, which concludes the verse. Between the two, there is a distinct tension connecting the internal throwing off of humiliation with the expansive command. And it is recognizing this tension, strung like a melancholic violin string and plucked just so, that is the poetic power of this piece. There is a refrain

Figure 4.1. Al Darwish performing "Kheir al-Shaghab" on May 20, 2016, at Metro Al Madina in Beirut. Courtesy of Chabaka Music and Beirut Records & Ent.

that can be shouted at the end: *madad, madad, madad!* This refrain could even be, in a very coarse description, *a call to riot*. That said, the piece is not, like DJ Sotusura recalled above, a call "to break shit." A listener invited to hear this piece is also a listener grieving, wholly aware of what has been lost. She is also a listener who is wrestling with herself, afraid, not daring to believe in the opening. I run until I cannot. The brown water churns and churns.

Later, I find a video of the guys performing the piece live in Beirut.[51] I focus on the sample, which I had ignored before, of Umm Kulthoum singing. She sings, "Give me my freedom and let go of me,"[52] and I hear in the recording what feels like the whole of the audience singing with their whole hearts, together, out loud, with the sample. Darwish takes the mic for his verse, drenched in sweat from bald head down. His eyes are closed, his body held in a palpable calm. He barely holds the mic—it almost just floats on the loose wire between his fingers. He rocks from one foot to the other as he spits the first half of his verse as if in prayer, as if in a trance. And it is unclear as he delivers the first lines if he is calling a listener in to do something or if he himself is praying. And this is the whole promise and possibility of filling the head and the transformative blending that tarab promises: the slippage between calling and listening that is stillness and the pleasure and release of yearning, which sometimes can look like meditative prayer.

It is fleeting. For the reprise, Darwish's eyes jump open, and the audience is moving with him. Soon he is above them, beyond them, the anger in his whole body bigger than the song, bigger than the stage. The chorus ends with a shouted *madad!* ... and the video cuts out.

* * *

"Kheir al-Shaghab" intervenes in liberal political discourse in Lebanon about the propriety of specific forms of protest. A debate with resonances in myriad other contexts, especially after the global protests of the summer of 2020, the question of violence as a strategy within political protest beleaguered the Lebanese political context in 2015 as it has others before and since. Among other things, Darwish and Nasserdayn's track intervenes with a symbolic middle finger to these debates about the respectability of political strategies. It is a holding onto the spirit of opening that the protests of 2015 against the sectarian system in Lebanon seemed to portend—not one reduced to a liberal politics of protest but a radical promise to imagine a chaotic collective otherwise. The song longs, like Muñoz writes, "for a moment outside of this current state of siege,"[53] where siege is not only the stalemate between protesters and the state but the blocks between each other and in our own minds that stop us from enacting collective power. When Darwish raps "*hayya ʿala al-shaʿb; hayya ʿala kheir al-shaghab*" ("heed the call of the people; heed the rising riot"), he is summoning the listener to that collective power of the people in its most powerful incarnation—the riot itself.

While it channels fury, the piece is not itself "a verse of anger." Nasserdayn's verse sets up the listener with a provocative series of invitations, repeating the informal *sar feek* (you can now) and a sequence of openings (you can move on, you can show your teeth, you can renounce a past, you can refuse to be called). Darwish responds to this series of openings with a recognition that it's not that easy, that a struggle awaits, or a *thawra ʿala al-nafs*—a revolution of oneself (playing on the Islamic concept of *jihad an-nafs*, or inward "struggle against temptation"). *The lowly, even if he eats the sun, will not find his way,* he continues. In other words, without shaking off humiliation, no amount of clarity or information about the current moment will do much toward the possibilities Nasserdayn identified. Overthrowing oneself is necessary.

In this, "Kheir al-Shaghab" calls an isolated listener and invites her to recognize, to borrow from Quashie, the wildness of her own interior.

In so doing, the song calls her to imagine collectivity otherwise. The hailing, the call, in Darwish's verse *hayya ʿala al-shaʿb* . . . is a call to come to the people. Together with the preceding line, *thawra ʿala al-nafs*, this twin invitation is a call to reimagine political action in the collective. Darwish's verse echoes Ernest Bloch when the latter writes, "One is alone with oneself. Together with others, most are alone even without themselves. *One has to get out of both*."[54] Building on Bloch, Muñoz suggests that "this getting out of oneself with and without others is an insistence on another mode in which one feels the collective."[55] This is the same move Darwish invites in this track. Darwish's verse is an invitation to collectivity and a kind of prayer for the materialization of a different shape of that collectivity. Central within these invitations is a call to recognize oneself, the ongoing struggle within oneself, and the obligation to that struggle one makes, that one makes in spite of oneself, and even that one hesitates to acknowledge one has made.

To understand Darwish's invitation, consider closely how his verse stages a sharp inversion of the Muslim call to prayer. Darwish's line *hayya ʿala al-shaʿb hayya ʿala kheir al-shaghab* (heed the call of the people; heed the rising riot) mirrors the lines of the adhan in *hayya ʿala salaa, hayya ʿala kheir al-ʿamal* (heed the call to prayer; heed your duty to perform the best of deeds[56]). The verse is clever and powerful for a number of reasons; central among these is how it figures the political action of the refrain that follows, the call for *madad, madad, madad* (succor, expansion, spreading).

Muslim believers responding to the call to prayer understand it is their duty and obligation to pray and do good deeds. The adhan doesn't tell them to do it; it reminds them of this duty: it is a call, an invitation addressed to believers. One can imagine many ways of playfully or forcefully telling a listener to riot. But Darwish's verse is significant in how it stages a reminder—like the call to prayer—of one's duties and obligations.[57] As such, the call Darwish makes in this track is not the rapper telling you to go into the street, to go "break shit" (recall DJ Sotusura in the chap. 3). The much more powerful invitation Darwish offers is instead *to heed the call from within*. It is addressed to a specific listener, and its call is an urgent one to engage the wolves and abandoned dogs roaming one's wild interior. In so doing, the potential of the expanding call for succor Darwish's verse ends on (*madad!*) emerges as a people self-actualized, overthrowing themselves, shaking off decades of humiliation: *that* is kheir al-shaghab, the rising riot that is the title of the track.

"Kheir al-Shaghab" is a resonant bookend to "Min al-Kaheff" ("From the Cave"), the Ramallah Underground track with which I opened this study (see intro) and that left me in tears in the subway in Harlem. In that piece, Asifeh raps, "I try to ignore her, but politics pulls at me. I tell her, 'Let go!' She tells me, 'I am part of you, you won't be able to resist me.'" In that piece, politics figures as a kind of muse (or demon) coming to haunt the listener, reminding her that she cannot disavow the part she always already plays in politics. Similarly, in "Kheir al-Shaghab," Darwish speaks to a pull to politics within the listener. The rallying cry in both "Kheir al-Shaghab" and "Min al-Kaheff" is not a call "to the street" but *to oneself*. As "Kheir al-Shaghab" in particular makes clear, this shift in address is not a disavowal of the material realities of the street or the urgent need to engage there. Both pieces understand and address a listener moving through waves of grief, apathy, fear, and hesitation . . . and call her in. There may not be hope, as Fakih told the hosts of *Sarde*. One has to struggle anyway. It is this dialectical pull to the political that gave me goosebumps.

To be clear, Darwish's play with the call to prayer and my description of him above as if almost in prayer are not a reinsertion of religion into my analysis. Quashie offers that prayer is "dreaming and self-assessment, wild motion rapt with possibility and ache, *a self-conversation* that is driven by the abundance of imagination."[58] And this combination of self-assessment and wild motion rapt with ache is precisely what Darwish's verse embodies. It is a meditation on politics as is that threatens to set fire. It is still and in motion. The verse is itself like Darwish's performance: quiet and inward and then aflame—like running while suspended in an in-between space.

"Kheir al-Shaghab" is for me a powerful example of the innovation in calling potential listeners, yearning, and the ache for being hailed otherwise in experimental rap in Arabic. It is as good an example as any of staging invitations to imagine collectivity otherwise. The piece invites sifting through sedimented layers. It offers aesthetic provocation (*istifzaz*, chap. 2) while drawing attention to a context of inescapable disgust (*qaraf*, chap. 1). And as it does so, it stages a slippage between calling and listening. Laced through the piece and its performance is the inseparability of the vocalization of the call and listening to it. *Heeding the call from within*. The cypher holds the invitation, the shouted command, and the open, vulnerable, otherwise wish. The cypher of the here and now right on top of the cypher to come.

The river, in its brown, spring flush, is rushing and gargling beside and below the highway. Running faster and faster against the traffic, the listener gives breath to all the anger and longing she is holding. The song ends, but her legs keep moving. She can barely feel them anymore. Above her, above the traffic, echoing in everything, *madad, madad, madad.*

Outro

POLITICS IN MOTION

In these final pages, I offer three meditations on motion, movement, and belonging. They all feature in whole or in part the work of Mazen El Sayed, the Lebanese rapper who goes by the name El Rass, whose fan base is eclectic. These three episodes point to the ways in which this music circulates: online, through networks of affiliation, through competition with other rappers, sustained in conversation with fans, and reverberating in protests and other political activities and performance spaces. These moments offer ways of thinking about the circulation of experimental rap and hip-hop in virtual spaces, at a remove from but intimately connected to the live concert.

1

In January 2020, during protests against corruption and sectarianism in Lebanon, a video circulated of a young woman protester approaching a line of police in riot gear, assembled behind plastic shields in Hamra, Beirut.[1] The video is shot from behind and only momentarily catches her face, covered up to her eyes with a handkerchief. The darkened street is empty around her, it is the empty space just in front of a police barricade. Green lasers dart through the gray-yellow, tear-gas clouded air. The woman walks purposefully toward the police line, passing overturned dumpsters. Her feet are laced into silver boots, a rhythmic swagger in her step. In her left hand she carries a handkerchief and a bag of onions, support against tear gas. In her right hand, she carries a portable speaker. Blaring from the speaker is El Rass's track "Shouf" ("Look"), released during the protests.[2] When she reaches the police cordon, she stops in front of it and faces the dark, amorphous mass of helmets and shields, the speaker still in her hand. The video gets shaky and then stops.

Outro: Politics in Motion | 111

Figure 5.1. A protester approaches a line of police carrying a portable speaker from which played El Rass's track "Shouf" in Hamra, Beirut, January 2020. Video by Makram Al-Halabi.

When El Rass shared the video, someone commented on it with concern for the young woman's safety, mistaking the portable speaker for a gallon of gasoline and the cloth and onions in her hand for a Molotov cocktail. Both El Rass and the tagged protester respond, bemused at the virtual friend's misreading of the video but respectful of his apprehension about her vulnerability in facing the police. In another comment, a friend responds, "If I knew that's what you were doing before I saw you yesterday, I would have slapped you!" The protestor agrees, she would have reconsidered if she knew what was to come. Her solo march happened on a night of considerable violence enacted by the police and internal security forces on unarmed protesters.

I have argued throughout this book that reading rap as "resistance" shrinks the possibilities available for discussing politics in process. I have suggested that the association of hip-hop in Arabic with early political iterations of the genre in the US amount to blackwashing the genre, or projecting US-centric ideas about nonviolence, creativity, and liberal protest. Instead, I have argued for the recognition of other models for reading both aesthetics and the potential shape of "collective effervescence" in experimental rap and hip-hop. I have contended instead that an aesthetics of istifzaz, or provocation, unsettling, and surprise, invites listeners to relate to politics as is differently and often results in reactions of quiet, stillness, and introspection. Far from the incitement to revolution or the rallying of crowds, the rap I have read closely in this book invites listeners to shift their relationship to politics. The resulting move is perceptible as a a shift in one's weight, relief.

On the face of it, this example of the woman facing the police cordon with a portable speaker blaring one of the scene's most prominent voices seems to present a contradiction. Alone, armed only with a rap recording, a young woman defies the state. Isn't this proof that rap does have its finger on the pulse of the street? That it *is* the soundtrack of revolution? That it provides the rhythm for uprising even a decade after the initial opening of the so-called Arab Spring?

The framework I have been building across these chapters should offer different tools to understand the circulation of this clip, the posture of the woman in it, and the composition of the track she carries with her. In the first part of this conclusion, I consider the circulation of this clip in order to offer a reading of the political salience of this rap that does not reduce the music performances of resistance. This should demonstrate that it is not only the selection of materials in the preceding chapters that has supported my arguments but a way of reading them.

The lyrics of this piece reference a collective we; El Rass raps, "We have become one people, so we have won." Yet, the protestor approaches the police cordon alone. Indeed, the most striking feature of the video during a night of harrowing displays of state violence is that the protester is alone. This speaks to the way in which, as I have argued, listening to this music interpellates the individual and invites her to imagine herself in different political constellations. While these have collective implications, they are often embodied in singular and solitary formations.

Equally striking is her stillness in the face of the crowded chaos ahead of and around her. Tear gas swirls in the air, other people rush away from the police, and yet her step is controlled, steady. Her arms by her sides, she does not speak. Relative to the movement around her, she offers a steady, quiet stillness: an echo in the street of the arms-folded expressions in different concert spaces (see chap. 2). While she carries a speaker, she herself is silent. In the video, her person is brimming with the kind of vibrant "interiority" Quashie identifies in other silent acts of political import.

The refrain of the song declares,

it's not going to go back how it was \\ مش رح ترجع تركب
it's not going to hurt again \\ مش رح ترجع تجرح
look how the country has spit you out there's \\ شوف البلد كيف بزقتكم بطل الكم مطرح
no space left for you

Even just within this short refrain, these lyrics reflect many of the themes discussed in previous chapters. El Rass speaks of the country spitting out its leaders and of a political situation understood as painful, damaging, disgusting. Sonically, the piece reflects the recent turn toward the aesthetics of global trap music. If the track "Shouf" became the sound of the October Revolution, trap has become the sound of rap in Ramallah, Amman, and Beirut since 2018.[3] This video at night, facing the dark mass of the police, reflects the darkness experienced by so many protesters during these chaotic, unnerving, and perilous encounters where the repression of the state mirrors the dark sound in the track itself (see chap 3.).

The first comment on the video El Rass shared is one of longing. Someone writes, "*Akhhh ya reit biqdar inzel*" ("Ohhhh, I wish I could go down [to the streets]"). The mediation of the music and protest produces a political expression of revolt that is also and primarily one of yearning. Of the twenty-nine comments on the post, this is one of two that El Rass himself "loves." A kind of solidarity emerges here where the speaker identifies himself as also on the receiving end of power. This wish to participate enacts a belonging to be that pivots the shared relationship from one primarily of disgust with al-wadaʿ to one fundamentally of co-presence. Critically, this is understood as a condition blocked (*I wish I could*), yet to be realized.

The second comment on the video is the one referred to above, about someone concerned for the woman's safety since "they [the police] are not differentiating between men and women, they're hitting everyone and imprisoning them." This one and the sequence following demonstrate that reverberating underneath the display of defiance recorded in the video is the real vulnerability of the protestor at the hands of the state. Once the woman is identified, El Rass tags her *al-bataleh* (the hero) in his post, but the discussion under it testifies to an intimate understanding of the violence encountered in the street. And so, importantly, this is not the celebration of nonviolence as a tool of political expression. It is acknowledgment of the real vulnerability of her person and the calculation of risk undertaken.

The circulation of the clip acts as a conductor for an affect of yearning connecting musicians and listeners that prominently figures in their relationship toward political conditions and events. The protestor imagines the track as a response to and a protection against the violence of the police. Others seeing the video of her playing the track long to be in the street. The rapper himself responds to others' responses in a kind of affirmation of the lyrics in the track. The protest illustrates the fundamentally solitary and introspective activity accompanying this rap music, embodied in quiet and stillness, even when it is used in loud and adrenaline-laden political events. Finally, the circulation of the video and the gap between what some viewers saw and what happened also draws out another dynamic I have been discussing. The man concerned for her safety saw an act of public protest and resilience manifest in a specific kind of revolt (gasoline and a Molotov cocktail). However, discussion with the protester revealed that instead the woman was armed with tools of defense: a cloth and onions to ward off the tear gas, and a chant that "it's not going to hurt again."

2

More than the scenes in Jordan or Palestine, the rap scene in Lebanon and specifically in Beirut has boasted more of a direct connection with protest. The #YouStink protests against municipal corruption in 2015 saw an initial marked outgrowth of this energy (see chap. 1). That summer, rap concerts became explicitly political and directly attached to street protest. I remember watching with surprise when, at the end of their concert at Metro Al Madina in Hamra on August 7, 2015, El Rass took the mic and delivered an impassioned diatribe to the gathered audience, urging them to join him in the streets the following day for a scheduled protest. The speech was uncharacteristically romantic, bordering on revolutionary melodrama (particularly surprising for an artist who usually casts himself as intellectual outsider), asking his audience to remember those who have less of a voice. He declared at one point, "If Lebanon isn't for all of us, it's for none of us!"; the speech culminated with audience and rapper repeating "revolution is in the street, not on the screen."[4]

This rapprochement between rap in Beirut and political protests in late 2015 are an important part of the history of rap in Beirut and in the region. They are important because of the engagement in both explicit politics and specific political strategy. However, moments of excitement and exhilaration—like the concert in 2015—largely do not survive the cycles of disgust, resignation, and cynicism that have come to characterize both politics and everyday life in Lebanon (what Ghassan Moussawi calls the tension of anxiety and despair in the term al-wadaʻ). The October Revolution of 2019 saw an even more robust representation of not only rappers but a host of independent musicians involved in the protests in Lebanon and performing live during sit-ins, street concerts, and other affiliated activities. The track "Shouf," just discussed, reflected the elation of the early days of the October Revolution in Lebanon, which saw a sequence of powerful displays of popular strength, anger, and bravery against the corruption and depravity of the Lebanese state.

But the articulation of political positions in rap is not limited to Lebanon. Nor is it restricted to an encouragement of protest. To be sure, since the start of the Syrian uprising (March 2011), rappers' declarations of specific political positions in their work and onstage has produced a range of reactions from listeners and fans. The rift among Syrian rappers as some chose to support the Assad regime against the uprising was just one of a series of public staking of political positions. Eslaam Jawaad's early support for Assad's regime against the protests divided hip-hop audiences in the Levant that were largely riding the enthusiasm of the uprisings. The affective and political backlash against Jawaad pinned the artist into a reactionary corner long before the Islamic State and other fundamentalist militias co-opted the Syrian uprising and turned other artists, previously sympathetic, against the opposition.[5] While the Syrian crisis has cast high stakes for the expression of solidarity, political motion around other questions have also led to the public staking of specific identities or positions. Considering this kind of navigation as essentially important in being able to craft the kinds of expressions that are able to *fill the head*, I explore the staking of political positions in a sequence of tracks exchanged between and collaborated on by the Lebanese rapper El Rass and the Jordanian rapper El Farʒi as its own kind of political movement.

January 2016 saw a short-lived but impassioned exchange of diss tracks that elaborated with nuance different aspects of solidarity, selling out, authenticity, and both the geographic and political location of rappers and their loyalty to their audiences. El Rass's "Watwateh," El Farʒi's "Washwasheh," and El Rass's "Habout Idtrari" stage an argument over where to locate the political that is literally in motion. The three tracks between former collaborators staged important debates in the development of political discourse within the scene.

El Rass's track "Watwateh" came out first.[6] He raps about the selling off of the *qadiyeh* (the issue): the Palestinian cause. The track proceeds as a cryptic but clear enough indictment of "giants"—people who make it big—and their distance from the Palestinian cause, asserting that "small people" are closer to the cause ("Glory to the dwarves, we are the issue"). El Rass aligns himself with the latter. A soft iteration of disgust, reflected in the metaphor of being "batlike," effectively underscores the piece. The track opens with a series of alliterative questions (*meen bitmathel 'ameen bitmathel bithasel lameen bitwasel*) [who do you represent, for whom are you performing, get it, who do you reach?] questioning an artist's or perhaps an activist's sense of audience and responsibility and the effect of that orientation.

In 2014, El Far3i relocated from Amman to London with the electro-mijwez group 47 Soul. The group's music is an electronic interpretation of "wedding music," *musiqah al-a'ras*, setting the *mijwiz* music of the *dabkeh* and other folk music of the Levant to hip dance beats. The group's approach to and take on the music has proved appealing to Arabs in the diaspora, Arabs in the Arab world, and foreigners. They have played to sold-out crowds in the UK, Europe, and the US.[7] 47 Soul's attempt at popularization of mijwiz music and El Far3i's relocation from Amman to London has not been without criticism. While Syrian wedding singer Omar Suleiman's popularity among hipster audiences that took to his mijwez-techno has for the most part not been interpreted as selling out, the "boy band" enthusiasm of 47 Soul and the accompanying poplike framing of the music has alienated El Far3i in particular from an audience that followed his solo lyrical rap work closely. The attitudes of 47 Soul's members—their obvious eagerness about the interest the new sounds received and their assertions about how their work reinvents while speaking for the *fellaheen* (peasantry)—has perhaps not really helped much. Their boyish enthusiasm about "making it" has been interpreted as condescending (if not plain absurd) by some of their colleagues, and accusations of "selling out" have accompanied the group's assertions about their own success. For example, in our interview, the Amman-based rapper Synaptik (whose family boasts famous Palestinian wedding singers) spoke at length about how he saw the 47 Soul project as a betrayal of local, traditional sounds and a selling out of these sounds to orientalist fantasies. In a comment on the discussion board of the collaboration track "E-stichrak" ("Orientalism") on Soundcloud, Synaptik wrote without explanation, "47 Soul" in early 2016. El Far3i responded, "Hmmm." This is to point to the latter's obvious awareness of how others have interpreted and received some of his new work. In our own interview, El Far3i spoke haltingly about his struggles to retain his former audiences and his eagerness to prove to them he was still the musician they respected.

El Far3i responded to El Rass's abstract musings in "Watwateh" as a personal affront. El Far3i clearly interpreted the "giants" El Rass ridiculed as himself. El Far3i's response scoffed at the extra-engaged politics of his former collaborator and poked fun at his pretentious alignment with the "little people" who are the real defenders of *al-qadiyeh* (Palestine). His retort, entitled "Washwasheh" ("Whisperings") plays alliteratively on El Rass's title ("Watwateh") and starts by spinning one of El Rass's lines "Glory to the heroes,"[8] rapping sarcastically, "Dear committed rapper that has been betrayed . . . where are you going?" The track pokes fun at the seriousness with which El Rass and others in Beirut (which he cynically calls "the city of rebellion") couched themselves in the midst of the #YouStink protests. "Wow, a café we want to build a fight with our dreams!" he mocks, drawing out the hypocrisy of progressive sociality others have also identified in Beirut (see chap. 1). Unlike those Lebanese rappers who also offered expressions of disgust with these forms of sociality, El Far3i invokes that hypocrisy not as reason *for* rebellion but reason why the protests were not able to really take off. Sonically, the vocals are not clear, and El Far3i's voice is low, as if he is whispering. But the barbs at El Rass are pointed accusations of intellectualism and elitism. As in the lines "*bihabouha el moukh shou bihabouha el moukh, w al-nokhbeh nokhbeh w li'nha aslee*" ("They love the brain, how they love the brain, and the elite remains elite because that is its origin"). Here, El Far3i plays on the word *moukh*, which means brain but also marrow, aligning those who like intellectual matters with an elite vantage point on society.[9] As discussed in chapter 1, this is similar to the critique Osloob leveled at rap that was "leaving the street" as it embraced more formal forms of Arabic poetry.

El Far3i's critique of the intellectual politics coming out of Beirut in 2016 were welcome, especially in the wake of a protest movement that by many accounts did stumble into the politics of middle-class respectability and accompanying exclusiveness that have played out in other cities worldwide.[10] But his personification of this problem in his former collaborator may have backfired. When El Rass responded to El Far3i's very explicit diss, he mobilized the wave of recent skepticism engendered by his work with 47 Soul. El Rass's response track, "Habout Idtrari" ("Emergency Landing"), denies categorically that he had El Far3i in mind while writing "Watwateh" and sprays a series of accusations back at his former collaborator, in the process revisiting many of the subjects they covered in their previous collaborations.[11]

The opening sample of El Rass's response, a dialogue, plays on this narrative of "making it." Heavily distorted sonically, the dialogue mocks a pursuit of authenticity and "making it" (the word used is *waselet*—literally, you've arrived], conjuring El Rass as the interviewed artist and El Far3i an orientalist called "Jimmy." The piece proceeds from here to respond to El Far3i's jibes, reciting back to him lyrics from their previous collaborations. Sonically, El Rass is louder (there is no whispering here), but the whole piece is couched in offended but sardonic laughter. The debate the rappers stage, despite the personal acrimony that they fling at each other, is an important deliberation of what counts as politics, who counts as political, and who is truly able to represent Palestine, the poor, and their musical traditions.

Debates about authenticity are a central feature of how rappers position themselves vis-à-vis their audiences (see chap. 2). Questions of travel, exile, and alienation appear in other tracks as well. "Fi al-Jaleed" stages negotiations of identity, community, engagement, and political commitment as the two MCs (El Rass and El Far3i) travel to Sweden and Denmark on tour (see the introduction).[12] As I gestured to in the opening pages of the book, one of the things that makes that piece interesting is that it gives voice to a range of perspectives in Europe, specifically of the Arab diaspora. El Rass raps, "In Stockholm I heard *ya ba* [a common interpellation] more than I heard ABBA," and El Far3i asserts, "Don't think that the knowledge of the homeland is geographic," pointing to a network of Syrian and Iraqi immigrants. His verse points to the important diasporic communities that also make up Europe. He acknowledges the switches and weakness of language accompanying these demographic movements: "It's ok my Arabic is weak ... but I still pronounce the *qaf*," offering an expression of pride even in what is usually considered a weak identity position (not knowing the language). In their verses and their attention to the experiences of Arabs in Europe, both rappers are clearly conscious of complicating positions voiced on a previous collaboration, "E-stichrak" ("Orientalism"). This lyrical work, in combination with the sounds of electronic musician Munma's scoring, produce an engaged interrogation of the positions and meaning of "Arab-ness," before the spectacular misery of the Syrian refugee crisis (the track was released in 2014).

"E-stichrak" (2013), the track both rappers referred to in 2016, constructs a character, "Jimmy," who arrives in the Arab world with an NGO job and in the name of making things better. He condescends, steals jobs, and changes the economic and demographic landscape. El Far3i raps, "Political science students coming from abroad change the demographic of Ramallah." The whole piece is underscored sonically with the whistling sound of a rocket. "E-stichrak" is based in Amman, Beirut, and Ramallah and features perspectives from those localities about the attitudes of those coming from abroad, including those Arabs who "return." "Fi al-Jaleed" flips these positions. In the latter, they point to questions of orientalism but from the position of Arabs in Europe. This series of tracks points to a healthy development of questions of inside/outside, diaspora and authenticity, and the politics attached to one's geographic position and mobility between these two MCs and in the scene in general.

The exchange over the several tracks discussed here is a good example of how rappers negotiate political positions without aligning themselves with parties, politicians, or ideologies. Moreover, the fluidity of these positions—as made especially clear by this exchange of diss tracks between rappers who used to collaborate—points to how politics in process, reflected lyrically and musically in this genre, is not an oscillation between fixed points (with one party or against it). Rather, these negotiations point to a wholly different kind of motion: wading through realities where there seem to be no options. It is this wading through and staking of positions (that then morph) that characterize political motion in addition to the obvious physical movement of rappers and their fans, whether in search of opportunities—concerts, degrees, jobs—or as immigrants, exiles, or refugees.

3

While I have focused my attention on the live concerts that are the intersections of urban change, orientalist representation, struggles over the right to the city, and changing perceptions about hip-hop and hip-hop culture, the vast majority of listener engagement with Arabic hip-hop and the MCs and producers who make it is not during live events but mediated through technology. SoundCloud, YouTube, Facebook, and Twitter were the primary sites for hosting and disseminating this material. This means that the primary mode of interaction between rappers and their listeners are comments on tracks and the virtual affectivity of likes, shares, and so on.

My emphasis in interviews on the live event often came as something of a surprise to musicians. They recognized that most of their interactions with fans are virtual at the same time that their assertions about the importance of the concert in "feeling with" their audience are genuine.

Negotiating the politics of positionality and negotiating physical space during years when parts of the Arab world are engulfed in occupation, siege, uprising, or war is also a question of determining the shape and rhythm of solidarity. Indeed, solidarity in these cases is often specifically about negotiating engagement when one cannot approach physically, as in the case of Lebanese and Syrians wishing to enact solidarity with Palestinians, whose territory they are forbidden from entering, and vice versa. In the most recent tracks I have discussed here, *how to express* that solidarity also emerged as a political navigation and an affective one. As such, my interlocutors also identified solidarity as politics in process: not something to be claimed but a process to engage in. The declaration of solidarity was not a statement but a negotiation of and active engagement with the options available. When I asked El Rass what solidarity meant to him and his work, if anything, he offered:

> To me, solidarity is the system of how you make sense of your belonging to different collectivities. You cannot just make sense by saying that you're in solidarity. Making sense involves a whole process of action, of release, of spreading the word, of questioning things, of being critical, of sometimes trying to get the morale back, of sometimes saying let's take two steps back so we can see the bigger image, sometimes people who are in the struggle are maybe depressed or down, you understand that maybe you have to take them to different kind of moods and thinking—I am thinking about the music here.[13]

El Rass offers a refreshingly active view of solidarity, one in which the individual who expresses solidarity must also act, and not only in ways sanctioned or prescribed by those with whom one expresses this political affinity. In this way, even a position becomes a process, one that, with and through technology, with and through technology, may even take advantage of that distance. Consider this social media exchange between a late-night supermarket checkout clerk in Ramallah and El Rass.

A photograph posted on Facebook in 2015 shows a grocery cashier's register with the screen open on a El Rass's SoundCloud profile (see fig. 5.4). The caption of the photo reads, "Because it's a duty to spread culture... The entire supermarket must listen to El Rass. Of course, people couldn't handle more than two tracks and asked to hear Elissa or Wael Kafouri [Lebanese

Figure 5.2. Exchange between a supermarket clerk in Ramallah and the rapper El Rass, July 11, 2015.

pop stars]." In response to the photograph in which he was tagged, El Rass's caption reads, "When the guy is working all night in a Ramallah supermarket and decides to make the customers listen to El Rass's tracks." Here, the virtual reality of the two computer screens—the one channeling El Rass's music into the supermarket and the one reflecting the aural soundscape and reactions of the supermarket back to El Rass—emerges as a horizon in which listeners and performers can meet despite the restrictions of space.

In the exchange above, the computer screen is figured as the primary medium through which listeners receive and exchange with musicians while it simultaneously draws the forbidden Lebanese voice into occupied Palestinian space. The clerk stages for the viewer expectation, hope, despair, solidarity, and humor—within the recognizably neoliberal framework of the all-night supermarket, no less. Because culture is a duty, the hourly employee tells us, he weaves in instruction, exposure, and acculturation through the tools available to him: the Wi-Fi and speaker system in the store. While he does not hope to change their opinions over*night* ("of course they could only stand two tracks before asking for Elissa"), he nonetheless deems the experiment successful enough to share it with a public audience—and to specifically bring it to the musician's attention. For his part, the musician is touched enough by the effort that he reposts it, with his own interpretation of the impact—political and aesthetic—of his own work. This exchange on social media frames a fluctuating spectrum of hope and despair that has anchored the affective political spectrum within which this study was composed. It also points to how technology, and social media in particular, is able to generate and transmit presence, substituting for the call-and-response of the live concert when geopolitics and logistics render such embodied exchanges impossible.

* * *

I thus draw this study of ongoing political processes, aesthetic experimentation, and lyrical invention to a close. The moments in which these pages were written affected the ways in which I interpreted what I heard expressed and negotiated online, in live concerts, and in my recorded and unrecorded interviews. The politics I observed and participated in stayed still only long enough to be captured in analysis (and sometimes not even that long). Nonetheless, in a world in as much flux as ours, listening has suggested this is perhaps all one can ask for. Having recorded what I heard, it is now for others to see what *fills the head*.

APPENDIX

خير الشغب
ناصردين الطفار، الدرويش

[ناصردين الطفار]
لا تنوشل أو تفتكر خبرية موت الملك كذب
مشّي الزجل لنحتفل نترقوص عنشيد الحزب
بكّي من فرح كلبك سرح، نام بفلا مات الذئب
صار فيك تقول مات أخي، الناضل عالدرب و ما ضل
فيك تبادر تنتخي، الضالل للأبد ما ضلّ
فيك تلبّق الوانك، فيك تفرجينا سنانك
فيك تقول أني الي اني معي اني مني فدا صرماية حدا
بطلت الكلمة تربط، فيك الجزمة ترفضا
فيك تقول اني مع اني ضد و يلعن كل شي و كل حدا
ناطر هالتراك من سنين، درويش و ناصردين
عموسيقى مريضة نزف الخبر لحلب و حمص و العين

[الدرويش]
ثورة على النفس
بس الذليل إذا أكل الشمس بيضل تايه
حيّ على الشعب، حي على خير الشغب
بآية عالغضب
الحق شرق، على شعر البلد اللي فرد
على صرخة ما في للأبد
حي على الناس مدد
ثورة على النفس
بس الذليل إذا أكل الشمس بيضل تايه
حيّ على الشعب، حي على خير الشغب
بآية عالغضب
الحق شرق، على شعر البلد اللي فرد
على صرخة ما في للأبد
حي على الناس
مدد مدد مدد مدد

"The Rising Riot"
"Kheir al-shaghab" is a play on a line in the Shi'a line to prayer (hayya 'ala kheir al 'amal) meaning "rise to do the best of deeds." The translation offered here is figurative and gestures to what heeding one's political obligations as gestured to in the track might portend.
Naserdayn al-Touffar and Al-Darwish

Translated by May Achour and Rayya El Zein with Huda Fakhreddine

[Nasserdayn al-Touffar]
Do not be confused or think the news of the King's death is a lie
Put on poetry: that's how we'll celebrate dancing to the Party's anthem

Crying from joy, the beaten dog inside you wandered off; sleeping in the wilderness, the Wolf died

You can now say, "My brother has passed on," the warrior from the path didn't stray

You can take the initiative, and choose yourself; the loser found his way

You now can mix and match your colors, you can reveal your fangs

You can declare, "I'm for me, I'm with me, devoted to none"

Since the commands no longer make sense, you can refuse the marching orders

You can declare, "I'm with, I'm against, and screw everything and everyone"

Awaiting this track for ages, Al-Darwish and Nasserdayn

Through sick music we deliver the breaking news to Aleppo, Homs, and Al-Ain

Al-Darwish
Overthrowing oneself

But a lowly dog will remain lost even if he eats the sun

Heed the call of the people: heed the rising riot

With a verse on anger

Truth has risen, on the feeling of the country that was set free

By the shout "There is no forever!"

Answer the call: *madad*[1]

Overthrowing oneself

But a lowly dog will remain lost even if he eats the sun

Heed the call of the people: heed the rising riot

With a verse on anger

Truth has risen, on the feeling of the country that was set free

By the shout "There is no forever!"

Answer the call:

Madad, madad, madad

NOTES

Intro: Learning to Listen

1. "Ramallah Underground—Min il Kaheff," YouTube video, 4:20, posted by Unknown SoldierMX, July 21, 2009, https://www.youtube.com/watch?v=A7EtoUO9V-c.
2. The chorus is Asifeh's voice mixed with both Muqata'a and Aswat's voices. (Personal correspondence, April 14, 2016).
3. Ted Swedenburg also writes about this track in particular in "Palestinian Rap: Against the Struggle Paradigm," in *Popular Culture in the Middle East and North Africa: A Postcolonial Approach*, edited by Walid El Hamamsy and Mounira Solimon (New York: Routledge, 2013), 17–32.
4. El Far3i uses the numeral 3 in the place of the Arabic letter ع in the orthography of his stage name, as is common in informal transliteration of Arabic.
5. "El Rass & Munma *el rass w munma fi el jaleed ma' el far' i*," YouTube video, 4:54, posted by Mo2amara, May 27, 2014, https://www.youtube.com/watch?v=sj2DHlAofeU.
6. Anna Tsing, *The Mushroom at the End of the World: On the Possibility of Life in Capitalist Ruins* (Princeton, NJ: Princeton University Press, 2015), 254–55.
7. Feeling as grounds for exploring political implications of contemporary, experimental music appears in Darci Sprengel's work on DIY musicians in Egypt. See Darci Sprengel, "Reframing the 'Arab Winter': The Importance of Sleep and a Quiet Atmosphere after 'Defeated' Revolutions," *Culture, Theory and Critique* 61 (2020): 246–66.
8. Ashon T. Crawley, *Blackpentecostal Breath: The Aesthetics of Possibility* (New York: Fordham University Press, 2017), 24, 82, 241, among others.
9. Staff, "El Général," in "The 2011 *TIME* 100," *TIME*, 2011, http://content.time.com/time/specials/packages/article/0,28804,2066367_2066369_2066242,00.html.
10. See, for example, George Lipsitz, *Dangerous Crossroads: Popular Music, Postmodernism, and the Poetics of Place* (London: Verso, 1994); Halifu Osumare, *The Hiplife in Ghana: the West African Indigenization of Hip-Hop* (Basingstoke, UK: Palgrave Macmillan, 2012); Marina Terkourafi, *The Languages of Global Hip-Hop* (New York: Bloomsbury Continuum, 2010); Laudan Nooshin, ed., *Music and the Play of Power in the Middle East, North Africa and Central Asia* (New York: Routledge, 2009); David McDonald, *My Voice Is My Weapon: Music, Nationalism, and the Poetics of Palestinian Resistance* (Durham, NC: Duke University Press, 2013); Tony Mitchell, *Global Noise: Rap and Hip-Hop Outside the USA* (Middletown, CT: Wesleyan University Press, 2002); Sunaina Maira, *Jil Oslo: Palestinian Hip-Hop, Youth Culture, and the Youth Movement* (Washington, DC: Tadween, 2013); Sujatha Fernandes, *Close to the Edge: In Search of the Global Hip-Hop Generation* (New York: Verso, 2011). For analysis of awareness of the persistence of these frameworks in popular culture and subculture of the region, see Walid El Hamamsy and Mounira Solimon, *Popular Culture in the Middle East and North Africa: A Postcolonial Outlook* (New York: Routledge, 2013); Tarik Sabry and Layal Ftouni, *Arab Subcultures: Transformations in Theory and Practice* (London: I. B. Tauris, 2017).

11. Nasser Kalaji, Jordanian producer with Immortal Entertainment, interview with the author, September 15, 2015, Amman.

12. For a discussion of how tropes of resistance limit understandings of power in rap in the Middle East and North Africa, see Cristina Moreno-Almeida, *Rap beyond Resistance: Staging Contemporary Power in Morocco* (London: Palgrave, 2017).

13. For a discussion of the Arena Battles, see "The Arena: The Middle East's First Official Rap Battle League with Nasser Shorbaji," *Status/al-wadaʿ*, August 16, 2018, https://www.jadaliyya.com/Details/37877. For recordings of the battles themselves see The Arena ME YouTube channel: https://www.youtube.com/@TheArenaME.

14. Hisham Aidi documents how blackwashing works as a tool of US empire vis-à-vis the Muslim world. See his *Rebel Music: Race, Empire, and the New Muslim Youth Culture* (New York: Pantheon, 2014). I have also elaborated how blackwashing works vis-à-vis rap in Arabic; see Rayya El Zein, "From Hip-Hop Revolutionaries to Terrorist Thugs: Blackwashing between the Arab Spring and the War on Terror," *Lateral* 5 (2016), https://csalateral.org/issue/5-1/hip-hop-blackwashing-el-zein.

15. See Chris Nickell and Adam Benkato, "On Blackness and the Nation in Arabic Hip-Hop: Case Studies from Lebanon and Libya," *Lateral* 10, no. 1 (2021), https://doi.org/10.25158/L10.1.14.

16. In early 2024, I am referring to the global solidarity protests against the genocide of Palestinians in Gaza and the occupied Palestinian territories and the acknowledgment of the unevenness of global solidarity with—even legibility of—genocidal violence in Sudan, the Congo, and elsewhere. See "Sudan: A Savage War and Toxic Information Battle," *The Listening Post,* April 27, 2024, https://www.aljazeera.com/program/the-listening-post/2024/4/27/sudan-a-savage-war-and-toxic-information-battle.

17. My understanding of the political is informed by Brazilian theater director Augusto Boal's understanding of catharsis. See Augusto Boal, *Theatre of the Oppressed*, trans. Charles A. and Maria Odilia Leal McBride (New York: Urizen, 1979).

18. Mouneer Bu Kolthoum, interview with the author, March 31, 2015, Amman.

19. Ibid.

20. Yael Navaro-Yashin, "'Life Is Dead Here': Sensing the Political in 'No Man's Land,'" *Anthropological Theory* 3 (2003): 107–25.

21. Navaro-Yashin, "Life Is Dead Here," 109.

22. Ibid.

23. Bu Kolthoum's August 2024 track is an excellent example of how the rapper has continued to develop this type of lyrical and musical work. See "Bu Kolthoum—Asef," 3:25 YouTube video, posted by Bu Kolthoum, August 15, 2024, https://www.youtube.com/watch?v=DoLl6unQ5Ko.

24. Stef Jansen, *Yearnings in the Meantime: 'Normal Lives' and the State in a Sarajevo Apartment Complex* (New York: Berghahn, 2015).

25. Tsing, *Mushroom*, 22.

26. Where the framework of the political depends on an Arendtian view of political subjectivity—where the performance of public speech and action signals the emergence of a political subject. See Hannah Arendt, *The Human Condition* (Chicago: University of Chicago Press, 1958).

27. Saba Mahmood, *Politics of Piety: The Islamic Revival and the Feminist Subject* (Princeton, NJ: Princeton University Press, 2004), 14.

28. Mahmood, *Politics of Piety*, 14; Lila Abu-Lughod, "The Romance of Resistance: Tracing Transformations of Power through Bedouin Women," *American Ethnologist* 17 (1990): 41–55.

29. Darci Sprengel, "More Powerful than Politics: Affective Magic in the DIY Musical Activism after Egypt's 2011 Revolution," *Popular Music* 2019, 54–72; Polly Withers, "Digital Feminisms in Palestinian Hip-Hop," *Global Hip-Hop Studies* 2, no. 2 (2021): 159–77; Polly Withers, "Ramallah Ravers and Haifa Hipsters: Gender, Class, and Nation in Palestinian Popular Culture," *British Journal of Middle East Studies* 48, no. 1 (2021): 94–113; Nadeem Karkabi, "Self-Liberated Citizens: Unproductive Pleasures, Loss of Self, and Playful Subjectivities in Palestinian Raves," *Anthropological Quarterly* 93, no. 4 (2020): 679–708; Christa Salamandra, *A New Old Damascus: Authenticity and Distinction in Urban Syria* (Bloomington: Indiana University Press, 2004).

30. Charles Hirschkind, *The Ethical Soundscape: Cassette Sermons and Islamic Counterpublics* (New York: Columbia University Press, 2009), and Brian Larkin, "Techniques of Inattention: The Mediality of Loudspeakers in Nigeria," *Anthropological Quarterly* 87, no. 4 (2014): 989–1015.

31. Viet Erlmann, ed., *Hearing Cultures: Essays on Sound, Listening, and Modernity* (Oxford: Berg, 2004), 2.

32. Steven Feld, *Sound and Sentiment: Birds, Weeping, Poetics, and Song in Kaluli Expression* (Durham, NC: Duke University Press, 1982). For an overview, see Tom Rice, "Listening," in *Keywords in Sound*, ed. David Novak and Matt Sakakeeny (Durham, NC: Duke University Press, 2015), 101. See also John Picker, *Victorian Soundscapes* (New York: Oxford University Press, 2003); Charles Hirschkind, *The Ethical Soundscape*; Alex E. Chávez, *Sounds of Crossing: Music, Migration, and the Aural Poetics of the Huapango Arribeño* (Durham, NC: Duke University Press, 2017); Ana María Ochoa Gautier, *Aurality: Listening and Knowledge in Nineteenth-Century Colombia* (Durham, NC: Duke University Press, 2014); Ziad Fahmy, *Street Sounds: Listening to Everyday Life in Modern Egypt* (Stanford, CA: Stanford University Press, 2020). The illegibility of some of this work as *sound studies* reflects recent critiques of persistent whiteness and Eurocentrism of both this field and neighboring ethnomusicology. That global hip-hop studies, feminist and Black feminist approaches to literature, or anthropology of Islam are less likely to engage a citational field of sound studies has less to do with the overlapping recognition of the potency of listening as metaphor and practice of political agency than a sense of the relevance of the citational field. For discussion, see Dylan Robinson, *Hungry Listening: Resonant Theory of Indigenous Sound Studies* (Minneapolis: University of Minnesota Press, 2020), and Jennifer Lynn Stoever, *The Sonic Color Line: Race and the Cultural Politics of Listening* (New York: New York University Press, 2016).

33. Hortense Spillers, "Mama's Baby, Papa's Maybe: An American Grammar Book," *Diacritics* 17, no. 2 (1987): 65–81, and *Black, White, and in Color: Essays on American Literature and Culture* (Chicago: University of Chicago Press, 2003), among others; Sylvia Wynter, "But What Does Wonder Do? Meanings, Canons, Too?: On Literary Texts, Cultural Contexts, and What It's Like to Be One/Not One of Us," *Stanford Humanities Review* 4 (1994): 1, and "Rethinking 'Aesthetics': Notes Towards a Deciphering Practice," in *Ex-iles: Essays on Caribbean Cinema*, ed. Mbye Cham (Trenton, NJ: Africa World Press, 1992), 238–79, among others; bell hooks, Ain't I a Woman?: Black Women and Feminism (Boston: South End Press, 1981), and Feminist Theory: From Margin to Center (Boston: South End Press, 1984); Audre Lorde, *Sister Outsider* (New York: Crossing Press, 1984), among others.

34. Kevin Quashie, *The Sovereignty of Quiet* (New Brunswick: Rutgers University Press, 2012); Crawley, *Black Pentecostal Breath*; Legacy Russell, "Digital Dualism and the Glitch Feminism Manifesto," *Society Pages*, December 10, 2012, https://thesocietypages.org/cyborgology/2012/12/10/digital-dualism-and-the-glitch-feminism-manifesto; Alexander G. Weheliye, *Habeas Viscus: Racializing Assemblages, Biopolitics, and Black Feminist Theories of the Human* (Durham, NC: Duke University Press, 2014).

35. See Imani Kai Johnson, *Dark Matter in Breaking Cyphers: The Life of Africanist Aesthetics in Global Hip-Hop* (Oxford University Press, 2023); Ediz Ozelkan, "Hip-Hop in Practice: the Cypher as Communicative Classroom," *Pedagogy, Culture & Society* 32 (3): 741–58. See also Mohamad Ali Nayal, "Music Politics after the Arab Uprisings, Part 1," *Jadaliyya*, June 8, 2022, https://www.jadaliyya.com/Details/44193/Music-Politics-After-the-Arab-Uprisings-Part-1.

36. Quote is Louis Althusser, "Ideology and Ideological State Apparatuses: Notes towards and Investigation," in *Lenin and Philosophy, and Other Essays*, trans. Ben Brewster (New York: Monthly Review, 1971), https://www.marxists.org/reference/archive/althusser/1970/ideology.htm. See Emilio Spadola, *The Calls of Islam: Sufis, Islamists, and Mass Mediation in Urban Morocco* (Bloomington: Indiana University Press, 2014); Brian Larkin, "Techniques of Inattention"; Patrick Eisenlohr, *Sounding Islam: Voice, Media, and Sonic Atmospheres in an Indian Ocean World* (Berkeley: University of California Press, 2018).

37. Kevin Quashie, *The Sovereignty of Quiet*; Ashon Crawley, *Blackpentecostal Breath*; A. G. Weheliye, *Feenin: R&B Music and the Materiality of BlackFem Voices and Technology* (Durham, NC: Duke University Press, 2023); and A. G. Weheliye, *Habeas Viscus*, among others. See also Fred Moten, *In the Break: Aesthetics of the Black Radical Tradition* (Minneapolis: Minnesota University Press, 2003).

38. Sianne Ngai, *Ugly Feelings* (Cambridge, MA: Harvard University Press, 2005).

39. Rana Issa, "Khatem Izdihar," *Al-Jumhuirryah*, February 12, 2021, https://aljumhuriya.net/ar/2021/12/02/%D8%AE%D8%A7%D8%AA%D9%85-%D8%A7%D8%B2%D8%AF%D9%87%D8%A7%D8%B1; Ghassan Moussawi, *Disruptive Situations: Fractal Orientalism and Queer Strategies in Beirut* (Philadelphia: Temple University Press, 2020); Tarek El-Ariss, *Trials of Arab Modernity: Literary Affects and the New Political*, (New York: Fordham University Press, 2013); Adania Shibli, *Minor Detail*, trans. Elisabeth Jaquette (New York: New Directions, 2020); Rima Najdi, https://rimanajdi.com/; Leila Sakr, *Arabic Glitch: Technoculture, Data Bodies, and Archives* (Stanford, CA: Stanford University Press, 2023).

40. Audre Lorde, *Sister Outsider*, 56.

41. Legacy Russell, "Digital Dualism and the Glitch Feminism Manifesto,".

42. bell hooks, "An Aesthetic of Blackness—Strange and Oppositional," *Lenox Avenue: A Journal of Interarts Inquiry* 1 (1995): 65–72.

43. Arjun Appadurai, *The Future as Cultural Fact: Essays on the Global Condition* (New York: Verso, 2013); Vincent Crapanzano, *Imaginative Horizons: An Essay in Literary-Philosophical Anthropology* (Chicago: Chicago University Press, 2004); Parla Ayse, *Precarious Hope: Migration and the Limits of Belonging in Turkey* (Stanford, CA: Stanford University Press, 2019).

44. Maurya Wickstrom, *Performance in the Blockades of Neoliberalism: Thinking the Political Anew* (London: Palgrave Macmillan, 2012); Lauren Berlant, "Cruel Optimism," in *The Affect Theory Reader*, ed. Melissa Gregg and Gregory J. Seigworth (Durham, NC: Duke University Press, 2010); Leila Tayeb, "Shahi al-Huriya: Militant Optimism and Freedom Tea,"

Communication and the Public 2, no. 2 (2017): 164–76; and Leila Tayeb, "Our Star: Amazigh Music and the Production of Intimacy in 2011 Libya," *Journal of North African Studies* 23, no. 5 (2018): 834–50.

45. Yael Navaro-Yashin, "'Life Is Dead Here': Sensing the Political in 'No Man's Land,'" *Anthropological Theory* 3 (2003): 107–25; Stef Jansen, *Yearnings in the Meantime: 'Normal Lives' and the State in a Sarajevo Apartment Complex* (New York: Berghahn, 2015); Sarah Sharma, *In the Meantime: Temporality and Cultural Politics* (Durham, NC: Duke University Press, 2014); Martin Frederiksen, *Young Men, Time, and Boredom in the Republic of Georgia* (Indianapolis, IN: Temple University Press, 2013); Ghassan Hage, "Waiting Out the Crisis: On Stuckedness and Governmentality," in *Waiting*, ed. Ghassan Hage (Carlton, VIC: Melbourne University Press, 2009), 97–106; Yakein Abdelmagid, "The Weight of Hope: Independent Music Production under Authoritarianism in Egypt," PhD diss., Duke University, 2018; Wickstrom, *Performance in the Blockades of Neoliberalism*.

46. *Antiphonal* refers to the dynamic of call-and-response. Johnson writes about breakdancing in hip-hop; Crawley writes about call-and-response in the Blackpentecostal tradition.

47. See Johnson, *Dark Matter*, 16; Crawley, *Blackpentecostal Breath*, 28.

48. See discussion in Rayya El Zein, "Call and Response, Radical Belonging, and Arabic Hip-Hop in 'the West," in *American Studies Encounters the Middle East*, ed. Alex Lubin and Marwan Kraidy (Chapel Hill, NC: University of North Carolina Press, 2016), 106–35.

49. See, among others, Deborah Kapchan, *Travelling Spirit Masters: Moroccan Gnawa Trance and Music in the Global Marketplace* (Middleton, CT: Wesleyan University Press, 2007); J. H. Shannon, *Among the Jasmine Trees: Music and Modernity in Contemporary Syria* (Middletown, CT: Wesleyan University Press, 2010); A. J. Racy, *Making Music in the Arab World: The Culture and Artistry of Tarab* (Cambridge, UK: Cambridge University Press, 2004); Richard C. Jankowsky, *Stambeli: Music, Trance, and Alterity in Tunisia* (Chicago: Chicago University Press, 2010).

50. Brad Weiss, *Street Dreams and Hip-Hop Barbershops: Global Fantasy in Urban Tanzania* (Bloomington: Indiana University Press, 2009); Hanan Toukan, *The Politics of Art: Dissent and Cultural Diplomacy in Lebanon, Palestine, and Jordan* (Stanford, CA: Stanford University Press, 2021); Jesse Weaver Shipley, *Living the Hiplife: Celebrity and Entrepreneurship in Ghanaian Popular Music* (Durham, NC: Duke University Press, 2013).

51. hooks, "An Aesthetic of Blackness," 71.

52. Raymond Williams, *Marxism and Literature* (Oxford, UK: Oxford University Press, 1977), 128–35.

53. Toukan, *The Politics of Art*.

54. See, for example, Saree Makdisi, "Laying Claim to Beirut: Urban Narrative and Spatial Identity in the Age of Solidere," *Critical Inquiry* 23 (1997): 660–705; C. Nagel, "Reconstructing Space, Re-Creating Memory: Sectarian Politics and Urban Development in Post-War Beirut," *Political Geography* 21 (2002): 717–25.

55. The Gulf wars and then US occupation of Iraq; following the 2011 uprisings, the counterrevolution in Egypt and civil war in Syria, Libya, Yemen; authoritarianism in UAE and KSA.

56. Following the US invasion of Iraq and the escalation of the Syrian civil war and the corresponding refugee crisis, the role of Amman in particular as host for international

humanitarian workers and Western students of Arabic (following the closure of Damascus to US students) blossomed. Beirut and Amman also saw real influxes in refugees from Syria, Libya, and Iraq in this period, adding to existing Iraqi and Palestinian refugee communities.

57. See, among others, Aseel Sawalha, "The Dilemmas of Conservation and Reconstruction in Beirut," in *The Emerging Asian City: Concomitant Urbanities and Urbanisms*, ed. Vinayak Bharne (Oxon, UK: Routledge, 2013), 148–57; and Craig Larkin, *Memory and Conflict in Lebanon: Remembering and Forgetting the Past* (Oxon, UK: Routledge, 2012).

58. The Abdali project shares designers and investors who backed the Solidere project, prominent among them the Saudi Arabian company Oger. (See, among others, Gildas Coignet, "Régénération urbaine ou dégénérescence de l'urbanité?: Le Projet de nouveau centreville d'Al-Abdali à Amman, Jordanie," *Annales de Géographie* 4 (2008): 42–61; and Sawalha, "The Dilemmas of Conservation and Reconstruction."

59. The project is a collaboration between Nablus-born businessman Bashar Masri and the country of Qatar. Despite being in Palestinian territory (Area A), it has been plagued with problems sourcing water since Israel controls the grid. See https://www.rawabi.ps/en/1503297758.

60. As Laleh Khalili has noted in the context of Beirut, "public" places are often laced with an implicit threat for women, and being in them may not always be a relaxing, much less liberating experience. She writes, "Rules of proper and decent behavior for women demand a certain degree of 'privacy' in public which is not easily provided by unsegregated spaces . . . where men's exuberant and sometimes aggressive behavior would threaten the women's ability to partake of a safe conviviality" (Laleh Khalili, "The Politics of Pleasure: Promenading on the Corniche and Beachgoing," *Society and Space* 34, no. 4 (2016): 583–600).

61. The remaking of public space in these ways largely excludes unaccompanied young men. For discussion of access to the sea for working-class fishermen in 'Ain al-Mreisseh and Solidere, see Aseel Sawalha, *Reconstructing Beirut: Memory and Space in a Postwar Arab City* (Austin: University of Texas Press, 2010), 69–88. For discussion of similar dynamics in Cairo, see Anouk de Koning, *Global Dreams: Class, Gender, and Public Space in Cosmopolitan Cairo* (Cairo: American University of Cairo Press, 2009). Martin Frederiksen writes of the dynamics of loitering in the social construction of the *birjeh* in post-Socialist Georgia. See Frederiksen, *Young Men, Time, and Boredom*.

62. See Rayya El Zein, "Toward a Dialectic of Discrepant Cosmopolitanisms," *Middle East Journal of Culture and Communication* 13, no. 2 (2020): 170–89.

63. Kareem Rabie, "Ramallah's Bubbles," *Jadaliyya*, January 18, 2013, http://www.jadaliyya.com/Details/27839/Ramallah's-Bubbles.

64. Sami Said, co-owner of the Ramallah restaurant pub Radio, formerly Beit Aneesah remarked, "I remember this period of like one month when maybe ten or fifteen broadcasts came out, and they all did the same report on the same theme, and that was 'Nightlife in Ramallah.' The first and the second one, we were pleased, whatever. But then we started to feel like something wrong was happening. [It's like people were surprised that], even though there's an Occupation, people are still living. What does this mean, *people are still living*? Like, what are we supposed to do, die? And then all of a sudden, we stopped hearing from these journalists. [And we were like,] what was that, you finished? Everything is fine because people go out at night? Look, it's our right to go out. And we want to go out. *And* we still have problems. It doesn't mean that everything is okay, that people are living normally" (Interview with the author, December 7, 2014, Ramallah). The media narrative Said identifies expresses

surprise that there could be such things as Palestinian nightlife, concerts, or social life under the Israeli occupation: It is an expression of wonder at and celebration of youthful Palestinian resilience against the odds. The Palestinian sociologist Lisa Taraki calls this an orientalist "wonderment that Palestinians are capable of intelligent lives" in Western and Israeli journalistic writings on Ramallah (Lisa Taraki, "Enclave Micropolis: The Paradoxical Case of Ramallah/Al-Bireh," *Journal of Palestine Studies* 37 [2008]: 11–12).

65. She'rap, interview with the author, August 26, 2014, Ramallah.

66. Kareem Rabie, *Palestine Is a Party and the Whole World Is Invited* (Durham, NC: Duke University Press, 2021); Tawfiq Haddad, *Palestine, Ltd.* (London: IB Tauris, 2016); Adam Hanieh, "The Internationalization of Gulf Capital and Palestinian Class Formation," *Capital and Class* 35, no. 1: 81–106. See also Nadeem Karkabi, "Staging Particular Difference: Politics of Space in the Palestinian Alternative Music Scene," *Middle East Journal of Culture and Communication* 6 (2013): 308–28.

67. Raed Serhan, Culture Manager for Red Bull, told me in 2015, "[Red Bull] labels every country in a tier. There's a 'tier three,' 'tier two,' 'tier one,' and 'cultural hotspot.' A country like Egypt, because of their theatre and music and film scene, they are a 'cultural hotspot.' Lebanon is a 'cultural hotspot' because of [its] nightlife. Since 2013, Jordan has been a 'culture tier two.' Before that it was dead: it was a 'tier three.' In the beginning of 2015, we moved into 'culture tier one.' Because of all the concerts and festivals, it's coming alive with music. So now the goal is becoming a 'cultural hotspot'" (Interview with the author, August 23, 2015, Amman). Mark LeVine writes of the important role Red Bull played in developing music venues in Pakistan. See Mark LeVine, *Heavy Metal Islam: Rock, Resistance, and the Struggle for the Soul of Islam*, second edition (Boston: MIT Press, 2022).

68. See Laleh Khalili, "The Politics of Pleasure."

69. El Rass, "Borkan Beirut," on the *Kachf el Mahjoub* (*Unveiling the Hidden*) album, released 2012. Lyrics translated by Moe Ali Nayel, published in "Exploring Popular Literature: Arabic Hip-Hop," *Shahadat* (Winter 2012): 64–69.

70. Ghassan Moussawi, *Disruptive Situations: Fractal Orientalism and Queer Strategies in Beirut* (Philadelphia: Temple University Press, 2021), 5–6.

71. Moussawi, *Disruptive Situations*, 5.

72. Moussawi, *Disruptive Situations*, 6.

73. Yael Navaro-Yashin, *The Make-Believe Space: Affective Geography in a Postwar Polity* (Durham, NC: Duke University Press, 2012), 17; Moussawi, *Disruptive Situations*, 5.

74. Ghassan Hage, "Waiting Out the Crisis: On Stuckedness and Governmentality," in *Waiting* (Melbourne: Melbourne University Press, 2009), 98.

75. Moussawi, *Disruptive Situations*, 5.

76. Sawalha, *Reconstructing Beirut*, Kindle locations 129–34.

77. In my fieldwork in 2014–15, I perceived that the limbo that Sawalha wrote about in the early 2000s was hardening; it was becoming darker, more cynical, more introverted, less hopeful. Disgust permeated many, many of my conversations: about local racism and local classism, especially about the lack of opportunities for young people, about the corruption and oligarchy of the government, about the lack of electricity and internet, about the lack of support for culture, about the stranglehold of NGO funding structures on art production (and other things), about the complicity of the diaspora or the dismal social prospects accompanying a move outside of the country, about sexism and patriarchy, about religious hypocrisy, and so on. Amine Younes, the owner of a chain coffeehouses who opened the first

local café (not an international chain) in Hamra in the 2000s (Younes café), told me about a shift he noticed in his café between 2006 and 2013: "People used to come, students or young professionals, spend half an hour, order something, and go to their work or back to their studies. Now, with social media and the Internet, people come and spend three or four hours on an espresso or a sandwich. Of course this affected us financially, but I'm not talking about this. Socially, the talk is different. There is pessimism. It's not always so serious, of course. But there used to be more positive vibes, people would be laughing. Now there's something negative in things. You can see it in people's faces. Like three years ago [2010], I started noticing this change. I cannot explain it. You have to see it, then you notice it. It's in their eyes. Their eyes are empty" (Interview with the author, August 28, 2013, Beirut).

78. Laith Al Huseini, public Facebook post, February 1, 2016, https://www.facebook.com/Synaptik808/posts/10153815341218903.

79. Julie Peteet writes, "Waiting and the trepidation it generates are shared experiences whether in Lebanon, Syria, Palestine, or Iraq." (Julie Peteet, "Closure's Temporality: The Cultural Politics of Time and Waiting," *South Atlantic Quarterly* 117, no. 1 [2018]: 62.)

80. Jansen, *Yearnings in the Meantime*, 173.

81. bell hooks, "An Aesthetic of Blackness," 65.

82. Laila Shereen Sakr, *Arabic Glitch: Technoculture, Data Bodies, and Archives* (Stanford, CA: Stanford University Press, 2023), 6.

83. Crawley, *Blackpentecostal Breath*.

84. Mark Fisher, "The Metaphysics of Crackle: Afrofuturism and Hauntology," *Dancecult: Journal of Electronic Dance Music Culture* 5, no. 2: 42–55.

85. Tsing, *Mushroom,* 22.

86. Ghassan Hage, *Alter-Politics: Critical Anthropology and the Radical Imagination* (Melbourne: Melbourne University Publishing, 2015), 94.

87. Based as it is on aural exposure to the language since birth and very little formal instruction.

88. Hage, *Alter-Politics*, 114.

1. Revolting

Raed Ghoneim is a Palestinian rapper who grew up in the refugee camps outside of Beirut. His stage name means "the voice of Gilgamesh" ("Istafrigh | Raed Ghoneim 'Sot Gilgamesh'" ("I Throw Up | Raed Ghoneim 'Voice of Gilgamesh'"), Sound Cloud audio recording, 4:57, posted by Gilgamesh, accessed January 23, 2021, https://soundcloud.com/sootgilgamesh/sont2e9dmty8); Sianne Ngai, *Ugly Feelings* (Cambridge, MA: Harvard University Press, 2007), 347; Rana Issa, "Khatem Izdihar," *Al-Jumhuirryah*, February 12, 2021, https://aljumhuriya.net/ar/2021/12/02/%D8%AE%D8%A7%D8%AA%D9%85-%D8%A7%D8%B2%D8%AF%D9%87%D8%A7%D8%B1.

1. Staff, "TIME 100: El Général," *TIME*, accessed April 28, 2018, http://content.time.com/time/specials/packages/article/0,28804,2066367_2066369_2066242,00.html.

2. See, for example, Staff, "How Rap Music Fueled and the Arab Uprisings," updated as "Hip-Hop Is the 'Wind and Sails' of Revolution," *NBC*, January 1, 2012, http://www.nbcnews.com/video/nbc-news/44506420; Caspar Llewellyn Smith, "Soundtrack to the Arab Revolutions," *The Guardian*, February 26, 2011, https://www.theguardian.com/music

/musicblog/2011/feb/27/arab-revolutions-protest-music; Arwa Damon, "The Lebanese Art Rockers Creating the Soundtrack to the Arab Spring," *CNN*, February 27, 2013, http://www.cnn.com/2013/02/27/world/meast/mashrou-leila-lebanon-rock/index.html; Morning Edition, "The Rap Songs of the Arab Spring," *NPR*, June 9, 2011, https://www.npr.org/sections/therecord/2011/06/09/137067390/the-rap-songs-of-the-arab-spring.

   3. Ted Swedenburg, "Fun^Da^Mental's Jihad Rap," in *Being Young and Muslim: New Cultural Politics in the Global South and North*, edited by Asef Bayat and Linda Herrera (Oxford: Oxford University Press, 2010), 291–308.

   4. Rayya El Zein, "From 'Hip-Hop Revolutionaries' to 'Terrorist-Thugs': 'Blackwashing' between the Arab Spring and the War on Terror," *Lateral* 5, no. 1 (2016), https://csalateral.org/issue/5-1/hip-hop-blackwashing-el-zein/.

   5. Ted Swedenburg, "Imagined Youths," *Middle East Research and Information Project* 245 (Winter 2007), http://www.merip.org/mer/mer245/imagined-youths.

   6. See Hisham Aidi, *Rebel Music: Race, Empire, and the New Muslim Youth Culture* (New York: Knopf Doubleday, 2014).

   7. Big Hass, *Re-Volt: A Hip-Hop Blog*, accessed March 12, 2016, http://revoltradio.blogspot.com.

   8. His enthusiasm for politics has since become more subdued. Personal correspondence with Big Hass, October 2015.

   9. Ted Swedenburg, "Palestinian Rap: Against the Struggle Paradigm," in *Popular Culture in the Middle East and North Africa*, ed. Mounira Solimon and Walid El Hamamsy, 17–32 (New York: Routledge, 2012); and Cristina Moreno-Almeida *Rap beyond Resistance: Staging Power in Contemporary Morocco* (London: Palgrave Macmillan, 2017).

   10. Laudan Nooshin, "Whose Liberation? Iranian Popular Music and the Fetishisation of Resistance," *Popular Communication* 15, no. 3 (2017): 163–91.

   11. Moreno-Almeida *Rap beyond Resistance*, 12.

   12. bell hooks, "An Aesthetic of Blackness—Strange and Oppositional," *Lenox Avenue: A Journal of Interarts Inquiry* 1 (1995): 65.

   13. Winfried Menninghaus, *Disgust: Theory and History of a Strong Sensation* (Albany, NY: SUNY University Press, 2003).

   14. Paul Geary, "The Production of Taste: Ecologies, Intersections, Implications," *Studies in Theatre and Performance* 40, no. 3 (2021): 281.

   15. Moreno-Almeida, *Rap beyond Resistance*, 12.

   16. Sianne Ngai, *Ugly Feelings* (Cambridge, MA: Harvard University Press, 2007), 345.

   17. Author's field notes, August 27, 2013. An earlier iteration of this analysis appeared in Rayya El Zein, "Resisting Resistance: On Political Feeling in Arabic Rap Concerts," in *Arab Subcultures: Transformations in Theory and Practice*, edited by Tarik Sabry and Layal Ftouni (London: IB Tauris, 2017): 87–112.

   18. Pierre Bourdieu, *Distinction: A Social Critique of the Judgment of Taste*, trans. Richard Nice (London: Routledge, 1984).

   19. Imani Kai Johnson, *Dark Matter in Breaking Cyphers: The Life of Africanist Aesthetics in Global Hip-Hop* (Oxford, UK: Oxford University Press, 2023), 12–13.

   20. Sara Ahmed, *The Cultural Politics of Emotion* (New York: Routledge, 2004), 94.

   21. Others have also noted the tension between protest from below (revolt) and the description of disgusting (revolting). In her book *Revolting Subjects: Social Abjection and Resistance in Neoliberal Britain*, British sociologist Imogen Tyler teases apart the symbolic

synonym I tripped on reading Big Hass's blog. In her analysis of the productive tension between political discourses of disgust and new mobilizations of protest in the UK, Tyler lays out two intersecting interpretations of "revolting." She suggests that there is productive intersectionality among groups cast out as "disgusting"—fearsome, pitiful, or otherwise abject (asylum seekers, Gypsies, the Irish Travellers, the homeless, and others)—and new protest movements rising up against the state (including Occupy Wall Street–type occupations, antiwar mobilization, and antieviction work). (Imogen Tyler, *Revolting Subjects: Social Abjection and Resistance in Neoliberal Britain* [London: Zed, 2013].)

22. Adam Faruqi assisted in the identification of musicological elements.

23. For more on the history of Palestinian refugees in Lebanon and the decades-long construction of these dynamics within Lebanese society, see Diana Allan, *Refugees of the Revolution: Experiences of Palestinian Exile* (Stanford, CA: Stanford University Press, 2013).

24. For Arabic lyrics and English translation by Rima Najdi and Faysal Bibi, see Rayya El Zein, ed., "Exploring Popular Literature: Arabic Hip-Hop," *ArteEast Shahadat* (Winter 2012): 74–81, https://issuu.com/arteeast/docs/shahadatwinter2012; the track itself is on the *Al-Tareeq Wahad Marsoum* (*One Way Decree*) album available on ReverbNation, accessed May 29, 2016, https://www.reverbnation.com/katibe5كتيبه/playlist/-4.

25. Osloob, interview with the author, September 3, 2013, Beirut.

26. Spelled with the aspirated hamza instead of the hard *qaf*.

27. Mary Douglas, *Purity and Danger: An Analysis of the Concept of Pollution and Taboo* (Oxon, UK: Routledge, 1966).

28. The private real estate company once run by former Lebanese Prime Minister Rafiq al-Hariri that was largely responsible for the reconstruction of downtown Beirut after the Lebanese Civil War (1975–90). Solidere has been the object of criticism for practices of property expropriation it mobilized to gain ownership of the downtown space, in addition to allegations of nepotism and corruption, among others.

29. "(Bu Nasserdyn al-Touffar w El Rass—nihna w a-zibl jeeran—video)" (Nasserdyn al-Touffar and El Rass—We Have Shit for Neighbors—Video (in Arabic)), YouTube video, 3:25, posted by Nasserdayn al touffar, August 31, 2015, https://www.youtube.com/watch?v=uTdlfAkwpJo&ab_channel=Naserdaynaltouffar.

30. Tarek El-Ariss, *Trials of Arab Modernity: Literary Affects and the New Political*, (New York: Fordham University Press, 2013), 53–87.

31. El-Ariss, *Trials of Arab Modernity*, 55.

32. Ibid., 75.

33. Julia Kristeva, *Powers of Horror: An Essay on Abjection*, trans. Leon S. Roudiez (New York: Columbia University Press, 1982).

34. Kristeva, *Powers of Horror*, 5.

35. Ibid., 2.

36. El-Ariss, *Trials of Arab Modernity*, 76, original emphasis.

37. Ahmed, *Cultural Politics of Emotion*, 91.

38. Lisa Wedeen has applied Berlant's concepts of a "good life" to political expression in Syria. Lisa Wedeen, "Ideology and Humor in Dark Times: Notes from Syria," *Critical Inquiry* 39 (2013): 841–73.

39. Berlant writes, "It may be a relation of cruel optimism, when, despite an awareness that the normative political sphere appears as a shrunken, broke, or distant place of activity among elites, members of the body politics return periodically to its recommitment ceremonies and scenes" (Lauren Berlant, *Cruel Optimism* [Durham, NC: Duke University Press, 2011], 227).

40. "Bu Nasser Touffar, El Rass (Prod. Jundi Majhul)—Beirut khaybetna," 5:18, YouTube clip, posted by Bu Nasser Touffar, January 11, 2013, https://www.youtube.com/watch?v=iPgDp2z3n-c.

41. The DshK is a Soviet-era machine gun.

42. "Beirut khaybetna—Naserdayn al-Touffar and El Rass (Intaj Wattar)" ("Beirut Disappointed Us—Nasrdayn al-Touffar and El Rass [Produced by Wattar]"), YouTube video clip, 5:18, posted by Naserdayn al touffar, January 11, 2013, https://www.youtube.com/watch?v=iPgDp2z3n-c&ab_channel=Naserdaynaltouffar.

43. This lyrical work is developing, but it is hardly representative of the entire scene. Raed Ghoneim's work, quoted in the epigraph to this chapter, is another example.

44. A video circulated on social media in 2015 captured the singing of this verse in the street and shows maybe half a dozen young men and at least one woman reciting the verse by heart. (See "Fi al-yom a-thaleth" ("On the Third Day"), YouTube video, 1:49, posted by Mak Man, August 24, 2015, https://www.youtube.com/watch?v=Gy45jFnNM50&ab_channel=MakMan.)

45. Rana Issa, "Khatem Izdihar."

2. *Istifzaz*

Palestinian rapper Muqata'a (also goes by the anglophone *boikutt*). "Qabl W Ba'l—*qabl w ba'l*," SoundCloud audio clip 5:15, posted by 'Muqata'a', 2014, accessed August 19, 2019, https://soundcloud.com/muqataa/qabl-w-bal; Legacy Russell, "Digital Dualism and the Glitch Feminism Manifesto," *Society Pages*, December 12, 2012, https://thesocietypages.org/cyborgology/2012/12/10/digital-dualism-and-the-glitch-feminism-manifesto.

1. Adam Faruqi assisted in the identification of musicological elements.

2. "Qabour al-Qarn": "Shua—Quboor Al Qarn (produced by Boikutt)," SoundCloud track, 2:02, posted by Shua, September 2014, https://soundcloud.com/shu-a-1/shua-quboor-al-qarn-produced-by-boikutt.

3. For another good example, see "Stormtrap—Zey ma sar mbare7," ("Stormtrap—As It Happened Yesterday") YouTube video, 3:21, posted by Ramallahunderground, June 10, 2010, accessed December 9, 2015, https://www.youtube.com/watch?v=ZAXczID4q4s8&ab_channel=Ramallahunderground. Arabic lyrics and their translation provided by the artist and published in Rayya El Zein, ed., "Exploring Popular Literature: Arabic Hip-Hop," *Shahadat* (Winter 2012): 54–59, http://issuu.com/arteeast/docs/shahadatwinter2012.

4. Marc Lamont Hill, *Beats, Rhymes, and Classroom Life: Hip-hop Pedagogy and the Politics of Identity* (New York: Teachers College Press, 2009), 4.

5. While I borrow the notion of a relational epistemology from global hip-hop, it is worthwhile to remind the reader that my attention in this research is on rap primarily and even rap in isolation from other cultural and artistic practices usually associated with hip-hop culture.

6. Henry Louis Gates Jr., "Foreword," in *The Anthology of Rap*, ed. Adam Bradley and Andrew DuBois (New Haven, CT: Yale University Press, 2010), xxii–xxix.

7. Hill, *Beats, Rhymes, and Classroom Life*.

8. Halifu Osumare, *The Africanist Aesthetic in Global Hip-Hop: Power Moves* (New York: Palgrave Macmillan, 2007), 15.

9. H. Samy Alim, *Roc the Mic Right: The Language of Hip-Hop Culture* (New York: Routledge, 2006).

10. Imani Kai Johnson, *Dark Matter in Breaking Cyphers: The Life of Africanist Aesthetics in Global Hip-Hop* (Oxford: Oxford University Press, 2023), 3.

11. Tarek El-Ariss, *Leaks, Hacks, and Scandals: Arab Culture in the Digital Age* (Princeton, NJ: Princeton University Press, 2018); Laura Marks, "Arab Glitch," in *Uncommon Grounds: New Media and Visual Practice in the Middle East and North Africa*, ed. Anthony Downey (London: I. B. Tauris, 2014), 256–71; Laila Shereen Sakr, *Arabic Glitch: Technoculture, Data Bodies, and Archives* (Stanford, CA: Stanford University Press, 2023), 6.

12. Sakr, *Arabic Glitch*, 2, emphasis added.

13. Sakr, *Arabic Glitch*, 2.

14. Russell, "Digital Dualism."

15. Rosa Menkman, *Glitch Studies Manifesto*, accessed December 8, 2023, http://amodern.net/wp-content/uploads/2016/05/2010_Original_Rosa-Menkman-Glitch-Studies-Manifesto.pdf.

16. See, for example, Jack L. Daniel and Geneva Smitherman, "How I Got Over: Communication Dynamics in the Black Community," *Quarterly Journal of Speech* 62 (1976): 26–39; Maggie Sale, "Call and Response as Critical Method: African American Oral Traditions in *Beloved*," *African American Review* 26 (1992): 41–50; Oliver Jackson, "Preface," in *Kuntu Drama*, ed. Paul Harrison (New York: Grove, 1974), ix–xiii; Geneva Smitherman, *Talkin' and Testifyin': The Language of Black America* (Detroit: Wayne State University Press, 1977); Robert Farris Thompson, *African Art in Motion: Icon and Act* (Los Angeles: University of California Press, 1974); Edward D. Miller, "Authoring the Occupation: The Mic Check, the Human Microphone, and the Loudness of Listening," in *Media Authorship*, ed. Cynthia Chris and David A. Gerstner (New York: Routledge, 2013), 180–93; and Alim, *Roc the Mic Right*, 54–56.

17. Thompson, *African Art in Motion*, 28.

18. Daniel and Smitherman, "How I Got Over," 33.

19. I have made different arguments about call-and-response in Arabic rap elsewhere. See Rayya El Zein, "Call and Response and Arabic Hip-Hop in 'the West,'" in *American Studies Encounters the Middle East*, ed. Marwan Kraidy and Alex Lubin (Chapel Hill: University of North Carolina Press, 2016), 106–35.

20. Adam Faruqi assisted in the identification and articulation of musicological forms.

21. I follow performance studies scholar Diana Taylor here in using *performatic* (referring to happenings in a live performance) to distinguish from the *performative* (a specific kind of speech or behavior that in its uttering brings something into being, theorized in the tradition of J. L. Austin or Judith Butler). Diana Taylor, *The Archive and the Repertoire: Performing Cultural Memory in the Americas* (Durham, NC: Duke University Press, 2003).

22. Louis Althusser, *Lenin and Philosophy and Other Essays*, trans. Ben Brewster (New York: Monthly Review Press, 2001), 111.

23. Russell, "Digital Dualism."

24. Ibid.

25. See, for example, Hill, *Beats, Rhymes, and Classroom Life*; John Jackson, *Real Black: Adventures in Racial Sincerity* (Chicago: University of Chicago Press, 2005); Alastair Pennycook, "Language, Localization, and the Real: Hip-Hop and the Global Spread of Authenticity," *Journal of Language, Identity & Education* 6, no. 2 (2007): 101–15; Alim, *Roc the Mic Right*; Halifu Osumare, *The Hiplife in Ghana: West African Indigenization of Hip-Hop* (New York: Palgrave Macmillan), 2012.

26. On the particularities of the formation "the Arab Street," see Terry Regier and Muhammad Ali Khalidi, "The *Arab Street*: Tracking a Political Metaphor," *Middle East Journal* 63, no. 1 (2009): 11–29.

27. For a fuller elaboration, see Tarik Sabry, *Cultural Encounters in the Arab World* (London: I. B. Tauris, 2010), especially 43–62.

28. The Palestinian rapper She'rap, interview with the author, August 26, 2014, Ramallah.

29. Testimonies like this one are the primary reason I do not find more recent assessments of pleasure or consumption "as resistance" under Occupation in the context of the growing middle class in Ramallah to be a compelling alternative to the asceticism of sumud. That is, my interlocutors were much more ready to disavow the existence of resistance at all in their work than they were to claim the presence of resistance in cultural activity not typically seen as such. (See Lisa Taraki, "Enclave Micropolis: The Paradoxical Case of Ramallah/Al-Bireh," *Journal of Palestine Studies* 37 [2008]: 9–14.)

30. Palestinian media scholar Helga Tawil-Souri suggests that in the context of Zionist policy, which declares, in the legacy of Golda Meir, that "Palestinians do not exist," every study of Palestinian people and culture that shows that they do is necessarily political. See Helga Tawil-Souri, "The Necessary Politics of Palestinian Cultural Studies," in *Arab Cultural Studies: Mapping the Field*, ed. Tarik Sabry (London: I. B. Tauris, 2012).

31. Simon Frith, *Performing Rites: On the Value of Popular Music* (Cambridge, MA: Harvard University Press, 1996), 3–20.

32. Here, Osloob is spouting some nonsense poetry in *fusha*, classical Arabic. The idea is that formal, flowery lines, regardless of how beautiful they are, don't connect with ordinary people or their lived experience.

33. Osloob, interview with the author, September 3 2013, Beirut.

34. El Rass (Mazen El Sayed), interview with the author, January 14, 2014, Beirut.

35. Russell writes, "Glitch refuses being categorized as subtext, it rejects being labeled as subversive, it does not speak for the marginal or the subaltern, as 'sub' as a prefix needs to be marked as a mode of acquiescence to our own exclusion front the canon, the academy, the Platonic ideal. The first step to subverting a system is accepting that the system will remain in place; that said, the glitch says fuck your systems!" (Russell, "Digital Dualism")

36. José Muñoz, *Cruising Utopia: The Then and There of Queer Futurity* (New York: New York University Press, 2009), 35.

37. "Shabjeed | Interview—shab jdeed | al-mqabaleh," YouTube video, 25:39, posted by Ma3azef, September 16, 2019, accessed March 3, 2024, https://www.youtube.com/watch?v=tvqRlsmFHwY.

38. "Shabjdeed—Ko7ol w 3atme," 3:15, posted by BLTNM, May 12, 2018, accessed April 28, 2024, https://www.youtube.com/watch?v=FN15PcYv8H0.

39. "Haykal—Sot Ramallah," 3:00, posted by Haykal, https://www.youtube.com/watch?v=03twPygAs8g, accessed April 28, 2024.

40. Haykal's track takes its name from an instrumental track by Ramallah Underground.

41. Russell, "Digital Dualism."

42. Menkman, *Glitch Studies Manifesto*.

43. Edward William Lane, *Arabic-English Lexicon*, Vol. 6. s.v. "فزّ," accessed November 6, 2024, http://lexicon.quranic-research.net/data/20_f/109_fz.html.

44. Menkman, Glitch Studies Manifesto.

3. Listening

Interview with the author, March 31, 2015, Amman.

1. Rosa Menkman, *Glitch Studies Manifesto*, 2009, http://amodern.net/wp-content/uploads/2016/05/2010_Original_Rosa-Menkman-Glitch-Studies-Manifesto.pdf.
2. Imani Kai Johnson, *Dark Matter in Breaking Cyphers: The Life of Africanist Aesthetics in Global Hip-Hop* (Oxford, UK: Oxford University Press, 2023), 12.
3. Johnson, *Dark Matter*, 32.
4. On Arabic rap and the global hip-hop cypher, see, for example, Lara Dotson-Renta, "Somos Sur: Translocal Hip-Hop and the Routes of Empire," *Muslim World* 111, no. 3: 2021; Janne Louise Andersen, "Transgressing Borders with Palestinian Hip-Hop," in *Palestinian Music and Song: Expression and Resistance since 1900*, ed. Moslih Kanaaneh et al. (Bloomington: Indiana University Press, 2013), 82–96; Alex Lubin, "Fear of an Arab Planet: The Sounds and Rhythms of Afro-Arab Internationalism," in *Arab American Literature and Culture*, ed. Alfred Hornung and Martina Kohl (Heidelberg, Germany: Universitätsverlag Winter, 2012), 243–63.
5. Charles Hirschkind, *The Ethical Soundscape: Cassette Sermons and Islamic Counterpublics* (New York: Columbia University Press, 2006).
6. Hirschkind, *The Ethical Soundscape*, 34.
7. Hirschkind, *The Ethical Soundscape*, 34, emphasis added.
8. Hirschkind, *The Ethical Soundscape*, 70. Hirschkind is interested in "the forms of public life this practice serves to uphold." He uses "disciplinary" in the sense of Michel Foucault's "technology of the self. "Hirschkind defines it as "a set of procedures by means of which individuals can work on their souls and bodies to achieve a distinct ethical or aesthetic form" (*The Ethical Soundscape*, 39).
9. Lara Deeb and Mona Harb, *Leisurely Islam: Negotiating Geography and Morality and Shi'ite South Beirut* (Princeton, NJ: Princeton University Press, 2013).
10. Jillian Schwedler, "Amman Cosmopolitan: Spaces and Practices of Aspiration and Consumption," *Comparative Studies of South Asia, Africa, and the Middle East* 30, no. 3 (2010): 547–62; Sarah A. Tobin, *Everyday Piety: Islam and Economy in Jordan* (Ithaca, NY: Cornell University Press, 2016).
11. Schwedler, "Amman Cosmopolitan," 549, 559.
12. Sawalha represented the local Jordanian production company and event platform MALAHI and the TBA Collective; Thorpe the Danish NGO Turning Tables; and Robinson the British NGO AptART. Malahi and TBA Collective, through Sawalha's work, were responsible for securing local services, many of which were donated to the festival free of charge. Red Bull Kuwait and Red Bull UAE sponsored artists traveling from those countries (Malikah and Sons of Yusuf). Turning Tables ended up not contributing directly to the festival. On AptART—which stands for "awareness and prevention through art"—and their sources of funding, see www.aptart.org, accessed November 7, 2024. The festival was supposed to rely predominantly on crowdfunding. However, both IndieGoGo and AfkarMENA campaigns were successful in raising only about half the funds requested (less than 42 percent of the $10,000 goal had been raised by October 1, 2015). The rest Sawalha paid largely out of pocket (Personal correspondence with Sawalha, January 19, 2016).
13. The Seven Hills Skatepark, run largely by Mohammed Zakaria, was built in December 2014 with the support of Make Life Skate Life, a Belgian/US NGO that collaborates with local

communities to build skate parks in developing countries. (Unrecorded conversations with the author. See also Hiba Dlewati, "Amman Skatepark a 'Melting Pot' for Locals and Refugees," *National Geographic*, October 14, 2015, https://news.nationalgeographic.org/amman-skatepark-a-melting-pot-for-locals-and-refugees/, among others.

14. The eight hip-hop acts were Malikah (Lebanon/UAE); Satti (Jordan); Almukhtar (Jordan); Sons of Yusuf (Kuwait); Synaptik and Jazz Tha Process (Jordan); Kazz Alomam (Jordan); Arab MC's (Jordan); and Bu Kolthoum (Syria/Jordan). Showcased artists also included DJs, beatboxers, and B-boy dancers. For the full lineup, see "The Word Is Yours Festival October 2: Street Art, Skateboarding, Live Rap, Beatboxing, DJ's, B-Boy Battle and Workshops!," hosted by "The Word Is Yours Festival," Facebook Event page, accessed January 21, 2016, https://www.facebook.com/events/400190190170359. Day two of the festival featured film screenings and artist and producer talk-backs. For the full lineup, see "The Word Is Yours—October 3: Artist Talks, Workshops, DJ Sets, Film Screenings, Street Art, Exhibitions," hosted by "The Word Is Yours Festival," accessed January 21, 2016, https://www.facebook.com/events/405036743027305.

15. The opening night concert was July 29, 2015. The concert was Tarabband, an Iraqi Swedish folk band. Tickets were 10 JDs. For a summary of acts at the festival, see http://al-balad.org/al-balad-music-festival/, accessed November 7, 2024.

16. Author's field notes, August 28, 2015.

17. Raed Asfour, interview with the author, August 16, 2015, Amman.

18. Ibid.

19. Ibid.

20. In the late 1990s, the municipality planted trees in the downtown plaza, which is historically home to the smaller Odeon theater and the larger Roman amphitheater. At night at that time, the plaza was unlit and dark. Asfour recalled that during their first efforts to host events in this space, people from outside the neighborhood (the target audience) largely refused to attend, and young men and boys from the neighborhood regularly threw stones at those who did. In 2012, the municipality cut down most of the trees and tiled the plaza, adding lights. It is now a popular shaʿbi space frequented by inhabitants of the neighboring hills of East Amman on every night of the week: families, young children, couples, and groups of young men alike. Asfour claims that the rapport between the artistic community, its audience, and the regular users of the space is improving, a status he described thusly: "They have to get used to the fact that there's [going to be] art there." He added, "Even if individuals are just hearing from the outside [of the theater], they are still hearing something different—not to say better or worse [than they would otherwise]—just different."

21. Christopher Parker elaborates that this is part of the Hashemite narrative as well: using Jordan's spectacular natural landscapes and ancient heritage as part of its specific appeal (specifically for its tourism industry) against whose backdrop its emergent modernity is all the more precious and spectacular. (Christopher Parker, "Tunnel-bypasses and Minarets of Capitalism: Amman as Neoliberal Assemblage, *Political Geography* 28[2009]:111–112.)

22. The one concert I did not attend was that of the Jordanian indie rock band Zaed Naes.

23. This cheaper ticket was a compromise with Muqataʿa, who requested a 5 JD donation as a condition for participating in the concert.

24. Khotta Ba, interview with the author, August 12, 2015, Amman.

25. The park is elevated above the street, making us visible to young and middle-aged men sitting outside a carpentry shop drinking coffee. Rana is not her real name.

26. Author's field notes, October 5, 2015.

27. My companion grew up in Amman. We spoke together in Arabic. Nonetheless, our activity cleaning up garbage indicated to the men across the street that we were not locals. They called out to us in broken English.

28. The police eventually convinced the religious authorities to back down by arguing that the event was mostly for *ajaneb* (foreigners). Needless to say, this insulted the (Arab) musicians and local participants, though they were simultaneously relieved the event could continue.

29. I suspect that at Jadal, a Syrian-run cafe and performance space, the crowd was much more self-selecting, less heterogeneous (predominantly Syrian), and familiar with his work. Here, in a context open to the public, the attention audiences spent on each other prevented an earnest engagement with the rappers and their work.

30. "Cosmopolitan international" is Schwedler's phrase. To be sure, Schwedler locates most aspiring cosmopolitan in the malls, traffic circles, and clubs of West Amman, not in East Amman. She doesn't address the negotiations of cosmopolitanism in shared public space, like the downtown plaza, that I am addressing here (Schwedler, "Amman Cosmopolitan.")

31. Rayya El Zein, "Toward a Dialectic of Discrepant Cosmopolitanisms," *Middle East Journal of Culture and Communication* 13, no. 2 (2020): 170–89.

32. Khotta Ba, interview with the author, August 12, 2015, Amman.

33. Hijazzi explained, "If you have one hundred people listening to you, that's not a fan base. Last year we did a concert . . . and put fourteen of the rappers with us on the label on stage. Fourteen people, and of them the biggest names in Amman, so they say of themselves. One hundred and fifty people came to the show. Fourteen people, that's ten percent of the crowd—on the stage. Don't tell me there's a fanbase. Where's the music scene? Where's the respect for this music? There isn't any." While the details vary, these comments are not limited to Amman. In Beirut, Osloob told me, "There's no music scene in Beirut. There's no movement [*haraka*]. There's no place for music. You know what's the dream of the musician in Beirut? To play with Ziad Rahbani and Fairouz. Of course, they're fine musicians, I respect them too. But there's no creativity in [this ambition]." (Interview with the author, September 3, 2013. For analysis of the Rahbani family musical legacy, see Christopher Stone, *Popular Culture and Nationalism in Lebanon: The Fairouz and Rahbani Nation* [Oxon, UK: Routledge, 2008].)

34. Brian Larkin, "Techniques of Inattention: The Mediality of Loudspeakers in Nigeria," *Anthropological Quarterly* 87, no. 4 (2014): 1007.

35. On the one hand, Larkin identifies the way in which anthropology of religion in the tradition of Talal Asad has approached the cultivation of attention as a religious practice. (Brian Larkin, "Techniques of Inattention: The Mediality of Loudspeakers in Nigeria," *Anthropological Quarterly* 87, no. 4 (2014): 989–1015). Charles Hirschkind's interlocutors in Cairo described the cultivation of attention as a repeated practice of learning how to "listen with a sensitive heart" (Hirshkind, *The Ethical Soundscape*, 70). On the other hand, Larkin identifies anthropologies of media that understand attention "as a quintessentially modern phenomenon defined as an activity of exclusion." (Larkin, "Techniques of Inattention," 996.) In societies characterized by the urban bombardment of mass media, European theorists of modernity like Simmel and Freud writing about turn of the (twentieth) century Berlin describe attention as "a process of ordering vision, defining what it is we choose to focus on and for how long" (Ibid.).

36. Larkin, "Techniques of Inattention," 1008.

37. Ibid.

38. Julia Elyachar, "The Political Economy of Movement and Gesture in Cairo," *Journal of the Royal Anthropological Institute* 17 (2011): 82–99.

39. Ghassan Moussawi, *Disruptive Situations: Fractal Orientalism and Queer Strategies in Beirut* (Philadelphia: Temple University Press, 2020).

40. Moussawi, *Disruptive Situations*, 5.

41. Menkman, *Manifesto*.

42. Mouneer Bu Kolthoum, interview with the author, March 31, 2015, Amman, emphasis added.

43. Hirschkind, *The Ethical Soundscape*.

44. El Rass (Mazen El Sayed), interview with the author, January 14, 2014, Beirut.

45. Hirschkind, *The Ethical Soundscape*, 28.

46. Following similar concerns, Darci Sprengel writes about the distinction between "loud" and "quiet" aesthetics and the political import of quiet "atmospheres" in Egyptian experimental art and music scenes following the 2011 revolution. See Darci Sprengel, "'Loud' and 'Quiet' Politics: Questioning the Role of 'the Artist' in Street Art Projects after the 2011 Egyptian Revolution," *International Journal of Cultural Studies* 23, no. 2 (2019): 208–26; and Darci Sprengel, "Reframing the 'Arab Winter': The Importance of Sleep and a Quiet Atmosphere after 'Defeated' Revolutions," *Culture, Theory and Critique* 61 (2020): 246–66.

47. Adam Faruqi assisted in the identification of musicological elements.

48. Hicham Ibrahim, the DJ who goes by Sotusura. Interview with the author, September 12, 2015, Amman.

49. See, for example, Sunaina Maira, *Jil Oslo: Palestinian Hip-Hop, Youth Culture, and the Youth Movement* (Washington, DC: Tadween, 2013); and David McDonald, *My Voice Is My Weapon: Music, Nationalism, and the Poetics of Palestinian Resistance* (Durham, NC: Duke University Press, 2013), among many others. *Slingshot Hip-Hop* (2008), dir. Jackie Reem Salloum.

50. Muqata'a (boikutt) and Asifeh (Stormtrap) both are still active in the rap scene in the region, though they are the subject of considerably less academic attention. Ted Swedenburg, "Palestinian Rap: Against the Struggle Paradigm," in *Popular Culture in the Middle East and North Africa*, ed. Mounira Solimon and Walid El Hamasy (New York: Routledge, 2013), 17–32.

51. See https://www.baselandruanne.com. I discuss some of their recent work in Rayya El Zein, "To Have Many Returns: Loss in the Presence of Others," *World Records* 4 (2020): https://worldrecordsjournal.org/to-have-many-returns-loss-in-the-presence-of-others/.

52. The younger generation of rappers in Ramallah agrees. The rapper Haykal told me, "The name *saleb wahed* (minus one) isn't really different from the phrase *Ramallah Underground*. It's almost a continuation of RU. We are -1 from Ramallah. It's the underground of Ramallah. We became a kind of a continuation of what the Ramallah Underground was." (Interview with the author, August 16, 2015, Amman.)

53. For thick description and analysis of DAM's concerts and their performance styles, see McDonald, *My Voice Is My Weapon*, 262–82.

54. He offered "more like comic" in English. (Interview with the author, August 16, 2015, Amman.)

55. Palestinian rapper Haykal, interview with the author, August 20, 2015, Amman.

56. Dakn interview with the author, Amman March 30, 2015.

57. The lyrics of "Meen Irhabi" have been transcribed and translated elsewhere; see, for example, Sunaina Maira, "'We Ain't Missing: Palestinian Hip-Hop: A Transnational Youth Movement," *CR: The New Centennial Review* 8 (2002): 177.

58. Dakn, interview with the author, March 30, 2015, Amman.

59. This identification of what was satisfying in listening to the music led in our conversations to a real disavowal of the populist aesthetics of a group like DAM and the ways in which the group imagines Palestinian politics and concert culture. Again, the thing to note here is that the three younger rapper-DJs identify a political process of listening in which they aligned themselves with one aesthetic over another.

60. Dakn, interview with the author, March 30, 2015, Amman.

61. Palestinian rapper Haykal, interview with the author, August 20, 2015, Amman.

62. "Ma Illi Horiyih (I don't have freedom)—DAM [with English translations] دام - حرية إلي ما," YouTube video 3:37, posted by Mr Palestinian Hiphop on July 8, 2013, https://www.youtube.com/watch?v=ooVdjKI68CU.

63. Palestinian rapper Haykal, interview with the author, August 20, 2015, Amman.

4. Yearning

1. My thanks to Lilian Volat for sharing this episode with me.

2. "Shaden Fakih: She Comes Again | Sarde (After Dinner) Podcast #121," 1:34:47, posted by Sarde After Dinner, October 11, 2023, https://www.youtube.com/watch?v=JwsOxP6LCQk.

3. Audre Lorde, *Sister Outsider: Essays and Speeches by Audre Lorde* (Berkeley, CA: Crossing, 2007), 153.

4. Lorde, *Sister Outsider*, 53.

5. Ashon T. Crawley, *Blackpentecostal Breath: The Aesthetics of Possibility* (New York: Fordham University Press, 2017), 25.

6. See Ali Jihad Racy, *Making Music in the Arab World: The Culture and Artistry of Tarab* (Cambridge, UK: Cambridge University Press, 2004), 202.

7. Michael Anthony Sells, *Early Islamic Mysticisms: Sufi, Qur'an, Mi'raj, Poetic and Theological Writings* (Mahwah, NJ: Paulis, 1996); Frederico García Lorca, "Theory and Play of the *Duende*," trans. A. S. Kline, accessed January 10, 2014, http://www.poetryintranslation.com/klineaslorcaduende.htm; Jane Sugarman, *Engendering Song: Singing and Subjectivity at Prespa Albanian Weddings* (Chicago: University of Chicago Press, 1997); Richard C. Jankowsky, *Stambeli: Music, Trance, and Alterity in Tunisia* (Chicago: University of Chicago Press, 2010); Deborah Kapchan, *Travelling Spirit Masters: Moroccan* Gnawa *Trance and Music in the Global Marketplace* (Middleton, CT: Wesleyan University Press, 2007).

8. See also Virginia Danielson, *The Voice of Egypt: Umm Kulthum, Arabic Song, and Egyptian Society in the Twentieth Century* (Chicago: University of Chicago Press, 1997); and Jonathan Shannon, *Among the Jasmine Trees: Music and Modernity in Contemporary Syria* (Middletown, CT: Wesleyan University Press, 2006).

9. A most welcome reflection from a fan came during the artist talks at the Word Is Yours Festival in Amman in October 2015. Discussion on the panel had turned to the subjects addressed in Arabic rap and the need to diversify subject matter. A young woman (half Jordanian, half German) sitting next to me turned and whispered, "What I like about Arabic rap is that it's not misogynistic. They insist on writing songs about their love lives, why? To make it misogynistic?"

10. Claudia Tate, *Psychoanalysis and Black Novels: Desire and the Protocols of Race* (Oxford, UK: Oxford University Press, 1998), 10. Also quoted in Kevin Quashie, *Sovereignty of Quiet*, 65.

11. Racy, *Making Music*, 14.

12. In Arabic, it is often invoked in relation to *saltanah*, or ecstasy, and *wajd*, religious ecstasy or trance (especially in the Sufi tradition), but is nonetheless distinct from both. Tarab need not have a spiritual connotation.

13. Charles Hirschkind, "The Ethics of Listening: Cassette-Sermon Audition in Contemporary Egypt," *American Ethnologist* 28, no. 3 (2001): 639.

14. Charles Hirschkind, *The Ethical Soundscape: Cassette Sermons and Islamic Counterpublics* (New York: Columbia University Press, 2006), 30.

15. Racy, *Making Music*, 203.

16. Al-Isfahani, Kitab al-Aghani (Book of Songs) qtd. in Gilbert Rouget, Music and Trance: A Theory of the Relations between Music and Possession, trans. Brunhilde Biebuyck (Chicago: University of Chicago Press, 1985) 260.

17. Al-Ghazzali, *On Music & Singing: Emotional Religion in Islam as Affected by Music and Singing: A Translation of the Ihya 'Ulm ad-Din of al-Ghazzali with Analysis, Annotation, and Appendices*, trans. Duncan Black MacDonald, *Journal of the Royal Asiatic Society of Great Britain and Ireland* 1901–1902, https://www.ghazali.org/articles/gz-music.pdf, 720.

18. Hicham Ibrahim, the DJ who goes by Sotusura. Interview with the author, September 12, 2015, Amman. Emphasis added.

19. Quashie, *Sovereignty*, 6.

20. Quashie, *Sovereignty*, 56.

21. Quashie, *Sovereignty*, 21.

22. Zora Neale Hurston, *Their Eyes Were Watching God* (New York: Harper & Row, 1990), 67. Quoted in Kevin Everod Quashie, "The Trouble with Publicness: Toward a Theory of Black Quiet," *African American Review* 43, no. 2–3 (2009): 336.

23. Hurston, *Their Eyes Were Watching God*, 67.

24. Quashie, *Sovereignty*, 8–9.

25. Quashie, *Sovereignty*, 9.

26. Quashie, *Sovereignty*, 71.

27. Quashie, *Sovereignty*, 72.

28. Quashie, *Sovereignty*, 67, emphasis added.

29. Ramallah Underground's track "Min al-Kaheff." For discussion, see the introduction.

30. Satti, interview with the author, August 20, 2015, Amman.

31. Khotta Ba (Majd Kamal), interview with the author, August 12, 2015, Amman.

32. "It is all the same, it's not getting better, one's plans get thwarted—so what's the point?" Samuli Schielke, *Egypt in the Future Tense: Hope, Frustration, and Ambivalence before and after 2011* (Bloomington: Indiana University Press, 2015), 27.

33. Khotta Ba, interview with the author, August 12, 2015, Amman.

34. Stef Jansen, *Yearnings in the Meantime:'Normal Lives' and the State in a Sarajevo Apartment Complex* (New York: Berghahn, 2015), 160; Ghassan Hage, "Waiting Out the Crisis: On Stuckedness and Governmentality" in *Waiting*, ed. Ghassan Hage (Melbourne: Melbourne University Press, 2009), 99.

35. Jansen, *Yearnings in the Meantime*, 159.

36. Lori Allen, *The Rise and Fall of Human Rights in Palestine: Cynicism and Politics in Occupied Palestine* (Stanford, CA: Stanford University Press, 2013); José Ciro Martínez and

Omar Sirri, "Of Bakeries and Checkpoints: Stately Affects in Amman and Baghdad," *Society and Space* 38, no. 5 (2020): 849–66.

37. Colin Mclaughlin-Alcock, "Cultivated Affects: The Artistic Politics of Landscape and Memory in Amman's Gardens," *Visual Anthropology Review* 36, no. 2 (2020): 275–95; Aseel Sawalha, *Reconstructing Beirut: Memory and Space in a Postwar Arab City* (Austin: University of Texas Press, 2010), 3.

38. A particularly good example is Leila Tayeb, "Shahi al-Huriya: Militant Optimism and Freedom Tea," *Communication and the Public* 2, no. 2 (2017): 164–76; and Leila Tayeb, "Our Star: Amazigh Music and the Production of Intimacy in 2011 Libya," *Journal of North African Studies* 23, no. 5 (2018): 834–50.

39. See, for example, Maria Frederika Malmstrom, *The Streets Are Talking to Me: Affective Fragments in Sisi's Egypt* (Berkeley: University of California Press, 2019).

40. Samuli Schielke, *Egypt in the Future Tense*.

41. Lisa Wedeen, "Ideology and Humor in Dark Times: Notes from Syria," *Critical Inquiry* 39, no. 4 (2013): 841–73.

42. See, among many others, Michael Stasik et al., "Temporalities of Waiting in Africa," *Critical African Studies* 12, no. 1 (2020): 1–9; Sarah Sharma, *In the Meantime: Temporality and Cultural Politics* (Durham, NC: Duke University Press, 2014); Martin Frederiksen, *Young Men, Time, and Boredom in the Republic of Georgia* (Philadelphia, PA: Temple University Press, 2016); James Ferguson, *Global Shadows: Africa in the Neoliberal World Order* (Durham, NC: Duke University Press, 2006); Brad Weiss, *Street Dreams and Hip-Hop Barbershops: Global Fantasy in Urban Tanzania* (Bloomington: Indiana University Press, 2009).

43. Louis Althusser, *Lenin and Philosophy and Other Essays*, trans. Ben Brewster (New York: Monthly Review, 2001), 111.

44. Jose Muñoz, *Cruising Utopia: The Then and There of Queer Futurity* (New York: New York University Press, 2009), 70, emphasis added.

45. C. L. R. James, *The Future in the Present: Selected Writings* (Westport, CT: Lawrence Hill and Co., 1977).

46. Muñoz, *Cruising*, 72.

47. "Bu Nasser Touffar Feat. Al Darwich (Prod. Hello Psychaleppo) - ريخ الشغب (Official Music Video)," 2:33 YouTube video posted by Bu Nasser Touffar, September 3, 2015, https://www.youtube.com/watch?v=Wy9hDrGFgcU#ddg-play.

48. For transcription and translation of the whole piece, see the appendix.

49. These lines are plays on the call to prayer, *hayya ʿala salaa* and in the call to prayer particular to the Shiʿa tradition, *hayya ʿala kheir al-ʿamal*.

50. For a full translation by May Achour, see the appendix. *Madad* is an invocation for support or succor typically used in Sufi religious contexts. It is not translated here as a prayer or a plea. It does not have a religious meaning in the context of the song, but it also is bigger than an ask or a plea. Indeed, it embodies the ache of yearning.

51. " المطحنة - الشغب خير " (Bu Nasser Touffar | (LIVE)," YouTube video, 6:12, posted by Bu Nasser Touffar, May 23, 2016, https://www.youtube.com/watch?v=HmOvOTK92UA.

52. The song is the classic "Al-Atlal" ("The Ruins"). See *"Umm Kulthoum—al-atlal -ʿateeni houriyati atlq ydayi,"* posted by Cherif Abidi, 6:30, November 28, 2017, https://www.youtube.com/watch?v=D2HFrt02Bxo. For English translation of the lyrics, see http://www.arabicmusictranslation.com/2007/11/oum-kalthoum-ruins-el-atlal-les-ruines.html.

53. Muñoz, *Cruising*, 72.

54. Ernest Bloch, *Traces*, quoted in Muñoz, *Cruising*, 69. Emphasis added.

55. Muñoz, *Cruising*, 69.

56. The second line, *hayya ʾala kheir al-ʿamal*, is specific to the Shiʿa call to prayer.
57. I am so very grateful to Huda Fakhreddine for thinking through this particular aspect of the resonance of this piece with me.
58. Quashie, *The Sovereignty of Quiet*.

Outro: Politics in Motion

1. Mazen El Sayed, (El Rass) public Facebook post, January 27, 2020, https://www.facebook.com/mazen.e.sayed.3/posts/10162843623255557.
2. "*Shouf—el rass*" ("Look—El Rass"), Soundcloud track, 2:24, accessed February 9, 2021, https://soundcloud.com/el-rass-the-head/46e13u8djxka.
3. Explicitly personified in Haykal's track "Sot Ramallah" ("Sound of Ramallah").
4. For interviews and recordings from this concert, see Moe Ali Nayel, "From Underground to Arabic Street Rap: Shad 3asab [Arabic]," *Jadaliyya's Status Hour* 3, no. 1 (Winter 2016), http://www.statushour.com/from-underground-to-arabic-street-rap-shad-3asab.html. For event promo and lineup, see "*Shed ʿAsab*" (Pulling Nerves), Facebook Event, posted by Metro Al Madina, August 7, 2015, https://www.facebook.com/events/1654745888075097.
5. See, for example, Greg Schick, "Eslaam Jawaad 'Dudd al-Nizam' (Syria)," in *Beats and Breath*, ed. Jackson Allers, accessed November 8, 2024, https://jacksonallers.wordpress.com/2011/05/05/syrian-revolutions-and-eslam-jawaads-response-%E2%80%9Cdudd-al-nizam%E2%80%9D-syria/.
6. "El Rass—Watwateh | intaj mouqataʿa" (El Rass—Being a Bat—Produced by Boikutt), SoundCloud audio recording, 3:34, posted by El Rass, January 2016, https://soundcloud.com/el-rass-the-head/wa6wa6a.
7. Nadeem Karkabi, "Electro-Dabke: Performing Cosmopolitan Nationalism and Borderless Humanity," *Public Culture* 30, no. 1 (2018): 173–96.
8. "El Far3i—washwasheh | El Far3i—Washwasheh," SoundCloud audio recording, 3:39, posted by El Far3i, February 2016, https://soundcloud.com/el-far3i/el-far3i-washwasheh.
9. The double meaning renders the "how they love the brain" as those who enjoy the intellectual engagement that El Rass can offer but also those who salivate over eating marrow, a treat. Readers will recall El Rass means "the head."
10. On the class makeup and class debate in and around the You Stink protests, see, for example, ʿAmr Mohsn, "'*Al hafleh*': ʿan nazret a-tabeqah al-wasta ila nfsha," *Al-Akhbar*, August 21, 2015, http://al-akhbar.com/node/241096. See also chapter 1.
11. "Habout idtrari" ("Emergency Landing"), SoundCloud audio recording, 5:15, posted by El Rass, February 2016, https://soundcloud.com/el-rass-the-head/dissornodiss.
12. "Fi al-Jaleed—maʿ el Far3i" ("In the Ice"—with El Far3i), SoundCloud audio recording, 4:50, posted by El Rass, 2015, https://soundcloud.com/el-rass-the-head/filjalid?in=el-rass-the-head/sets/adb. This track is on the album *Adam, Darwin, and the Penguin*, released May 24, 2014.
13. El Rass, interview with the author, January 14, 2014, Beirut.

Appendix

1. *Madad* is a Sufi supplication for succor. Here, Darwish invokes a prayer, an expansion, a spreading . . .

BIBLIOGRAPHY

Abdelmagid, Yakein. "The Weight of Hope: Independent Music Production under Authoritarianism in Egypt." PhD diss., Duke University, 2018.
Abu-Lughod, Lila. "The Romance of Resistance: Tracing Transformations of Power through Bedouin Women." *American Ethnologist* 17 (1990): 41–55.
Ahmed, Sara. *The Cultural Politics of Emotion*. New York: Routledge, 2004.
Aidi, Hisham. *Rebel Music: Race, Empire, and the New Muslim Youth Culture*. New York: Knopf Doubleday, 2014.
"Al-Atlal" (The Ruins). See "*Umm Kulthoum – at-atlal -'ateeni houriyati atlq ydayi*," posted by Cherif Abidi, 6:30, November 28, 2017. https://www.youtube.com/watch?v=D2H Frto2Bxo.
Al-Ghazzali. *On Music & Singing: Emotional Religion in Islam as Affected by Music and Singing: A Translation of the Ihya 'Ulm ad-Din of al-Ghazzali with Analysis, Annotation, and Appendices*. Translated by Duncan Black MacDonald. *Journal of the Royal Asiatic Society of Great Britain and Ireland*: 1901–02. https://www.ghazali.org/articles/gz-music.pdf.
Alim, H. Samy. *Roc the Mic Right: The Language of Hip-Hop Culture*. New York: Routledge, 2006.
Allen, Lori. *The Rise and Fall of Human Rights in Palestine: Cynicism and Politics in Occupied Palestine*. Stanford, CA: Stanford University Press, 2013.
Althusser, Louis. *Lenin and Philosophy and Other Essays*. Translated by Ben Brewster. New York: Monthly Review, 2001.
Andersen, Janne Louise. "Transgressing Borders with Palestinian Hip-Hop." In *Palestinian Music and Song: Expression and Resistance since 1900*. Edited by Moslih Kanaaneh et al, 82–96. Bloomington: Indiana University Press, 2013.
Arendt, Hannah. *The Human Condition*. Chicago: University of Chicago Press, 1958.
Appadurai, Arjun. *The Future as Cultural Fact: Essays on the Global Condition*. New York: Verso, 2013.
Ayse, Parla, *Precarious Hope: Migration and the Limits of Belonging in Turkey*. Stanford, CA: Stanford University Press, 2019.
"*Beirut khaybetna—Naserdayn al-Touffar and El Rass (Intaj Wattar)*" ("Beirut Disappointed Us—Nasrdayn al-Touffar and El Rass (Produced by Wattar)"). YouTube video clip, 5:18, posted by Naserdayn al touffar, January 11, 2013. https://www.youtube.com/watch?v=iPgDp2z3n-c&ab_channel=Naserdaynaltouffar.
Berlant, Lauren. *Cruel Optimism*. Durham, NC: Duke University Press, 2011.
Big Hass. *Re-Volt: A Hip-Hop Blog*. Accessed March 12, 2016. http://revoltradio.blogspot.com.
Boal, Augusto. *Theatre of the Oppressed*. Translated by Charles A. and Maria Odilia Leal McBride. New York: Urizen, 1979.
Bourdieu, Pierre. *Distinction: A Social Critique of the Judgment of Taste*. Translated by Richard Nice. London: Routledge, 1984.

"Bu Nasserdyn al-Touffar w El Rass—nihna w a-zibl jeeran—video" (Nasserdyn al-Touffar and El Rass—We Have Shit for Neighbors—Video (in Arabic)). YouTube video, 3:25, posted by Naserdayn al touffar, August 31, 2015. https://www.youtube.com/watch?v=uTdlf AkwpJo&ab_channel=Naserdaynaltouffar.

"Bu Nasser Touffar Feat. Al Darwich (Prod. Hello Psychaleppo) - خبر الشغب (Official Music Video)," 2:33 YouTube video posted by Bu Nasser Touffar, September 3, 2015. https://www.youtube.com/watch?v=Wy9hDrGFgcU#ddg-play.

"Bu Nasser Touffar, El Rass (Prod. Jundi Majhul)—*Beirut khaybetna*." YouTube clip, 5:18, posted by Bu Nasser Touffar, January 11, 2013. https://www.youtube.com/watch?v=iPgDp2z3n-c.

Chávez, Alex E. *Sounds of Crossing: Music, Migration, and the Aural Poetics of the Huapango Arrivebeño*. Durham, NC: Duke University Press, 2017.

Coignet, Gildas. "Régénération urbaine ou dégénérescence de l'urbanité?: Le Projet de nouveau centre-ville d'Al-Abdali à Amman, Jordanie." *Annales de Géographie* 4 (2008): 42–61.

Crapanzano, Vincent. *Imaginative Horizons: An Essay in Literary-Philosophical Anthropology*. Chicago: Chicago University Press, 2004.

Crawley, Ashon T. *Blackpentecostal Breath: The Aesthetics of Possibility*. New York: Fordham University Press, 2017.

Damon, Arwa. "The Lebanese Art Rockers Creating the Soundtrack to the Arab Spring." *CNN*, February 27, 2013. http://www.cnn.com/2013/02/27/world/meast/mashrou-leila-lebanon-rock/index.html.

Daniel, Jack, and Geneva Smitherman. "How I Got Over: Communication Dynamics in the Black Community." *Quarterly Journal of Speech* 62 (1976): 26–39.

Danielson, Virginia. *The Voice of Egypt: Umm Kulthum, Arabic Song, and Egyptian Society in the Twentieth Century*. Chicago: University of Chicago Press, 1997.

Deeb, Lara, and Mona Harb. *Leisurely Islam: Negotiating Geography and Morality and Shi'ite South Beirut*. Princeton, NJ: Princeton University Press, 2013.

de Koning, Anouk. *Global Dreams: Class, Gender, and Public Space in Cosmopolitan Cairo*. Cairo: American University of Cairo Press, 2009.

Dimon, Jamie. "El Général: 2011 Time 100" *TIME*. Accessed April 28, 2024. https://content.time.com/time/specials/packages/article/0,28804,2066367_2066369_2066242,00.html.

Dlewati, Hiba. "Amman Skatepark a 'Melting Pot' for Locals and Refugees." *National Geographic*. October 14, 2015. https://news.nationalgeographic.org/amman-skatepark-a-melting-pot-for-locals-and-refugees/.

Dotson-Renta, Lara. "Somos Sur: Translocal Hip-Hop and the Routes of Empire." *Muslim World* 111, no. 3 (2021): 376–96.

Douglas, Mary. *Purity and Danger: An Analysis of the Concept of Pollution and Taboo*. Oxon, UK: Routledge, 1966.

Eisenlohr, Patrick. *Sounding Islam: Voice, Media, and Sonic Atmospheres in an Indian Ocean World*. Berkeley: University of California Press, 2018.

El-Ariss, Tarek. *Trials of Arab Modernity: Literary Affects and the New Political*. New York: Fordham University Press, 2013.

"*El Far3i—washwasheh* | El Far3i—Washwasheh." SoundCloud audio recording, 3:39. Posted by El Far3i, February 2016. https://soundcloud.com/el-far3i/el-far3i-washwasheh.

El Hamamsy, Walid, and Mounira Solimon. *Popular Culture in the Middle East and North Africa: A Postcolonial Outlook*. New York: Routledge, 2013.

"El Rass—Watwateh | intaj mouqata'a" (El Rass—Being a Bat—Produced by Boikutt)." SoundCloud audio recording, 3:34. Posted by El Rass, January 2016. https://soundcloud.com/el-rass-the-head/wa6wa6a.

"El Rass & Munma el rass w munma fi el jaleed ma' el far'i." YouTube video, 4:54. Posted by Mo2amara, May 27, 2014. https://www.youtube.com/watch?v=sj2DHlAofeU.

Elyachar, Julia. "The Political Economy of Movement and Gesture in Cairo." *Journal of the Royal Anthropological Institute* 17 (2011): 82–99.

El Zein, Rayya. "Call and Response and Arabic Hip-Hop in 'the West.'" In *American Studies Encounters the Middle East*, edited by Marwan Kraidy and Alex Lubin, 106–35. Chapel Hill: University of North Carolina Press, 2016.

———, ed. "Exploring Popular Literature: Arabic Hip-Hop." *ArteEast Shahadat* Winter (2012). https://issuu.com/arteeast/docs/shahadatwinter2012.

———. "From 'Hip-Hop Revolutionaries' to 'Terrorist-Thugs': 'Blackwashing' between the Arab Spring and the War on Terror." *Lateral* 5, no. 1 (2016). https://csalateral.org/issue/5-1/hip-hop-blackwashing-el-zein.

———. "Toward a Dialectic of Discrepant Cosmopolitanisms." *Middle East Journal of Culture and Communication* 13, no. 2 (2020): 170–89.

Erlmann, Viet, ed. *Hearing Cultures: Essays on Sound, Listening, and Modernity*. Oxford, UK: Berg, 2004.

Fahmy, Ziad. *Street Sounds: Listening to Everyday Life in Modern Egypt*. Stanford, CA: Stanford University Press, 2020.

Feld, Steven. *Sound and Sentiment: Birds, Weeping, Poetics, and Song in Kaluli Expression*. Durham, NC: Duke University Press, 1982.

Ferguson, James. *Global Shadows: Africa in the Neoliberal World Order*. Durham, NC: Duke University Press, 2006.

Fernandes, Sujatha. *Close to the Edge: In Search of the Global Hip-Hop Generation*. New York: Verso, 2011.

"Fi al-yom a-thaleth" ("On the Third Day"). YouTube video, 1:49. Posted by Mak Man, August 24, 2015. https://www.youtube.com/watch?v=Gy45jFnNM50&ab_channel=MakMan.

"Fi el Jaleed—ma' el Far3i" ("In the Ice"—with El Far3i). SoundCloud audio recording, 4:50. Posted by El Rass, 2015. https://soundcloud.com/el-rass-the-head/filjalid?in=el-rass-the-head/sets/adb.

Fisher, Mark. "The Metaphysics of Crackle: Afrofuturism and Hauntology." *Dancecult: Journal of Electronic Dance Music Culture* 5 (2): 42–55.

Frederiksen, Martin. *Young Men, Time, and Boredom in the Republic of Georgia*. Philadelphia, PA: Temple University Press, 2016.

Frith, Simon. *Performing Rites: On the Value of Popular Music*. Cambridge, MA: Harvard University Press, 1996.

Gates, Henry Louis, Jr. "Foreword." In *The Anthology of Rap*, edited by Adam Bradley and Andrew DuBois, xxii–xxix. New Haven, CT: Yale University Press, 2010.

Gautier, Ana María Ochoa. *Aurality: Listening and Knowledge in Nineteenth-Century Colombia*. Durham, NC: Duke University Press, 2014.

Geary, Paul. "The Production of Taste: Ecologies, Intersections, Implications." *Studies in Theatre and Performance* 40, no. 3 (2021): 280–91.

"*Habout idtrari*" ["Emergency Landing"]. SoundCloud audio recording, 5:15. Posted by El Rass, February 2016. https://soundcloud.com/el-rass-the-head/dissornodiss.

Haddad, Tawfiq. *Palestine, Ltd.* London: I. B. Tauris, 2016.
Hage, Ghassan. *Alter-Politics: Critical Anthropology and the Radical Imagination.* Melbourne: Melbourne University Publishing, 2015.
———. *Waiting.* Carlton, VIC: Melbourne University Press, 2009.
Hanieh, Adam. "The Internationalization of Gulf Capital and Palestinian Class Formation." *Capital and Class* 35, no. 1: 81–106.
"Haykal—Sot Ramallah." YouTube video, 3:00. Posted by Haykal, December 14, 2019. https://www.youtube.com/watch?v=o3twPygAs8g.
Hill, Marc Lamont. *Beats, Rhymes, and Classroom Life: Hip-hop Pedagogy and the Politics of Identity.* New York: Teachers College Press, 2009.
Hirschkind, Charles. *The Ethical Soundscape: Cassette Sermons and Islamic Counterpublics.* New York: Columbia University Press, 2006.
———. "The Ethics of Listening: Cassette-Sermon Audition in Contemporary Egypt." *American Ethnologist* 28, no. 3 (2001): 623–49.
hooks, bell. "An Aesthetic of Blackness—Strange and Oppositional." *Lenox Avenue: A Journal of Interarts Inquiry* 1 (1995): 65–72.
———. *Ain't I a Woman?: Black Women and Feminism.* Boston: South End Press, 1981.
———. *Feminist Theory: From Margin to Center.* Boston: South End Press, 1984.
Hurston, Zora Neale. *Their Eyes Were Watching God.* New York: Harper & Row, 1990.
Issa, Rana. "Khatem Izdihar." *Al-Jumhuirryah*, February 12, 2021. https://aljumhuriya.net/ar/2021/12/02/%D8%AE%D8%A7%D8%AA%D9%85-%D8%A7%D8%B2%D8%AF%D9%87%D8%A7%D8%B1.
"Istafrigh | Raed Ghoneim 'Sot Gilgamesh'" ("I throw up | Raed Ghoneim 'Voice of Gilgamesh'"). SoundCloud audio recording, 4:57. Posted by Gilgamesh. Accessed January 23, 2021. https://soundcloud.com/sootgilgamesh/sont2e9dmty8.
Jackson, John. *Real Black: Adventures in Racial Sincerity.* Chicago: University of Chicago Press, 2005.
Jackson, Oliver. "Preface." In *Kuntu Drama*, ed. Paul Harrison, ix–xiii. New York: Grove, 1974.
James, C. L. R. *The Future in the Present: Selected Writings.* Westport, CT: Lawrence Hill and Co., 1977.
Jankowsky, Richard C. *Stambeli: Music, Trance, and Alterity in Tunisia.* Chicago: University of Chicago Press, 2010.
Jansen, Stef. *Yearnings in the Meantime: 'Normal Lives' and the State in a Sarajevo Apartment Complex.* New York: Berghahn, 2015.
Johnson, Imani Kai. *Dark Matter in Breaking Cyphers: The Life of Africanist Aesthetics in Global Hip-Hop.* Oxford, UK: Oxford University Press, 2023.
Kapchan, Deborah. *Travelling Spirit Masters: Moroccan Gnawa Trance and Music in the Global Marketplace.* Wesleyan, CT: Wesleyan University Press, 2007.
Karkabi, Nadeem. "Electro-Dabke: Performing Cosmopolitan Nationalism and Borderless Humanity." *Public Culture* 30, no. 1 (2018): 173–96.
———. "Self-Liberated Citizens: Unproductive Pleasures, Loss of Self, and Playful Subjectivities in Palestinian Raves." *Anthropological Quarterly* 93, no. 4 (2020): 679–708.
———. "Staging Particular Difference: Politics of Space in the Palestinian Alternative Music Scene." *Middle East Journal of Culture and Communication* 6 (2013): 308–28.
Katibe 5. *A-Tareeq Wahad Marsoum [One Way Decree].* ReverbNation. Accessed May 29, 2016. https://www.reverbnation.com/katibe5%D9%83%D8%AA%D9%8A%D8%A8%D9%87/song/10699957---.

Khalili, Laleh. "The Politics of Pleasure: Promenading on the Corniche and Beachgoing." *Society and Space* 34, no. 4 (2016): 583–600.
Kraidy, Marwan. "A Heterotopology of Graffiti." Proceedings of the Conference "Inverted Worlds: Cultural Motion in the Arab Region." Beirut, October 4–18, 2012. http://www.perspectivia.net/publikationen/orient-institut-studies/2-2013/kraidy_graffiti.
Kristeva, Julia. *Powers of Horror: An Essay on Abjection*. Translated by Leon S. Roudiez. New York: Columbia University Press, 1982.
Larkin, Brian. "Techniques of Inattention: The Mediality of Loudspeakers in Nigeria." *Anthropological Quarterly* 87, no. 4 (2014): 989–1015.
Larkin, Craig. *Memory and Conflict in Lebanon: Remembering and Forgetting the Past*. Oxon, UK: Routledge, 2012.
LeVine, Mark. *Heavy Metal Islam: Rock, Resistance, and the Struggle for the Soul of Islam*. Second Edition. Boston: MIT Press, 2022.
Lipsitz, George. *Dangerous Crossroads: Popular Music, Postmodernism, and the Poetics of Place*. London: Verso, 1994.
Lorca, Frederico García. "Theory and Play of the *Duende*." Translated by A. S. Kline. Accessed January 10, 2014. http://www.poetryintranslation.com/klineaslorcaduende.htm.
Lorde, Audre. *Sister Outsider: Essays and Speeches by Audre Lorde*. Berkeley, CA: Crossing, 2007.
Lubin, Alex. "Fear of an Arab Planet: The Sounds and Rhythms of Afro-Arab Internationalism." In *Arab American Literature and Culture*, edited by Alfred Hornung and Martina Kohl, 243–63. Heidelberg, Germany: Universitätsverlag Winter, 2012.
Mahmood, Saba. *Politics of Piety: The Islamic Revival and the Feminist Subject*. Princeton, NJ: Princeton University Press, 2004.
"Ma Illi Horiyih (I Don't Have Freedom)—DAM [with English translations] ما إلي حرية – دام." YouTube video, 3:37. Posted by Mr Palestinian Hiphop, July 8, 2013. https://www.youtube.com/watch?v=ooVdjKI68CU.
Maira, Sunaina. *Jil Oslo: Palestinian Hip-Hop, Youth Culture, and the Youth Movement*. Washington, DC: Tadween, 2013.
———. "'We Ain't Missing: Palestinian Hip-Hop: A Transnational Youth Movement." *CR: The New Centennial Review* 8 (2002): 161–92.
Makdisi, Saree. "Laying Claim to Beirut: Urban Narrative and Spatial Identity in the Age of Solidere." *Critical Inquiry* 23 (1997): 660–705.
Malmstrom, Maria Frederika. *The Streets Are Talking to Me: Affective Fragments in Sisi's Egypt*. Berkeley: University of California Press, 2019.
Martínez, José Ciro, and Omar Sirri. "Of Bakeries and Checkpoints: Stately Affects in Amman and Baghdad." *Society and Space* 38, no. 5 (2020): 849–66.
Mazen El Sayed. Facebook post. January 27, 2020. https://www.facebook.com/mazen.e.sayed.3/posts/10162843623255557.
McDonald, David. *My Voice Is My Weapon: Music, Nationalism, and the Poetics of Palestinian Resistance*. Durham, NC: Duke University Press, 2013.
McLaughlin-Alcock, Colin. "Cultivated Affects: The Artistic Politics of Landscape and Memory in Amman's Gardens." *Visual Anthropology Review* 36, no. 2 (2020): 275–95.
Menkman, Rosa. *Glitch Studies Manifesto*. Accessed December 8, 2023. http://amodern.net/wp-content/uploads/2016/05/2010_Original_Rosa-Menkman-Glitch-Studies-Manifesto.pdf.
Menninghaus, Winfried. *Disgust: Theory and History of a Strong Sensation*. Albany, NY: SUNY, 2003.

Miller, Edward D. "Authoring the Occupation: The Mic Check, the Human Microphone, and the Loudness of Listening." In *Media Authorship*, edited by Cynthia Chris and David A. Gerstner, 180–93. New York: Routledge, 2013.

Mitchell, Tony. *Global Noise: Rap and Hip-Hop Outside the USA*. Middletown, CT: Wesleyan University Press, 2002.

Mohsn, ʿAmr. "'Al hafleh': ʿan nazret a-tabeqah al-wasta ila nfsha." *Al-Akhbar*, August 21, 2015. http://al-akhbar.com/node/241096.

Moreno-Almeida, Cristina. *Rap beyond Resistance: Staging Power in Contemporary Morocco*. London: Palgrave Macmillan, 2017.

Morning Edition. "The Rap Songs of the Arab Spring." *NPR*, June 9, 2011. https://www.npr.org/sections/therecord/2011/06/09/137067390/the-rap-songs-of-the-arab-spring.

Moten, Fred. *In the Break: Aesthetics of the Black Radical Tradition*. Minneapolis: Minnesota University Press, 2003.

Moussawi, Ghassan. *Disruptive Situations: Fractal Orientalism and Queer Strategies in Beirut*. Philadelphia: Temple University Press, 2020.

Muñoz, José. *Cruising Utopia: The Then and There of Queer Futurity*. New York: New York University Press, 2009.

Nagel, C. "Reconstructing Space, Re-Creating Memory: Sectarian Politics and Urban Development in Post-War Beirut." *Political Geography* 21 (2002): 717–25.

Navaro-Yashin, Yael. "'Life Is Dead Here': Sensing the Political in 'No Man's Land.'" *Anthropological Theory* 3 (2003): 107–25.

———. *The Make-Believe Space: Affective Geography in a Postwar Polity*. Durham, NC: Duke University Press, 2012.

Nayel, Moe Ali. "From Underground to Arabic Street Rap: Shad 3asab [Arabic]." *Jadaliyya's Status Hour* 3, no. 1 (Winter 2016). https://soundcloud.com/status-7/from-underground-to-arabic-street-rap-shad-3asab-arabic.

Nayel, Mohamad Ali. "Music Politics after the Arab Uprisings, Part 1." *Jadaliyya*, June 8, 2022. https://www.jadaliyya.com/Details/44193/Music-Politics-After-the-Arab-Uprisings-Part-1.

Ngai, Sianne. *Ugly Feelings*. Cambridge, MA: Harvard University Press, 2007.

Nickell, Chris, and Adam Benkato. "On Blackness and the Nation in Arabic Hip-Hop: Case Studies from Lebanon and Libya." *Lateral* 10, no. 1 (2021).

Nooshin, Laudan, ed., *Music and the Play of Power in the Middle East, North Africa and Central Asia*. New York: Routledge, 2009.

———. "Whose Liberation? Iranian Popular Music and the Fetishisation of Resistance." *Popular Communication* 15, no. 3 (2017): 163–91.

Osumare, Halifu. *The Africanist Aesthetic in Global Hip-Hop: Power Moves*. New York: Palgrave Macmillan, 2007.

———. *The Hiplife in Ghana: The West African Indigenization of Hip-Hop*. Basingstoke, UK: Palgrave Macmillan, 2012.

Ozelkan, Ediz. "Hip-Hop in Practice: the Cypher as Communicative Classroom." *Pedagogy, Culture & Society* 32, no. 3: 741–58.

Parker, Christopher. "Tunnel-Bypasses and Minarets of Capitalism: Amman as Neoliberal Assemblage." *Political Geography* 28 (2009): 110–20.

Pennycook, Alastair. "Language, Localization, and the Real: Hip-Hop and the Global Spread of Authenticity." *Journal of Language, Identity & Education* 6, no. 2 (2007): 101–15.

Peteet, Julie. "Closure's Temporality: The Cultural Politics of Time and Waiting." *South Atlantic Quarterly* 117, no. 1: 43–64.

Picker, John. *Victorian Soundscapes.* New York: Oxford University Press, 2003.
"Qabl W Ba'l—qabl w ba'l." SoundCloud audio clip, 5:15. Posted by Muqata'a, 2014. https://soundcloud.com/muqataa/qabl-w-bal.
Quashie, Kevin. *The Sovereignty of Quiet: Beyond Resistance in Black Culture.* New Brunswick, NJ: Rutgers University Press, 2012.
———. "The Trouble with Publicness: Toward a Theory of Black Quiet." *African American Review* 43, no. 2–3 (2009): 329–43.
Rabie, Kareem. *Palestine Is a Party and the Whole World Is Invited.* Durham, NC: Duke University Press, 2021.
———. "Ramallah's Bubbles." *Jadaliyya*, January 18, 2013. http://www.jadaliyya.com/Details/27839/Ramallah's-Bubbles.
Racy, Ali Jihad. *Making Music in the Arab World: The Culture and Artistry of Tarab.* Cambridge, UK: Cambridge University Press, 2004.
"Ramallah Underground—Min il Kaheff." YouTube video, 4:20. Posted by UnknownSoldier-MX, July 21, 2009. https://www.youtube.com/watch?v=A7EtoUO9V-c.
Regier, Terry, and Muhammad Ali Khalidi. "The *Arab Street*: Tracking a Political Metaphor." *Middle East Journal* 63, no. 1 (2009): 11–29.
Rice, Tom. "Listening." In *Keywords in Sound*, edited by David Novak and Matt Sakakeeny, 99–111. Durham, NC: Duke University Press, 2015.
Robinson, Dylan. *Hungry Listening: Resonant Theory of Indigenous Sound Studies.* Minneapolis: University of Minnesota Press, 2020.
Rouget, Gilbert. Music and Trance: A Theory of the Relations between Music and Possession. Translated by Brunhilde Biebuyck. Chicago: University of Chicago Press, 1985.
Russell, Legacy. "Digital Dualism and the Glitch Feminism Manifesto." *Society Pages*, December 10, 2012. https://thesocietypages.org/cyborgology/2012/12/10/digital-dualism-and-the-glitch-feminism-manifesto.
Sabry, Tarik. *Cultural Encounters in the Arab World.* London: I. B. Tauris, 2010.
Sabry, Tarik, and Layal Ftouni. *Arab Subcultures: Transformations in Theory and Practice.* London: I. B. Tauris, 2017.
Sakr, Laila Shereen. *Arabic Glitch: Technoculture, Data Bodies, and Archives.* Stanford, CA: Stanford University Press, 2023.
Salamandra, Christa. *A New Old Damascus: Authenticity and Distinction in Urban Syria.* Bloomington: Indiana University Press, 2004.
Sale, Maggie. "Call and Response as Critical Method: African American Oral Traditions in *Beloved*." *African American Review* 26 (1992): 41–50.
Salloum, Jackie Reem, dir. *Slingshot Hip-Hop.* 2008.
Salti, Rasha. "Urban Scrolls and Modern-Day Oracles: The Secret Life of Beirut's Walls." *Third Text* 22 (2008): 615–27.
Sawalha, Aseel. *Reconstructing Beirut: Memory and Space in a Postwar Arab City.* Austin: University of Texas Press, 2010.
———. "The Dilemmas of Conservation and Reconstruction in Beirut." In *The Emerging Asian City: Concomitant Urbanities and Urbanisms*, edited by Vinayak Bharne, 148–57. Oxon, UK: Routledge, 2013.
Schick, Greg. "Eslaam Jawaad 'Dudd al-Nizam' (Syria)." On *Beats and Breath*. Accessed November 8, 2024. https://jacksonallers.wordpress.com/2011/05/05/syrian-revolutions-and-eslam-jawaads-response-%E2%80%9Cdudd-al-nizam%E2%80%9D-syria/.
Schielke, Samuli. *Egypt in the Future Tense: Hope, Frustration, and Ambivalence before and after 2011.* Bloomington: Indiana University Press, 2015.

Schwedler, Jillian. "Amman Cosmopolitan: Spaces and Practices of Aspiration and Consumption." *Comparative Studies of South Asia, Africa, and the Middle East* 30, no. 3 (2010): 547–62.

Sells, Michael Anthony. *Early Islamic Mysticisms: Sufi, Qur'an, Mi'raj, Poetic and Theological Writings*. Mahwah, NJ: Paulis, 1996.

"Shabjeed | Interview—shab jdeed | al mqabaleh." YouTube video, 25:39. Posted by Ma3azef. Accessed March 3, 2024. https://www.youtube.com/watch?v=tvqRlsmFHwY.

"Shabjdeed—Ko7ol w 3atme." YouTube video, 3:15. Posted by BLTNM, May 12, 2018. https://www.youtube.com/watch?v=FN15PcYv8Ho.

"Shaden Fakih: She Comes Again | Sarde (After Dinner) Podcast #121." YouTube video, 1:34:47. Posted by Sarde After Dinner, October 11, 2023. https://www.youtube.com/watch?v=JwsOxP6LCQk.

Shannon, Jonathan. *Among the Jasmine Trees: Music and Modernity in Contemporary Syria*. Middletown, CT: Wesleyan University Press, 2006.

Sharma, Sarah. *In the Meantime: Temporality and Cultural Politics*. Durham, NC: Duke University Press, 2014.

"Shed 'Asab" ("Pulling Nerves"). Facebook Event. Posted by Metro Al Madina, August 7, 2015. https://www.facebook.com/events/1654745888075097.

Shibli, Adania. *Minor Detail*. Translated by Elisabeth Jaquette. New York: New Directions, 2020.

Shipley, Jesse Weaver. *Living the Hiplife: Celebrity and Entrepreneurship in Ghanaian Popular Music*. Durham, NC: Duke University Press, 2013.

"Shouf—el rass" ("Look—El Rass"). SoundCloud track, 2:24. Accessed February 9, 2021. https://soundcloud.com/el-rass-the-head/46e13u8djxka.

Smith, Caspar Llewellyn. "Soundtrack to the Arab Revolutions." *Guardian*, February 26, 2011. https://www.theguardian.com/music/musicblog/2011/feb/27/arab-revolutions-protest-music.

Smitherman, Geneva. *Talkin' and Testifyin': The Language of Black America*. Detroit: Wayne State University Press, 1977.

Spadola, Emilio. *The Calls of Islam: Sufis, Islamists, and Mass Mediation in Urban Morocco*. Bloomington: Indiana University Press, 2014.

Spillers, Hortense. *Black, White, and in Color: Essays on American Literature and Culture*. Chicago: University of Chicago Press, 2003.

———. "Mama's Baby, Papa's Maybe: An American Grammar Book." *Diacritics* 17, no. 2 (1987): 65–81.

Sprengel, Darci. "'Loud' and 'Quiet' Politics: Questioning the Role of 'the Artist' in Street Art Projects after the 2011 Egyptian Revolution." *International Journal of Cultural Studies* 23, no. 2 (2019): 208–26.

———. "'More Powerful than Politics': Affective Magic in the DIY Musical Activism after Egypt's 2011 Revolution." *Popular Music*, January 3, 2019.

———. "Reframing the 'Arab Winter': The Importance of Sleep and a Quiet Atmosphere after 'Defeated' Revolutions." *Culture, Theory and Critique* 61 (2020): 246–66.

Stasik, Michael et al. "Temporalities of Waiting in Africa." *Critical African Studies* 12, no. 1 (2020): 1–9.

Stoever, Jennifer Lynn. *The Sonic Color Line: Race and the Cultural Politics of Listening*. New York: New York University Press, 2016.

Stone, Christopher. *Popular Culture and Nationalism in Lebanon: The Fairouz and Rahbani Nation*. Oxon, UK: Routledge, 2008.
"Sudan: A Savage War and Toxic Information Battle." *Listening Post*, April 27, 2024. https://www.aljazeera.com/program/the-listening-post/2024/4/27/sudan-a-savage-war-and-toxic-information-battle.
Sugarman, Jane. *Engendering Song: Singing and Subjectivity at Prespa Albanian Weddings*. Chicago: University of Chicago Press, 1997.
Swedenburg, Ted. "Fun^Da^Mental's Jihad Rap." In *Being Young and Muslim: New Cultural Politics in the Global South and North*, edited by Asef Bayat and Linda Herrera, 291–308. Oxford: Oxford University Press, 2010.
———. "Imagined Youths." *Middle East Research and Information Project* 37 (2007). http://www.merip.org/mer/mer245/imagined-youths.
———. "Palestinian Rap: Against the Struggle Paradigm." In *Popular Culture in the Middle East and North Africa*, edited by Mounira Solimon and Walid El Hamamsy, 17–32. New York: Routledge, 2012.
Taraki, Lisa. "Enclave Micropolis: The Paradoxical Case of Ramallah/Al-Bireh." *Journal of Palestine Studies* 37 (2008): 9–14.
Tate, Claudia. *Psychoanalysis and Black Novels: Desire and the Protocols of Race*. Oxford, UK: Oxford University Press, 1998.
Tawil-Souri, Helga. "The Necessary Politics of Palestinian Cultural Studies." In *Arab Cultural Studies: Mapping the Field*, edited by Tarik Sabry. London: I. B. Tauris, 2012.
Tayeb, Leila. "*Nduwash bel Malgy*: Performing the Civil in Post-Revolution Libya." Talk at the Sijal Institute, Amman, Jordan, August 12, 2015.
———. "Our Star: Amazigh Music and the Production of Intimacy in 2011 Libya." *Journal of North African Studies* 23, no. 5 (2018): 834–50.
———. "Shahi al-Huriya: Militant Optimism and Freedom Tea." *Communication and the Public* 2, no. 2 (2017): 164–76.
Taylor, Diana. *The Archive and the Repertoire: Performing Cultural Memory in the Americas*. Durham, NC: Duke University Press, 2003.
Terkourafi, Marina. *The Languages of Global Hip-Hop*. New York: Bloomsbury Continuum, 2010.
"The Arena: The Middle East's First Official Rap Battle League with Nasser Shorbaji." *Status/al-wada'*, August 16, 2018. https://www.jadaliyya.com/Details/37877.
"The Word Is Yours—Hip-Hop in the Middle East." *IndieGoGo*. Accessed January 18, 2016. https://www.indiegogo.com/projects/the-word-is-yours-hip-hop-in-the-middle-east#/story.
Thompson, Robert Farris. *African Art in Motion: Icon and Act*. Los Angeles: University of California Press, 1974.
Tobin, Sarah A. *Everyday Piety: Islam and Economy in Jordan*. Ithaca, NY: Cornell University Press, 2016.
Toukan, Hanan. *The Politics of Art: Dissent and Cultural Diplomacy in Lebanon, Palestine, and Jordan*. Stanford, CA: Stanford University Press, 2021.
Tsing, Anna. *The Mushroom at the End of the World: On the Possibility of Life in Capitalist Ruins*. Princeton, NJ: Princeton University Press, 2015.
Tyler, Imogen. *Revolting Subjects: Social Abjection and Resistance in Neoliberal Britain*. London: Zed, 2013.

Wedeen, Lisa. "Ideology and Humor in Dark Times: Notes from Syria." *Critical Inquiry* 39 (2013): 841–73.
Weheliye, A. G. *Feenin: R&B Music and the Materiality of BlackFem Voices and Technology.* Durham, NC: Duke University Press, 2023.
———. *Habeas Viscus: Racializing Assemblages, Biopolitics, and Black Feminist Theories of the Human.* Durham, NC: Duke University Press, 2014.
Weiss, Brad. *Street Dreams and Hip-Hop Barbershops: Global Fantasy in Urban Tanzania.* Bloomington: Indiana University Press, 2009.
Wickstrom, Maurya. *Performance in the Blockades of Neoliberalism: Thinking the Political Anew.* London: Palgrave Macmillan, 2012.
Williams, Raymond. *Marxism and Literature.* Oxford, UK: Oxford University Press, 1977.
Withers, Polly. "Digital Feminisms in Palestinian Hip-Hop." *Global Hip-Hop Studies* 2, no. 2 (2021): 159–77.
———. "Ramallah Ravers and Haifa Hipsters: Gender, Class, and Nation in Palestinian Popular Culture." *British Journal of Middle East Studies* 48, no. 1 (2021): 94–113.
Wynter, Sylvia. "But What Does Wonder Do? Meanings, Canons, Too?: On Literary Texts, Cultural Contexts, and What It's Like to Be One/Not One of Us." *Stanford Humanities Review* 4 (1994): 1.
———. "Rethinking 'Aesthetics': Notes Towards a Deciphering Practice." In *Ex-iles: Essays on Caribbean Cinema*, edited by Mbye Cham, 238–79. Trenton, NJ: Africa World Press, 1992.

INDEX

Note: Page numbers in italics indicate figures.

abjection: al-wada' and, 18; constitutive disgust and, 30–31, 39–40; desire and, 30, 39, 40; distancing from, 35, 39; hailing to, 34; heroes of, 36; stereotypes of, 35, 36, 87, 136n21; stickiness of, 37

Abu-Lughod, Lila, 9

aesthetics: of alienation, 60; becoming and, 11, 21, 29, 33, 43; of concert venues, 48; connecting spaces, 3; digital, 47; of disgust, 21, 28–29, 30, 40, 46, 52; disinterest in, 64; dominance of, 14; experimental invitation and, 10; of global trap, 113; innovation and, 61–62; invitation into the cypher and, 57, 85; political, 27, 28–29, 30, 33, 43; populist, 55, 144n59; of provocation, 29, 60, 111–12; of resistance, 22, 63; sha'bi, 53, 54, 55, 59; specific to Arabic, 54, 55; strategies of hailing and, 52; of venues, 12, 16, 32, 48, 57

affect: al-wada' and, 18; as analytic tool, 11; authenticity and, 6; the cypher as relation and, 33; disavowing the political and, 7; engagement and, 21–22, 50; exchange and, 32–33; of hope, 40; inattention and, 66; intimacy and, 21, 50; istifzaz and, 61–62; listening and, 1–2, 91, 92 (*see also* tarab); lyrics and, 2, 22, 33, 101; malaise and, 18–19; movement between, 94; ranges of, 28; relations to politics and, 14; scholarly attention to, 100–101; in speech, 8; spitting and, 33; surprise and, 2, 33, 90, 94; tension and, 71–72; transnational, 19–20; virtual, 119; yearning/longing and, 7, 22, 91, 114. *See also* desire; despair; disgust; hope; tarab

agency: calls into the cypher and, 76, 98; detached from progressivism, 9; ethnography and, 8; inattention as, 78; the interior as alternative to, 96; listening as, 9, 65; motion and, 20; in music making/listening, 11; political, 8, 22, 28, 89, 95, 98, 129n32; reason and, 93; resistive, 44; yearning as, 10, 22, 89, 99

Al-Balad Festival, 67–69, *69*, 70–71, *71*, *74–75*, 79, 82

alienation, 21, 36, 50, 60, 91, 118

Alim, H. Samy, 46

Allen, Lori, 100–101

Althusser, Louis, 10, 76, 97, 98, 101

al-wada' (the situation): abjection and, 18; anxiety and, 115; Beirut and, 18, 66, 79; corruption as part of, 79; despair and, 18, 115; disgust with, 113; disruption and, 66, 79, 82; exhaustion and, 18, 100, 115; experimental rap intervening in, 99; inattention and, 79, 82–83; temporality of, 18; waiting and, 99–101

Al-'Arabi, Abu Said b., 94, 95

"Amal Hayati" (U. Kulthoum), 83, 84, 86, 91, 105

Amman: Al-Balad Festival in, 67–69, *69*, 70–71, *71*, *74–75*, 79, 82; concert etiquette and, 77; cosmopolitanism in, 67, 75; cultural reputation of, 17, 19, 142n33; development in, 15; downtown plaza of, 141n20; forces shaping creative scene, 13–14, 17, 19 (*see also* Red Bull); Jadal venue in, 50, 74, 142n29; refugees in, 132n56; Satti, 73, 82, 99–100, 141n14; Seven Hills Skatepark, 68, 72, *74*, *75*, 79, 141n13; Synaptik, 19, 116; Word Is Yours Festival in, 67, 68, 72–74, *74*, *75*, 79, 82. *See also* Bu Kolthoum; El Far3i; public space; Satti

anger: disgust and, 29, 34, 38, 43, 84; revolution and, 115; transmitted/shared, 95, 106, 109; yearning and, 89, 92, 104

159

anticipation: frustration and, 52, 99; of the future, 18, 79; the glitch and, 48, 52–53, 61, 63, 66–67; of hailing otherwise, 23; of irritation, 35; shared, 52; of surprise, 35
anxiety, 17, 18, 19, 43, 79, 99, 100, 115
Arabic, 20–21, 25, 27, 54, 55, 118, 139n32
Arabs: anti-Black racism and, 5, 28; diaspora of, 5, 12, 24, 25, 84, 118, 119, 133n77; identity and, 21, 89, 118; left-wing politics and, 42; literary modernity and, 39; millennial culture and, 22, 47, 78, 100; racism against, 2 (*see also* orientalism); turath (heritage) and, 54, 59
Arab Spring, the, 26, 112
Arab Uprisings, the, 3, 24–25, 26, 28, 89
Arab world, the: disgust and, 26, 31; millennial, 22, 40, 47, 48, 78, 100; NGO presence in, 14, 119, 133n77, 140n12, 141n13. *See also* al-wada'
Arab youth, 3, 5, 25, 27, 28
Arendt, Hannah, 128n26
Asfour, Raed, 68, 69–70, 71, 141n20. *See also* Al-Balad Festival
Asifeh (Stormtrap), 1, 84, 85, 108, 143n50. *See also* Ramallah Underground
attention: careful listening and, 61, 82, 92, 101; competition for, 74, 75, 75, 78, 80; as a continuum, 78; cultivation of, 9, 66, 77, 81, 89, 93, 142n35; disruption and, 66, 76; filling the head and, 63; ideals of, 66, 81–82; invitations into the cypher and, 61; istifzaz and, 49; religious listening practices and, 65; still listening and, 12, 22, 51, 81, 82, 83, 84, 97; still movement and, 11; yearning and, 22, 89. *See also* inattention; listening
attention, embodied: concert goers/observers and, 76, 80; shapes of, 22; stillness as, 66, 81, 82, 94, 96, 97, 114. *See also* sedimentation
audiences: acknowledgement of listening by, 35; different listening and, 22, 85; disciplining the behavior of, 76–77, 88; disdain for, 21; distracted, 80; expectations of, 53, 77, 80, 83; filtered, 34, 36, 49–52, 54, 60; frustrating of, 49; heterogenous, 34, 36, 48–49, 142n29; lyric expectations and, 60, 83 (*see also* glitch, the); potential, 108;

rappers' disappointment with, 63; rappers engaging with, 56, 61–62, 81, 85, 92, 95; violence in, 73; vocalizing approval, 31, 32–33. *See also* concert goers; concert observers
authenticity, 53–60; affect and, 6; critique of, 6; declarations of, 59; embodiment of, 57–58; Haykal and, 53–54, 59; identity and, 46, 47, 52, 60; performance of, 46, 52; pursuit of, 118; Shab Jdeed and, 57–58; sha'bi and, 53; the street and, 53, 56; US rap and, 56

Balad Festival. *See* Al-Balad Festival
becoming: aesthetics and, 11, 21, 29, 33, 43; coconstituted, 90; listening and, 80–81; political, 20, 31, 33, 43–44, 76; relational, 11; yearning as, 47
Beirut: al-wada'/disruption and, 66, 79; bombings in, 17–18, 32; café culture in, 66, 117, 133n77; corruption and, 14, 38, 79; cultural reputation of, 18, 142n33; failure of the left in, 41–42; forces shaping creative scene, 13–14; graffiti in, 36–38, 37, 43; ideals of, 38–39; Katibeh 5 Fête de la Musique performance in, 35–36; liberalism in, 42, 79; malaise in, 18; Osloob and, 17–18, 142n33; post–civil war development in, 15 (*see also* Solidere); pretension to cosmopolitanism and, 40; refugees in, 132n56; romanticization of, 41, 42; as schizophrenic, 17–18; sectarian politics in, 14, 103, 106, 110; tourism in, 17; #YouStink protests in, 38, 103, 106, 114–15, 117. *See also* Hamra, Beirut
"Beirut Khaybetna" ("Beirut, Our Disappointment," N. al-Touffar, El Rass, and Wattar), 41–42, 137n44
Bekaa', 32–33, 34, 36. *See also* al-Touffar, Jaafar
belonging: building, 46; call-and-response and, 12; in difference, 57; evasive, 103; filtering and, 54; frameworks of, 21–22, 61, 120 (*see also* identity); imagined, 38–39; material incarnations of, 102; otherwise, 11, 94, 95; populist, 59; questions of, 52; yearning and, 10, 23, 35, 90, 113. *See also* collectivity; identity; solidarity

Berlant, Lauren, 41, 101, 137n39
Big Hass (Hass Dennaoui), 28, 29, 136n21
Black people: blackwashing and, 111; culture assimilated, 27; discrimination/racism against, 4, 5, 28; feminism and, 8, 9, 10, 48, 129n32; the interior and, 95–96, 97; meaning-making in rap and, 46–47; organization and resistance by, 27, 95, 97; overlap of present and future and, 102–3; rap as nonviolent protest and, 3, 4; shared oppression with Palestinians, 4, 5
Bloch, Ernest, 107
blockage, 11, 14, 17, 18, 31, 113. *See also* suffocation
BLTNM, 49, 57, 59, 60. *See also* Shab Jdeed
boredom, 11, 91–92, 100–101
breakdancing, 10, 33, 46, 64, 68, 80
Bu Kolthoum: coming to listen and, 63, 80–81, 82, 83; feeling as sensing the political, 6–7; rejection of political narratives and, 5–6, 8; Word Is Yours Festival performance, 73

Cairo, 1, 26, 65, 78, 142n35. *See also* Egypt
call-and-response: belonging and, 12; as calling into the cypher, 36; creating community and, 48; designed glitches and, 60; distaste initiating, 29; effective, 81; as hailing otherwise, 23, 90; irritation and, 21, 29; isolation and, 48–49, 50; as political movement, 11–12; as populist, 52. *See also* hailing
class: barriers to cultural events and, 70, 71; bourgeois, 17; disgust and, 34; elite, 56, 67, 117, 137n39; grievance and, 32; hipster, 32, 33, 56, 116; oligarchy, 37–38, 133n77; taste and, 30, 54, 56; tensions of, 74, 133n77; working, 16, 57–58, 65, 75. *See also* cosmopolitanism
class, middle: biases of, 71; enacted, 67, 75; leisure consumption and, 15, 16, 54, 70; othering lower classes, 32–33; the "Ramallah Bubble" and, 17, 132n64; respectability politics of, 117
collectivity: in concerts, 9; the cypher and, 64; of experience, 33; feeling of, 107; fleeting, 57; implications of, 112; inability to create, 36; istifzaz and, 46, 61; longing for, 34; otherwise, 46, 107, 108; resilience and, 60; shared anticipation and, 52; virtual, 9, 120–22, *121*; waiting and, 19, 38. *See also* belonging; cypher, the (invitation into); solidarity
concert goers: awareness of observers, 68, 69, 72–73, 74–75; clothing choices of, 68–69; dispossessing space from observers, 70, 71; distancing from observers, 72; embodied attention and, 76, 80; organizer distinction from observers, 69–70; refusing calls into the cypher, 56–57, 66
concert observers: awareness of goers, 68–69, 72–73, 74–75; dispossession of public space and, 70, 71; distancing from goers, 72; embodied attention and, 76, 80; organizer distinction from goers, 69–70; refusing calls into the cypher, 66, 70–72, 74, 75, 76–77
concert venues: ability to connect and, 73–74, *74*; aesthetics of, 48; Al-Balad Festival and, 67, 68–69, *69*, 70–72, *71*; cultural industries and, 16; expectations of audiences, 67; homogeneity and, 56; inattention as engagement in, 66; interactions outside, 31–32, 64–65, 71–72, 75, 79–80; Jadal, 50, 74, 142n29; La Wain Pub, 50–52, *51*, 61; Metro Al Madina, 31, 32, 34, *105*, 114; physical cyphers and, 64; receptiveness to hip-hop in, 55; Seven Hills Skatepark, 68, 72, *74*, *75*, 79, 141n13; sha'bi society and, 53, 55; unfilled, 70–71; Younes café, 133n77. *See also* public space
conservativeness, 4, 37, 40, 67, 69
contamination, 37, 40, 41. *See also* disgust
corruption: alienation and, 91; Beiruti, 14, 38, 79; disgust and, 38, 40, 133n77; protest against, 38, 40, 103, 106, 110–11, *111*, 114–15, 117; Tunisian, 26. *See also* Solidere
cosmopolitanism: aspiration to, 67, 75, 142n30; embrace of, 56; exclusion and, 32–33, 34; public space and, 75, 82, 142n30; rejection of, 37–38, 40, 41, 75; taste and, 15, 17, 57. *See also* class

Crawley, Ashon T., 3, 11–12
cultural production: alternative, 14, 99; Amman as regional center of, 19, 142n33; Beirut as regional center of, 18, 142n33; comparative, 13; felt impossibility of, 19; filling the head and, 8; infrastructure for, 14, 15, 16; opportunities for, 16; political ethnography and, 97–98; refusal of romanticizing, 9; stereotyped, 54; traditional, 46; whitewashing of, 27
cynicism, 19, 45–46, 100–101, 115, 117, 133n77
cypher, the: coconstruction of, 64; collectivity and, 64; contribution to, 65; embodiment in, 10, 22, 47; layering within, 66 (*see also* sedimentation); the performance space and, 10, 33, 47, 64; possibility and, 101, 102; skating through, 78, 83; spitting into, 33; struggle and, 103; wetness and, 33, 36, 49
cypher, the (invitation into): aesthetics and, 57, 85; agency and, 76, 98; call-and-response as, 36; the cypher of the here and now and, 11, 23, 90, 102, 109; the cypher to come and, 11, 23, 90, 102, 109; disgust and, 10, 35; frustration and, 29, 47–48, 55, 60; glitch and, 47–48; istifzaz and, 10, 49, 57, 61, 88; kinds of, 84, 85, 102; meaning-making and, 46–47; otherwise, 90, 91, 97, 102, 109; pleasure and, 50; political, 43–44, 48; selective/filtered, 21; spitting and, 33, 36, 46, 49; stillness and, 81, 85–86, 97, 98; successful, 57. *See also* interpellation; listening, practices of; refusal, of calls into the cypher

Dakn, 85–86
DAM (Tamer Nafar, Suhell Nafar, and Mahmoud Jreri): audience communication and, 85; as hip-hop school, 84–85, 86; lyrical meaning and, 87; the Second Intifada and, 84; style and subjects of, 54, 85, 86, 144n59; "Ma Ili Hurriyyeh" ("I Don't Have Freedom"), 87; "Meen Irhabi" ("Who's the Terrorist?"), 86
dancing: breakdancing, 10, 33, 46, 64, 68, 80; musical styles and, 52, 86, 116; as opposed to listening, 51, 80, 83; religious opposition to, 73, 142n28

Daniel, Jack L., 48
al-Darwish: "Kheir al-Shaghab" ("The Rising Riot," with Nasserdayn Al-Touffar), 102–3, 104–7, *105*, 146n50
Deeb, Lara, 66
depoliticization, 4, 27
desire: abjection and, 30, 39, 40; to be rid of disgust, 40; distinct from yearning, 30; for kinds of attention/engagement, 66, 77, 81–82, 83, 92; to know otherness, 24; for the political, 41, 91, 108; providing power, 11; quiet and, 95–96; unspecified, 7, 92, 94
despair: al-wadaʿ and, 18, 115; hope and, 19, 99, 121, 122
difference: aesthetic, 85; in audience response, 81; belonging in, 57; concert goer vs. concert observer, 68, 70, 72; felt, 60, 69; material, 18, 56; in participation, 68; strength in, 34
disappointment, 19, 32, 40, 41–42, 44, 63, 101
disdain, 5, 6, 20–21, 35
disengagement, 22, 46, 49, 50, 52
disgust (qaraf): aesthetics of, 21, 28–29, 30, 40, 46, 52; with al-wadaʿ, 18, 113; anger and, 29, 34, 38, 43, 84; with the Arab world, 26, 31; calls into the cypher and, 10, 36; class and, 34; constitutive, 30–31, 39–40, 43, 46; corruption and, 38, 40, 133n77; desire to be rid of, 40; disavowing hope and, 40; disgusted listeners and, 46; distancing from objects of, 38, 40; embodiment of, 32, 33, 36; exhaustion and, 37, *37*, 38, 40, 60, 100, 115; expelling romanticism/idealism, 40–41; frustration and, 29, 38, 42, 44; generational, 42–43; graffiti and, 36–38, *37*, 43; hailing and, 29, 46; hip-hop and, 38, 40; with mainstream politics, 87; met with disgust, 31, 34, 43; performance of, 21, 29, 33, 46; politics of, 34, 36, 113; as refusal, 30, 36, 41; release and, 29, 30, 31, 38, 101; revolution wordplay and, 28, 34, 136n21; with romanticizing oppression, 5–6; spitting expressing, 40, 46; as sticky, 34, 40; with tropes of abjection, 34–35, 41; yearning and, 84. *See also* distaste
disruption, 10, 18, 47–48, 66, 76, 79, 82–83

distancing: from abjectness, 35, 39; between concert goers and observers, 72; embodiment of, 59; of heart and mind, 93; from hype, 61–62, 81, 83; from objects of disgust, 38, 40; political, 4, 6, 116; from the popular, 53–54, 55, 59, 60; from resistance, 54, 64, 82, 99, 139n29; from stereotypes, 35, 54, 59; from the street, 53–54, 55, 117. *See also* release

distaste: call-and-response initiated by, 29; distrust and, 33; embodiment of, 32, 33, 36; hailing initiated by, 29; irritation and, 32, 33; physical expression of, 32–33; politics of, 32, 40, 113; reaction to, 35. *See also* disgust

DJ Sotusura. *See* Sotusura

Douglas, Mary, 37

Egypt, 1, 100, 131n55, 133n67, 143n46. *See also* Cairo

El-Ariss, Tarek, 10, 39–40, 47

El Far3i: diss exchange with El Rass, 115–19; as selling out, 116–17; "E-stichrak" ("Orientalism," with El Rass and Munma), 116, 118–19; "Fi al-Jaleed" ("In the Ice," with El Rass), 2, 118, 119; "Washwasheh" ("Whisperings"), 115, 117

El Rass (Mazen El Sayed): Al-Balad Festival performance, 70–71; characterization of Beirut, 18; concert call to protest, 114; disgust for politicized romanticism, 41; diss exchange with El Far3i, 115–19; meaning of solidarity and, 120; sha'bi contexts and, 56, 57; social media and, 110, 111, 113, 120–21, *121*, 122; stillness and, 81, 82, 83; "Beirut Khaybetna" ("Beirut, Our Disappointment," with Nasserdayn al-Touffar and Wattar), 41–42, 137n44; "E-stichrak" ("Orientalism," with El Far3i and Munma), 116, 118–19; "Fi al-Jaleed" ("In the Ice," with El Far3i), 2, 118, 119; "Habout Idtrari" ("Emergency Landing"), 115, 117–18; "Nihna w al-zibl jeeran" ("We Are Neighbors with Dung," with Nasserdayn al-Touffar), 38–39; "Shouf" ("Look"), 110–11, 112, 113–14; "Watwateh," 115, 116, 117, 118

Elyachar, Julia, 78

embodiment: of alternative sensibility, 47; of authenticity, 57–58; in the cypher, 10, 22, 47; of disgust/distaste, 32, 33, 36; of distance, 59; engagement and, 9; of feeling, 10–11; of inattention, 78; political, 47; of political motion, 88, 90; of release, 92; singular formations of, 112, 114; sites of, 96; taste and, 30; of trickster identity, 46; of yearning, 31, 94, 146n50. *See also* listening, embodied; stillness

embodiment, of attention: concert goers/observers and, 76, 80; shapes of, 22; stillness as, 66, 81, 82, 94, 96, 97, 114

emotion: interpellation and, 61; political, 6, 24; produced by listening, 29, 30, 65, 92, 93–94, 98, 101; produced by making music, 29, 30; as researcher, 24, 25. *See also individual emotions*

engagement: active, 63–64, 65; affective, 21–22, 50; desire for kinds of, 66, 77, 81, 83, 92; embodied, 9; ideal, 81–82, 83; inattention and, 66, 82–83; intellectual, 94, 147n9; inviting, 50, 52, 80, 86–87; negotiation of, 118, 120, 121; political, 1–2, 3–4, 5, 6, 114–15 (*see also* interpellation: political); selective, 56; social, 25; virtual, 119–20. *See also* listening

Erlman, Viet, 9

"E-stichrak" ("Orientalism," El Far3i, El Rass, and Munma), 116, 118–19

ethnomusicology, 8, 12, 48, 90, 129n32

exhaustion (inhak): al-wada' and, 18, 100, 115; disgust and, 37, *37*, 38, 40, 60, 100, 115; frustration and, 100, 103; inversion of, 101; longing and, 92

Fairouz, 38, 142n33

Fakih, Shaden, 89, 108

fear, 42, 61, 95–96, 100, 108, 136n21

Feld, Steven, 9

feminism, 43; Black, 8, 9, 10, 48, 129n32

"Fi al-Jaleed" ("In the Ice," El Far3i and El Rass), 2, 118, 119 filling the head: changing perspective and, 86, 87–88, 96–97; cultural production and, 8; experience as political process, 29; felt location of, 98; hailing as, 62 (*see also* cypher, the (invitation into); interpellation); identities and, 115; individual-collective experience and, 33; as pleasure, 31, 60, 87, 90, 101, 106; political release and, 21, 31, 106; possibility of, 106; as reception metaphor, 2–3; search for music for, 38, 98; stillness and, 65, 82; tarab and, 93–94; yearning and, 53, 90

filtering, 21, 34, 36, 49–52, 54, 59, 60

frustration: al-wadaʿ and, 18; anticipation/excitement and, 52, 99; calling into the cypher and, 29, 47–48, 55; disgust and, 29, 38, 42, 44; exhaustion and, 100, 103; of expectation, 46, 49, 60; invitation into the cypher and, 29, 47–48, 55; of listening, 31, 49–50; malaise and, 99–100; rappers', 73–74, 80

future, the: affective relation to, 14; anticipation of, 18, 79; building, 12; collective attitudes toward, 101; the cypher to come and, 11, 23, 90, 102, 109; hope for, 14–15, 19; inseparable from history, 44; interpellation and, 103; as in motion, 11; not offered, 45–46, 59; overlap with the present, 18, 102–3; yearning and, 7, 22, 89. *See also* waiting

Geary, Paul, 30 al-Ghazzali, Muhammad ibn Muḥammad Al-Tusiyy, 92, 94, 95

glitch, the: anticipation and, 48, 52–53, 61, 63, 66–67; communality and, 22; designed, 60; dialectic of, 47; divergent experience of, 63, 79; invitation into the cypher and, 47–48; listening for, 23; pleasure and, 45, 48, 52, 61; refused expectations and, 59, 60, 139n35; reinterpretation and, 28; theory of, 11, 45, 47, 59, 139n35; unsuccessful interpellation and, 10, 60

graffiti: on Dbayeh road, 36–38, *37*, 43; in hip-hop, 46, 68

"Habout Idtrari" ("Emergency Landing," El Rass), 115, 117–18

"Hadini iza feek" ("Hold Me Back If You Can," Katibeh 5), 34–36

Hage, Ghassan, 11, 18, 24, 25, 100

hailing: to abjection, 34; aesthetic strategies of, 52; disgust and, 29, 46; emotion and, 61; as filling the head, 62; initiated by disgust/distaste, 29; movement and, 61; of power, 47; refusal of, 9, 56–57; selective, 34; solitude and, 61. *See also* call-and-response; cypher, the (invitation into); interpellation

hailing, otherwise: anticipation of, 23; call-and-response as, 23, 90; to the collective, 107; satisfaction in, 98; subjectivity and, 95; yearning for, 10, 11, 23, 90–91, 98, 108

Hamra, Beirut: café culture in, 133n77; as hostile to young women, 31, 33, 79; as liberal, 41, 79; Metro Al Madina in, 31, 32, 34, *105*, 114; protest in, 110–11, *111*. *See also* Beirut

Harb, Mona, 66

al-Hariri, Rafiq, 14, 15, 16, 136n28. *See also* Solidere

Hayawan Nateq (Muqataʿa), 49, 50–52, *51*; "Al-Missfah" ("The Filter"), 49–50

Haykal: authenticity and, 53–54, 59; being hailed otherwise and, 95, 98; distancing and, 53–55; stylistic rap distinctions and, 85, 87–88, 96–97, 143n52; "Sot Ramallah" ("The Sound of Ramallah"), 58–59

heart, the (qalb), 92–93, 95, 98, 142n35

hijab. *See* veiling

al-Hijazi, Mohammed, 77, 142n33

Hill, Marc Lamont, 46

hip-hop: anti-Black racism and, 5, 28; authenticity and, 53, 56; Big Hass and, 28, 29, 136n21; epistemology of, 46–47, 49, 111–12, 137n5; global, 24, 34, 46, 47, 49, 56, 64, 81, 137n5; racialization and, 27, 111; schools of, 84–85, 86; umma/Nation, 46–47, 56–57; US, 59; virtual circulation of, 110–11, 113, 119–22. *See also* Al-Balad Festival; rap, experimental; Word Is Yours Festival; *individual artists*

hip-hop studies, 10, 33, 42, 47, 53, 64, 81, 129n32

Hirschkind, Charles: attentive listening and, 80; disciplinary practice and, 61, 92–93, 98, 140n8, 142n35; embodiment and, 9, 92–93; ethic of listening and, 96; listener agency and, 65; sedimentation and, 85

hooks, bell, 9, 11, 13, 21, 29

hope: affect of, 40; anthropology of, 11; of connection, 49, 122; cruel optimism and, 41, 137n39; despair and, 19, 99, 121, 122; disavowal of, 40, 41, 89, 108, 133n77; fragile, 100; the future and, 14–15, 19; overlap with longing, 92, 99; political, 28; static, 19, 22, 89

hype: distancing from, 61–62, 81, 83; excess of, 77; failure of, 52; hip-hop schools and, 84–85; populism and, 52

identity: Arab, 21, 89, 118; authenticity and, 46, 47, 52, 60; consumption and, 67; filing the head and, 115; imperialism and, 27–28; invitations to listen and, 52; localized, 54; negotiation of, 118; Palestinian, 54–55; public staking of, 115; racialized, 27; trickster, 46; weak, 118. *See also* belonging

ideology, 39, 47, 52, 119

impossibility, 19, 31, 43, 66, 103. *See also* possibility

inattention: affect and, 66; as agency, 78; al-wada' and, 79, 82–83; attention perceived as, 80; audience violence and, 73; cultivation of, 9, 66, 76–77, 78, 79, 82; as embodied listening, 79, 80; engagement and, 66, 82–83; as political, 76; refusal and, 78; as skating through the cypher, 78, 83; use of space and, 74, 74. *See also* attention

inclusion, 33, 67, 70–71

interference, 45, 46–47, 49, 50, 52, 63, 66–67. *See also* glitch, the

interior, the: as alternative to agency, 96; as alternative to subjectivity, 96; Black life and, 95–96, 97; defining, 96; motion and, 98–99, 108; possibility and, 95, 98; quiet and, 95–96, 98, 99; stillness and, 112 (*see also* quiet); wildness of, 97, 107

interpellation: authority and, 10, 76; into the cypher, 23, 90–91; emotion and, 61; the future and, 103; infelicitous, 10, 49, 60; modes of, 21–22, 52, 61; political, 31, 52, 62, 76, 93, 97, 112; role of, 86, 118; spectrum of, 29; theory of, 9, 76, 97. *See also* cypher, the (invitation into); hailing

irritation, 21, 29, 32, 33, 34, 35, 60, 73

Islam: call to prayer and, 78, 107–8; forms of listening and, 65, 78, 82, 92–93, 142n35; forms of stillness and, 97; stereotypes of, 27; temptation and, 106; youth potential and, 27

Islamic State, 16, 115

Israel: attack on Gaza, 89; Lod as inside, 84; the Nakba and, 42; Oslo Accords and, 14–15, 17, 58, 59; Palestinian economic reliance and, 87–88; Palestinian genocide by, 25, 102, 128n16; Palestinians moving through, 58; Ramallah development and, 15; relationship with Jordan, 17; Six Day War and, 14; Zionism and, 86, 139n30. *See also* Ramallah, Occupation of

Issa, Rana, 10, 26, 42, 43–44

istifzaz (provocation): attention and, 49; authenticity and, 53–59; collectivity and, 46, 57, 61; constant disruption and, 79; epistemology of, 21–22, 46, 47, 49–52, 60, 111–12 (*see also* filtering); invitation into the cypher and, 10, 47, 48–49, 57, 60, 61–62, 88; listening and, 22, 47, 52, 60, 61; materializing, 63 (*see also* filtering; glitch, the: anticipation and; interference); "Khaleeni 'Ayeesh" ("Let Me Live," Ramallah Underground) and, 83–84, 86, 87–88

Jaafar. *See* al-Touffar, Jaafar

Jansen, Stef, 8, 11, 100

Jawaad, Eslaam, 115

Johnson, Imani Kai, 10, 12, 33, 47, 64

Jordan: cultural assessment of, 133n67; Hashemite monarchy and, 4, 141n21; Khotta Ba, 70–71, 77, 82, 100; lifting of martial law in, 14; relationship with Israel/US, 17; Roman history and, 67, 68, 69, 70, 141n20; secret police in, 7, 70; DJ Sotusura, 22, 84–85, 95, 105, 107. *See also* Amman; El Far3i

al-Kalaji, Nasser, 3–4
Katibeh 5: camp studios of, 24; disgust and, 35, 41; performance in Beirut, 35–36; select audience of, 34; "Hadini iza feek" ("Hold Me Back If You Can"), 34–36. *See also* Osloob
"Khaleeni ʿAyeesh" ("Let Me Live," Ramallah Underground), 83–84, 85–86
Khalili, Laleh, 132n60
"Kheir al-Shaghab" ("The Rising Riot," Al-Darwish and N. al-Touffar), 102–3, 104–7, 105, 146n50
Khotta Ba, 70–71, 77, 82, 100
"Kohl wa ʿAtmeh" ("Charcoal and Darkness," Shab Jdeed), 58, 59
Kristeva, Julia, 39–40. *See also* abjection
Kulthoum, Umm: "Amal Hayati," 83, 84, 86, 91, 105

Larkin, Brian, 9, 78, 142n35
Lebanon: Jaafar al-Touffar, 31, 32–33, 34, 36, 41; Bekaaʿ and, 32–33, 34, 36; civil war in, 14, 42, 136n28; as cultural hotspot, 133n67; diaspora of, 15, 24, 39–40; Malikah, 73–74, 82, 140n12; October Revolution, 13, 113, 115; Palestinians in, 17–18, 34–36, 42, 132n56, 134 ch. 1 pre-note (*see also* Osloob); pop music in, 120; protest in, 40, 103, 106, 110–11, *111*, 114–15; state failure of, 37–38; stereotyped women in, 41. *See also* al-Hariri, Rafiq; al-Touffar, Nasserdayn; Beirut; El Rass; Solidere
Left, the. *See* politics, left-wing
liberalism, 4, 9, 27–28, 42, 79, 106, 111
Lispector, Clarice, 26, 31
listening: acknowledgment of, 35; as active, 65–66; affective response and, 1–2, 91, 92; careful attention and, 61, 82, 92, 101; as cocreating, 63–64; as culturally and politically situated, 9; within the cypher, 47; of different audiences, 22, 85; frustration of, 31, 49–50; infelicitous, 64; in Islam, 65, 78, 82, 92–93, 95, 98, 142n35; istifzaz and, 22, 47, 52, 60, 61; motivations for, 2–3; patterns of interaction and, 49; politically, 3, 8, 29–30, 48, 62, 144n59; politics of, 29; 50; quiet and, 98; self-selection into, 56; slippage with calling, 108–9; stillness and, 11, 80, 85–86, 88, 96, 97; tarab and, 91, 92. *See also* attention; cypher, the (invitation into); inattention; stillness; yearning
listening, embodied: as attention, 9, 80, 94; the cypher to come and, 23; as inattention, 79, 80; as sifting, 66 (*see also* sedimentation). *See also* attention, embodied; stillness
longing: acknowledged, 38; as active, 22, 89; affective, 91–92, 100, 109; alienation and, 91; for collectivity, 34, 113; release and, 94–95, 106; separate from love, 91–92; for something worth believing in, 42; tarab and, 91, 92, 94; without hope, 89. *See also* yearning
Lorde, Audre, 9, 11, 89, 90
lyrics: affect and, 2, 22, 33, 101; audience expectations and, 60, 83 (*see also* glitch, the); development within hip-hop, 55, 57, 87; experimentation and, 4, 6, 59; patterns of exchange and, 18, 118; release and, 95, 101. *See also* disgust; distaste; longing; *individual works*

Mahmood, Saba, 8–9
"Ma Ili Hurriyyeh" ("I Don't Have Freedom," DAM), 87
Malikah, 73–74, 82, 140n12
"Meen Irhabi" ("Who's the Terrorist?," DAM), 86
Menkman, Rosa, 59–60, 61, 63, 79
migrants, 5, 34, 37–38, 118, 119. *See also* refugees
"Min al-Kaheff" ("From the Cave," Ramallah Underground), 1–2, 45, 108
"Al-Missfah" ("The Filter," Muqataʿa), 49–50
Moreno-Almeida, Cristina, 28, 29
motion: agency and, 20, 112; constant, 29, 57, 94; emotional, 84, 91, 92–93, 94, 100, 106; listening practices and, 7; "not moving well enough" and, 100; political, 7, 11–13, 62, 76, 88, 115–16, 119; public space and, 16, 72, 73, 78, 132n60, 141n20, 142n30; rappers', 31, 73–74, 105–6; relational, 90; rhythmic,

21, 60, 76, 80, 110; stillness/quiet as, 23, 66, 90, 95–96, 98, 108; trajectories of, 25, 119; yearning and, 11, 19. *See also* blockage; motion; stillness

Moussawi, Ghassan, 10, 18, 66, 79, 82–83, 115

Munma: "E-stichrak" ("Orientalism," with El Farʒi and El Rass), 116, 118–19

Muñoz, José, 57, 88, 90, 102–3, 106, 107

Muqataʿa: Al-Balad Festival performance, 70–71, 142n23; *Hayawan Nateq*, 49, 50–52, *51*; "Al-Missfah" ("The Filter"), 49–50; "the shitty beat's in your shitty face"("Bastafazzak ʿa beat kharra zay wijjak"), 45, 47, 61. *See also* Ramallah Underground

Muslims. *See* Islam

narratives: of discomfort, 35; dominant, 6, 34; of "making it," 58, 116, 118; of modernity, 39; orientalist, 26–27, 132n64; of pan-Arabism, 40; political, 6, 87, 88, 141n21; populist, 5, 45–46, 88; of rap revolt, 3, 28; reductive, 8

Nasserdayn. *See* al-Touffar

Al-Nather, 49, 50, 58, 85, 86

Navaro-Yashin, Yael, 6–7, 11, 18

neoliberalism, 11, 14, 27, 67, 101, 121

Ngai, Sianne, 10, 26, 30–31

NGOs, 14, 15, 17, 119, 133n77, 140n12, 141n13

noise, 47–48, 52, 59

orientalism, 2, 7, 26–27, 116, 118, 119, 132n64

Oslo Accords, 14–15, 17, 58, 59

Osloob: Beirut and, 17–18, 142n33; classical Arabic and, 139n32; perception of Palestinians in Lebanon and, 35–36; performance with Jaafar, 31, 32; shaʿbi society and, 55–56, 57, 117. *See also* Katibeh 5

Osumare, Halifu, 46

Palestine: cynicism and, 100–101; deadening reference to struggle and, 5–6; Gaza, 45, 89, 128n16; Oslo Accords and, 14–15, 17, 58, 59; schools of hip-hop from, 84–85, 86; Second Intifada in, 16, 24, 84; solidarity with, 4, 5, 116, 118; West Bank, 13, 14, 58, 59, 83–84 (*see also* Ramallah)

Palestinians: as abject, 35, 36, 87; anti-Palestinian sentiment, 5, 35–36; diaspora of, 24, 83–84, 86; Israeli genocide of, 25, 102, 128n16; Rana Issa, 10, 26, 42, 43–44; Katibeh 5's audience as, 34; narratives of, 45–46, 84, 139n30, 144n59; popular expectations of, 5, 54; Rami GB, 54; rap making the cause legible, 4; Right of Return and, 41; Sheʿrap, 17, 53–54, 55, 59; Sot Gilgamesh, 26, 31, 134 chap. 1 pre-note. *See also* DAM; Haykal; Katibeh 5; Ramallah Underground; Shab Jdeed; Shuaʿa

Parker, Christopher, 141n21

patience (sabr, sumud), 45–46, 59. *See also* resilience; resistance

performance: of authenticity, 46, 52; the cypher as the space of, 10, 33, 47, 64; disdain for the audience and, 21; of disgust, 21, 29, 33; lack of connection and, 35–36, 73–74; meaning-making and, 46–47; in public space, 66, 67, 68, 70, 72, 73, 74, 82; rapper's frustration and, 73–74, 80; rappers' motion and, 31, 73–74, 105–6; refusal of etiquette and, 31, 32–33; of resistance, 8, 83–84, 87, 96, 97; styles and, 84–87, 96–97, 143n52; tarab and, 91; vs. virtual engagement, 119–20. *See also* Al-Balad Festival; concert venues; Word Is Yours Festival

performance studies, 8, 9, 138n21

pleasure: calls into the cypher and, 50; constitutive disgust and, 30; enactment of, 67; filling the head as, 31, 60, 87, 90, 101, 106; the glitch and, 45, 48, 52, 61; invitation into the cypher and, 50; philosophy and, 29; as power, 89–90; release and, 92–93, 101, 106; stillness and, 83

police: public protest and, 110, 111, *111*, 112, 113, 114; public space and, 16, 70, 73, 78, 142n28; secret, 7, 70; shared oppression by, 4; subjectivation and, 76

political being, 96, 97, 98

political economies, 8, 14, 48

political engagement, 1–2, 3–4, 5, 6, 114–15. *See also* interpellation: political

political positions, 28, 115, 119
political relation, 7, 8, 11, 88, 114
politics: aesthetics and, 27, 28–29, 30, 33, 43; affect and, 7, 14; agency and, 8, 22, 28, 89, 95, 98, 129n32; antiracist, 4–5; becoming and, 20, 31, 33, 43–44, 76; as boring, 91–92; call to, 108; class and, 67; depoliticization and, 4, 27; desire for the political, 41, 91, 108; of distaste, 32, 40, 113; explicit connection to, 114–15; as is, 62, 91, 97, 101, 108, 111–12; left-wing, 27, 38, 41–42, 43; of listening, 29, 50; listening politically and, 3, 8, 29–30, 48, 62, 144n59; motion and, 7, 11–13, 62, 76, 88, 110–12, 115, 119 (*see also* stillness); narratives of, 6, 87, 88, 141n21; political possibilities, 29, 66, 95; popular, 57; populist, 52, 88; posturing and, 41–42; in process, 111, 119, 120; refusal of rupture and, 43; refusing frameworks of, 3–4, 5–6, 8, 20–21, 57–58, 80, 99–100; relation otherwise and, 91, 97, 112; sectarian, 14, 103, 106, 110; sensing the political, 6–7, 11; sociality of, 99–100; subjectivity and, 78, 90, 93, 94, 95, 96, 98, 128n26; what counts as, 118; yearning as political relation, 7, 104–5, 113, 114
popular, the (sha'bi): aesthetics of, 55, 59; authenticity and, 53; bringing rap to sha'bi spaces and, 55, 59; distancing from, 53–54, 55, 59, 60; resistance and, 59; society, 55–56, 57, 117; "Kheir al-Shaghab" ("The Rising Riot," al-Touffar and Al-Darwish) and, 102
possibility: the cypher and, 101, 102; of filling the head, 106; of glitchy interpellation, 60; layers of, 10; ongoingness of, 90; political, 29, 66, 95; prayer and, 99, 108; promise of, 13; of violence, 78. *See also* impossibility
precarity, 14, 16, 79, 82–83
present, the, 14, 18, 102–3. *See also* al-wada'; future, the
private spaces. *See* concert venues
protest: concert venues and, 110–11, *111*, 114; against corruption, 38, 40, 103, 106, 110–11, *111*, 114–15, 117; exhaustion and, 100; as ground for creativity, 28; liberalism and, 106, 111; nonviolence and, 3, 4; as not all life, 97; propriety and, 106; riots and, 102, 105, 106; solitude and, 112, 114; student encampments and, 102, 103; #YouStink protests, 38, 103, 106, 114–15, 117. *See also* revolution; violence: state provocation. *See* istifzaz
public space: movement and action in, 16, 72, 73, 78, 132n60, 141n20, 142n30 (*see also* inattention); performance in, 66, 67, 68, 70, 72, 73, 74, 82; policing of, 16, 70, 73, 78, 142n28; privatization of, 15, 16. *See also* concert venues

"Qaboor al-Qarn" (Shua'a), 45–46
Quashie, Kevin, 90, 95–97, 98, 99, 107, 108, 112

racialization, 4, 27, 40
racism, 2, 4–5, 28, 133n77
Racy, Ali Jihad, 92, 93–94
Ramallah: BLTNM, 49, 57, 59, 60; Dakn, 85–86; as de facto capital, 15; development in, 15, 132n59; El Rass's music in a supermarket in, 120–21, *121*; forces shaping creative scene, 13–14; La Wain Pub in, 51, *51*, 52, 61; Al-Nather, 49, 50, 58, 85, 86; outsiders in, 119; political suffocation in, 17; the "Ramallah Bubble" and, 17, 132n64. *See also* Haykal; Palestine; Ramallah Underground; Shab Jdeed
Ramallah, Occupation of: blockage and, 14; everyday life in, 59, 83–84, 132n64, 139n29; precarity and, 16; the "Ramallah Bubble" and, 17, 132n64; refusing as narrative, 58, 83, 84
Ramallah Underground: Asifeh (Stormtrap), 1, 84, 85, 108, 143n50; Haykal and, 85, 87–88, 96–97, 143n52; as hip-hop school, 84–85, 86; resilience and, 87–88; the Second Intifada and, 84; "Khaleeni 'Ayeesh" ("Let Me Live"), 83–84, 85–86; "Min al-Kaheff" ("From the Cave"), 1–2, 45, 108. *See also* Muqata'a; Osloob; saleb wahed collective

rap, experimental: avoidance of turath and, 54; being hailed otherwise and, 108; constitutiveness of decay and, 40; dark humor and, 46; disdain and, 20–21; feeling blended with reason in, 93; filtering and, 59 (*see also* Muqataʿa); intervening in al-wadaʿ, 99; invitation to possibility and, 102; istifzaz epistemology and, 21, 47, 49, 52, 111–12; listening as a practice and, 48, 52, 61, 63–64, 85; opportunities for producing, 16; popularity and, 53; still attention and, 81, 84, 97; struggle and, 103; virtual circulation of, 23, 110–11, 113, 119–22. *See also* hip-hop; *individual artists*

Red Bull, 17, *74*, 133n67, 140n12

refugee camps, 17–18, 34, 36, 42, 134 chap. 1 pre-note

refugees, 34, 37, 101, 118, 119, 132n56. *See also* migrants

refusal: of aspiring cosmopolitanism, 75; of communication, 55; disgust as, 30, 36, 41; disruption and, 79; the glitch and, 59, 60, 139n35; inattention and, 78; to listen, 22, 65; of narratives, 6, 58; of optimism, 40, 43; of performance etiquette, 31, 32–33; of politeness, 35; of political frameworks, 3–4, 5–6, 8, 20–21, 57–58, 80, 99–100; of rejection, 74; of resistance frameworks, 3–4, 53–54; of rupture, 43; of topics, 5–6, 8

refusal, of calls into the cypher: across demographics, 61; concert goers and, 56–57, 66; concert observers and, 66, 70–72, 74, 75, 76–77; effect on others and, 67; inattention and, 78; listening practices and, 63, 76–77; permission and, 106

release: articulation of the unarticulated and, 94–95; disgust and, 29, 30, 31, 38, 101; filling the head and, 21, 32, 101, 106; lyrics and, 95, 101; pleasure and, 92–93, 101, 106; solidarity and, 120; from tension, 38, 83, 90; through performance, 7; through practices of listening/tarab, 92–93, 94; without rupture, 21, 31; yearning/longing and, 8, 94–95, 106. *See also* pleasure

religion: opposition to Word Is Yours Festival and, 73. *See also* Islam

resignation, 19, 100, 101, 115

resilience (sabr, sumud): as asceticism, 139n29; collectivity and, 60; resistance and, 114; tropes of, 45–46, 59, 60, 87–88, 132n64. *See also* patience; resistance

resistance (mouqawameh): aesthetics of, 22, 63 (*see also* disgust; istifzaz); agency and, 9, 44; Black, 27, 95, 97; capacity for, 87; chants of, 34; distance/distancing from, 40, 43–44, 53–54, 64, 82, 99, 139n29; ethic of, 96; frameworks of, 3–4, 83–84, 95, 96; performance of, 8, 83–84, 87, 96, 97; political agency and, 8, 28; romanticization of, 3–4, 21, 28–29, 59; Second Intifada and, 16, 24, 84, 86; shaʿbi and, 59; simplistic understanding of, 8, 28, 29, 111, 112; traditional readings of, 12, 28, 64, 95. *See also* patience; resilience

revolution: anger and, 115; chants of, 34, 114; counterrevolution and, 13, 24–25, 131n55; disgust and, 28, 34, 42, 136n21; hypocrisy and, 41; Lebanese (2019, the October Revolution), 13, 113, 115; popular (2011), 1, 13, 28 (*see also* Arab Spring, the; Arab Uprisings, the); romanticization of, 3–4, 26, 27, 28, 114; of the self, 102, 104, 106–8. *See also* struggle

romanticization: of Beirut, 41, 42; disavowal of, 40–41; as oppression, 5–6; refusal of, 9; of resistance, 3–4, 21, 28–29, 59; of revolution, 3–4, 26, 27, 28, 114

rupture, 21, 31, 43–44

Russell, Legacy, 11, 48, 52, 59, 139n35

Said, Edward, 26–27
Said, Sami, 132n64
Sakr, Leila, 10, 22, 47
saleb wahed collective, 21, 49, 59, 85, 143n52. *See also* Ramallah Underground
Sarde (After Dinner), 89, 108
Satti, 73, 82, 99–100, 141n14
Sawalha, Aseel, 18, 133n77
Sawalha, Shermine, 68, 73, 140n12. *See also* Word Is Yours Festival
Schielke, Samuli, 100, 145n31
Schwedler, Jillian, 66, 75, 142n30

Second Intifada, 16, 24, 84, 86
sedimentation, 65–66, 81–82, 83–88, 97
selling out, 42, 115, 116
Serhan, Raed, 133n67
Seven Hills Skatepark, 68, 72, 74, 75, 79, 141n13. *See also* Word Is Yours Festival
Al-Isfaahani, 94
Shab Jdeed, 57–58; "Kohl wa 'Atmeh" ("Charcoal and Darkness"), 58, 59. *See also* BLTNM
She'rap, 17, 53–54, 55, 59
Al-Shidyaq, Ahmed Faris, 39–40
"Shouf" ("Look," El Rass), 110–11, 112, 113–14
Shua'a: "Qaboor al-Qarn," 45–46
Smitherman, Geneva, 48
sociality, 5, 16, 18, 41, 99–100, 117
solidarity: in being subject to power, 113; declarations as shallow, 27–28; diss tracks and, 115; imaginaries of, 47; meaning of, 120; as negotiating engagement, 120, 121; with Palestine, 4, 5, 120, 128n16; release and, 120; simplistic understanding of, 8; staging of, 54; stakes of expressing, 115. *See also* belonging; collectivity
Solidere, 14, 15, 38–39, 132n58, 136n28. *See also* al-Hariri, Rafiq
Sot Gilgamesh (Raed Ghoneim), 26, 31, 134 chap. 1 pre-note, 137n43
"Sot Ramallah" ("The Sound of Ramallah," Haykal), 58–59
Sotusura (Hicham Ibrahim), 22, 84–85, 95, 105, 107
Southwest Asia and North Africa (SWANA), 4, 26–27
Spillers, Hortense, 9, 96
spitting: affect and, 33; as alienating, 36, 49; calls into the cypher and, 33, 36, 46, 49; as connective, 36; enunciation and, 33; expressing disgust, 40, 46; as invitation, 33; on the left's failures, 41–42; lyrical, 32, 81; politics of distaste and, 32, 40, 113; as rejection of a place, 33; subject position and, 30–31. *See also* aesthetics: of disgust
spitting back, 30–31, 34
stability, 14, 15, 16, 17, 18, 79
stagnation, 19, 31, 66, 79, 82–83, 99

static, 47–48, 49, 52
stillness: as active, 97; cocreated, 65; cultivating, 84, 85–86; El Rass and, 81, 82, 83; as embodied attention, 66, 81, 82, 94, 96, 97, 114; feeding back to rappers, 82; filling the head and, 65, 82; interiority and, 112; invitation into the cypher and, 81, 85–86, 97, 98; listening and, 11, 85–86, 88, 96, 97; as motion, 11, 23, 66, 90, 98; needed for listening, 11, 80; pleasure and, 83; as political motion, 88, 90, 98; sedimentation through listening and, 66, 84; waiting and, 97. *See also* listening, embodied; sedimentation
street, the (al-share'): authenticity and, 53, 56; distancing from, 53–54, 55, 117; fluidity of, 57; material realities of, 102, 108, 112 (*see also* public space); violence and, 113; work of bringing music to, 55
struggle: call into, 31; the cypher and, 103; deadening reference to, 5–6; diluted, 42; expectation of, 28; invoking, 5–6; over space, 4, 119 (*see also* public space); as persistence, 89, 108; personal, 6, 103, 106, 107, 120; reduction to, 29; regional, 5. *See also* protests; revolution
subject formation, 9–10, 22, 76, 97. *See also* interpellation
subjectivity: agentive, 8; alternatives to, 96, 98; emergent, 29; hailing otherwise and, 95; liberal, 28; political, 78, 90, 93, 94, 95, 96, 98, 128n26; relational, 101; spitting back and, 30–31
suffocation, 7, 19, 30–31, 40, 43, 99. *See also* blockage
surprise: affective, 2, 33, 90, 94; anticipated, 35; knowing the world otherwise and, 47; listener expectation and, 60, 88; the miraculous and, 82; as negative or positive, 50; staging, 46; stereotypes and, 132n64. *See also* istifzaz
SWANA (Southwest Asia and North Africa), 4, 26–27
Swedenburg, Ted, 4, 27, 28
Synaptik (Laith Al Huseini), 19, 116
Syria: anti-Syrian discrimination, 5; civil war in (Syrian Uprising), 5, 6, 7, 16, 32, 115;

Damascus, 5, 6, 7, 32, 132n56; diaspora of, 2, 5, 6; the "good life" in, 101; rappers supporting Assad regime, 115; romanticized victimization of, 5–6. *See also* Al-Darwish; Bu Kolthoum; Munma

tarab, 12, 84, 91, 92–93, 94, 106, 145n12
Taraki, Lisa, 132n64
taste, 15, 17, 30, 54, 56, 57
Tate, Claudia, 92
Tawil-Souri, Helga, 139n30
Taylor, Diana, 138n21
tension: of abjection, 39; affective, 71–72; class-based, 74–75, 133n77; cultivating stillness and, 84; disgust with, 18, 113; recognition of, 105; release from, 38, 83, 90; of revolt/revolting, 136n21. *See also* al-wadaʿ
terrorism, 16, 27, 32, 86
Thompson, Robert Farris, 48
ticket prices, 51, 68, 70–71, 142n23
time, 11, 18–19, 101, 121. *See also* future, the; present, the; waiting
Tobin, Sarah, 67
Touffar. *See* al-Touffar, Jaafar; al-Touffar, Nasserdayn
al-Touffar, Jaafar, 31, 32–33, 34, 36, 41
al-Touffar, Nasserdayn: "Beirut Khaybetna" ("Beirut, Our Disappointment," with El Rass and Wattar), 41–42, 54, 137n44; "Kheir al-Shaghab" ("The Rising Riot," with Al-Darwish), 102–3, 104–7, 146n50; "Nihna w al-zibl jeeran" ("We Are Neighbors with Dung," with El Rass), 38–39
Toukan, Hanan, 13–14
Tsing, Anna, 3, 23
Tunisia, 1, 26, 70, 91
Tyler, Imogen, 136n21

United States, the: Black and brown resistance in, 27, 111; Black and brown youth in, 4; 47 Soul in, 116; invasion of Iraq by, 131n55, 132n56; military actions in Syria, 32; Palestinian diaspora in, 25; Palestinian liberation visible in, 5, 102; political narratives of, 6; political potential of Arab-Muslim youth and, 27; politics of disgust in, 34; rap authenticity in, 56; rappers in, 3, 111; relationship with Jordan and Israel, 17

veiling, 31, 68, 79
violence: in audiences, 73; everyday, 18, 79; question of, 106; state, 32, 111, 112, 113, 114 (*see also* police); terrorism and, 16, 27, 32, 86

wadaʿ. *See* al-wadaʿ
waiting, 11, 19, 38, 50, 59, 97, 99–101
"Washwasheh" ("Whisperings," El Far3i), 115, 117
"Watwateh" (El Rass), 115, 116, 117, 118
Wedeen, Lisa, 101
West, the: modernity in, 39; orientalism of, 2, 7, 26–27, 116, 118, 119, 132n64; philosophy in, 9, 30, 98; political ties with, 17; press of, 4, 132n64; students from, 132n56
Williams, Raymond, 13
Word Is Yours Festival, 67, 68, 72–74, *74, 75,* 79, 82
Wynter, Sylvia, 9

yearning: affect and, 7, 22, 114; as agency, 10, 22, 89; anger and, 89, 92, 104; attention and, 22, 89; as becoming, 47; for being hailed otherwise, 10, 11, 23, 90–91, 98; for being otherwise, 99; belonging and, 10, 23, 35, 90, 113; connecting listeners and musicians, 38, 114; disgust and, 84; distinct from desire, 30; filling the head and, 53, 90; the future and, 7, 22, 89; as informed by other feelings, 89; motion and, 11, 19; as political agency, 22, 89; as political relation, 7, 104–5, 113, 114; relation to time, 11; release and, 8, 106
Younes, Amine, 133n77
youth: Arab, 3, 4, 5, 25, 27, 28, 67, 132n64; Arabic-speaking, 20–21, 25, 27; cultures of, 3, 4, 8, 12, 84; US Black and brown, 3, 4, 5

RAYYA EL ZEIN is an independent writer and researcher. She holds a PhD in Theatre and Performance from the Graduate Center at the City University of New York.

For Indiana University Press

Tony Brewer, Artist and Book Designer
Anna Garnai, Production Coordinator
Sophia Hebert, Assistant Acquisitions Editor
Samantha Heffner, Marketing and Publicity Manager
Katie Huggins, Production Manager
David Miller, Lead Project Manager/Editor
Bethany Mowry, Acquisitions Editor
Dan Pyle, Online Publishing Manager
Jennifer Witzke, Senior Artist and Book Designer